68-11434 (5/8/69)

WAR AND AFTERMATH

1914–1929

WAR AND AFTERMATH 1914–1929

by Pierre Renouvin

Translated by Rémy Inglis Hall

1817

HARPER & ROW, PUBLISHERS

NEW YORK, EVANSTON, AND LONDON

The translator wishes to thank Mr. Stephen Lax for his kind assistance in the preparation of the manuscript.

This book was originally published in French under the title *Les Crises du XXe Siècle De 1914–1929*. © Librairie Hachette, 1957.

FIRST EDITION

LIBRARY OF CONGRESS CATALOG CARD NUMBER: 68-11954

C-S

Contents

[v]

BOOK II: THE PEACE SETTLEMENT

BOOK III: EUROPE AND THE WORLD
BETWEEN 1920 AND 1929

General Introduction

The predominant position that Europe had occupied in the affairs of the other continents during the first years of the century was seriously undermined by the First World War. Ten years after this conflict, and after a long convalescence, the nations of Europe had still only partially recovered their former pre-eminence. The study of international relations during this first stage in the "decline of Europe" is thus more than ever inseparable from that of the material, social, intellectual and moral transformations which were brought about and accelerated by the war. Of course, this study is not and cannot be a history of contacts between civilizations. It can only be a history of relations between states, although it should never overlook the explanations to be found in the fundamental forces behind these relations.

Historical research is much more difficult for this period of the history of international relations than in the previous period. The public archives are on the whole inaccessible to researchers. The large editions of documents that permitted the historian to follow the details of diplomatic activity during the last years of the nineteenth century and the beginning of the twentieth century, and to discern, at least partially, the intentions of the governments, are rarely to be found in the case of the First World War or of the postwar period.

For the study of the First World War there exists no collection of documents taken from French or British archives. The collection of Russian documents that gives valuable information on the policies of the other Entente Powers is limited to the czarist period. The edition of the American documents, valuable for the study of United States neutrality, covers the world situation only after the entry into the war. The Italian and German archives have yielded few documents. The Austro-Hungarian archives have been opened to few historians.

For the study of the period between 1919 and 1929, the British documents currently being published are of great importance, and the publications of the United States State Department supply much useful information. However, the collection of documents taken from the Italian archives consists only of four volumes at the present time, while similar collections are not available to the historical researcher in either France, Germany or the U.S.S.R. Moreover, there are few critical studies of the policies of these countries.

There are several works on the study of collective behavior and the tendencies of public opinion, but they are limited to the peace conference and to the postwar period. The press, subject to censorship during the war, can offer the historian no valid information on the currents of public opinion.

Economic and financial questions have been amply explored, because the history of the 1914–1918 war has given rise to numerous works in this field, many of them firsthand reports, under the auspices of the Carnegie Endowment, and because the publications of the League of Nations Labor Bureau offer abundant statistical information. However, there is still insufficient data concerning the international movement of capital.

Therefore, this book can only be an outline. It cannot presume to give satisfactory answers to all of the questions that come to mind. Its only ambition is to focus on what is already known without omitting to point out the gaps in this knowledge, to try to bring the essential interpretations to light, and to suggest hypotheses that might become the subject of further research.

P. R.

October, 1960

BOOK

I

THE FIRST WORLD WAR

Introduction to Book I

What should be the scope of a history of the First World War in the framework of a study of international relations?

The military and naval vicissitudes of a struggle in which the greatest nations of Europe and then of the world were pitted against one another take center stage. However, the development and the outcome of this struggle were largely determined by the entry into the war of new powers or by the defection of belligerent states. One must therefore concentrate on the foreign policy decisions of the belligerent or neutral governments.

Naturally enough, each belligerent country was forced to adapt its foreign policy to the military situation. But the war effort in each country was linked to that nation's political aims and the extent of its determination to fulfill them. The nature of the war aims, that is to say the desired objectives, sometimes decided military and naval operations. Often they led a government to reject from the outset the possibility of a negotiated peace that would prevent it from attaining all its desired goals. The predilections of statesmen and the role played by political leaders in making these decisions were by no means negligible factors, especially since the war allowed them more freedom of action than would have been the case in peacetime. Their actions were nevertheless restricted by the condition of their nation's morale:

a strength of national tradition, an awareness of national interests, and a sense of unity within the population. Diplomacy courts disaster when it overlooks these fundamental factors. Reactions or impulses varied according to the significance of the conflict: was a nation engaged in a struggle for its existence, or was it merely seeking to increase its political strength or to stimulate its economic expansion? These reactions also depended on the national temperament, on a people's spirit of sacrifice and discipline, on the conflicts that might exist between the "national minorities" and the state, and finally on economic and social conditions. Enemy propaganda was eager to exploit any conflict or weakness.

In their political decisions the governments of the belligerent states are also obliged to bear in mind the exigencies of a war of coalition, not only because the defection of one of the allies would considerably alter the complexion of the war, but also because the military and diplomatic collaboration between allies could be frustrated by the inability to adjust to one. These compromises among the interests of allies could be reached successfully only after difficult negotiations; in working out plans of operation, it was not unusual for each to try to have prevail the solutions that would assure him, at the least risk, a "war map" favorable to his political aims. Further, one ally might consider limiting its war effort as much as possible and allowing the burden of the conflict to fall on the other partners, so that at the time of the peace negotiations it would have a reserve of fresh troops, which would assure it the position of authority in the interallied councils.

Thus, a study of foreign policies of the belligerent states should explore all of these considerations and calculations.

The balance of military, naval, and economic forces was decisively changed by the entry of new belligerents into the war. In most cases, with one important exception, such intervention by a neutral state was the result of extended discussions and hard bargaining. A neutral state would have good reason to make sure that a common victory would serve its interests before committing itself to the sacrifices and hazards of war. For their part, the belligerent governments were perfectly delighted to make promises that would be fulfilled at the expense of the enemy, although they were more reserved when it was a question of territories that attracted other neutral states. They were even more so when they themselves were called upon to provide the compensation. In such matters the dexterity of diplomatic action had its own value, which was not negligible. However, negotiations were dominated above all by the "war map" and the possibilities opened up by the hazards of war: political history was closely linked to military history.

It is equally important to examine the motives determining the actions of the neutral powers as it is to study the negotiations themselves. Here again, an explanation is more often than not to be found in the public mood and in the economic interests of each of these nations. Once again we must attempt to evaluate the importance of each.

Finally, this progression from neutrality to belligerent intervention, important as it was, must not overshadow another major aspect of this study. Although the European war spread throughout the world, it directly affected only a part of humanity— granted, that part that had played the leading role in world affairs for several centuries. What were the consequences of the conflict in those countries that were only spectators of the struggle, or that made declarations of war but did not in fact participate in the hostilities, and in those regions of the world—Asia, Africa, Latin America—where the great European powers had established their political domination or economic influence? To what extent did the agony of Europe undermine European prestige in colonial territories or damage the foundations of Europe's economic domination in the "new countries"? What opportunities did the war afford to the great competitors of the nations of Europe?

This is the vantage point from which we must examine the history of international relations between 1914 and 1918.

The Underlying Forces

From the first days of August to the last days of September 1914, the attention of the whole world was focused on the battles being fought in France, eastern Prussia, and Galicia. Every government and high command believed it would be a short war. Economically, the belligerents expected to live on their reserves, while their armies in a few glorious days would decide the outcome of the conflict: thus, they made no attempt to call upon the material resources that the neutral powers could offer them. There was as yet no apparent difficulty in maintaining high morale. Each government's watchword of "sacred union" ["holy alliance" for the Central Powers, *entente cordiale* for the Allies] was accepted by all the parliaments—even by members of the International, with the single exceptions of a few British worker deputies and a handful of Russian Socialist extremists; and it had not yet been questioned by such minorities as the Slavs in Austria-Hungary, the Poles in Russia, or the nationalists of southern Ireland. In the end the diplomatic effort directed toward the European neutrals met with cool reserve. Even the Turkish government, which had signed a treaty of alliance with Germany on August 2, 1914, hesitated about actually going to war. During these few weeks, despite the agitation that the war provoked in the collective psychology of neutrals, the contacts between the peoples of the world seemed reduced to those established by the use of weapons.

However, after the battle of the Marne and the failure of the German plan of operation which should have, according to General von Moltke, settled the outcome "within a period of six weeks," the belligerents found themselves, during the autumn of 1914, faced with the prospect of a long struggle, whose issue would depend no longer solely upon military or naval strength: the preservation of morale and the question of foreign economic exchanges once again became an important concern for all the governments. At the same time they became increasingly aware of matters relating to the strengthening or extension of coalitions.

The Countries at War

What was the balance of strength between the belligerent states when it became apparent that a long war lay ahead?

The two Central Powers, Germany and Austria-Hungary, had approximately 120,000,000 inhabitants, while their adversaries— Russia, Great Britain, France, Belgium, and Serbia—had 238,-000,000, without counting the population of their colonies. This numerical disproportion, of little importance in a short war, becomes more important in the light of a long one, where the consistent maintenance of manpower is of major concern. Of course, the effective use of manpower depends upon the condition of the armaments and, as a result, on the capacity of industrial production; it also depends upon the social structure, which facilitates or hinders the recruiting of ranks in the army; finally it is linked to the state of the country's morale and to the consent it more or less willingly gives to the war effort.

The manpower available to Germany and Austria-Hungary at the beginning of the war was numerically comparable to that of the enemy. During the first great battles they deployed almost 150 divisions of infantry, not counting the territorials; while the Allied forces had drawn up approximately 170, whose weapons were inferior, particularly in heavy artillery. At the outset the prospect of a prolonged struggle did not concern them, since they had far from called upon their total resources of manpower. In October of 1914 and May of 1915, the German general staff brought 18 newly formed divisions to the front, and the Austro-Hungarian general staff brought 16. Only by the end of 1916 did a shortage of manpower begin to be felt.

The continuity of the war effort appeared to be assured without any trouble, for although the Austro-Hungarian high command often complained about the cutting behavior of the top German generals, they declined and, save on rare occasions, bowed to their superiority. During the first two years of the war the harmony of political action was undisturbed, for the routine of maintaining an alliance for thirty-five years had established solid traditions, and it was all the easier to adjust "war aims" in that the geographical areas of interest were different: Germany had no designs on the Balkans which were, at the beginning of the war, the only area of interest to Austro-Hungarian policy. Only toward the end of 1916 did the fate of the Polish territories within the Russian empire provoke Vienna and Berlin to lengthy disputes, whose atmosphere nevertheless remained that of a business conference, lacking any feeling of nationalistic passion.

Finally, the economic collaboration that the war had obliged the two countries to establish paved the way for a customs union which could, in the future, reinforce the material interests of the alliance. Friedrich Naumann's *Mitteleuropa* was published in October of 1915 and within a few months had sold 100,000 copies. Although it was opposed in Germany by the great munitions manufacturers and exporters out of concern about reprisals that the other powers might take against the Austro-German economic bloc after the war—although it provoked objections from Austrian industrialists who feared German competition—its central thesis commanded the attention of the two governments and was the subject of long technical discussions. During the rest of the war, this point of view contributed a new source of strength to the Austro-German alliance.

The weak points of the alliance were, on the one hand, the difficulty of bringing about the cooperation of two nations whose populations had totally different emotional outlooks, and on the other, the threat that weighed on their foreign economic relations. The contrast between the state of morale in the two allied empires was evident. In Germany the bulk of the population was animated by an active patriotism, a deep belief in national grandeur, an innate sense for discipline, a spirit of sacrifice in the interest of the state and a vigorous military tradition. Doubtless, the presence of alien national groups within the empire—Poles in Prussia, Danes in northern Schleswig, Alsace-Lorrainers—who were situated near the frontiers and who were almost complete strangers to the national life, might in the future constitute an element of weakness. But these "national minorities"—five million people—comprised only 7 per cent of the total population of the empire; distributed over a large area, separated by their particular mentalities and their social structures, they were unable to offer effective resistance to the state. The imperial government counted on rigorous administrative measures and police surveillance to stifle any attempted protest.

In Austria-Hungary, on the other hand, where only the presence of the administrative machine maintained a fiction of cohesiveness among disparate populations, before 1914 it was hardly a question of fighting a "national war." Although the minority groups did not express secessionist aspirations, except on rare occasions, the European war offered the opportunity of shaking off the German or the Magyar yoke to those who retained an active ethnic identification.

Was it possible for the imperial and royal government to ignore the fact that the Slavs—Poles and Ruthenians in Galicia, Bohemians, Czechs and Slovaks in the northern regions of Hungary, Slovenes in Istria and Styria, Croats and Serbs of southern Hungary—constituted close to 49 per cent of the total population of the Dual Monarchy; that even if the Poles were thoroughly hostile toward Russia, certain intellectual Czech circles and the Serbian Orthodox clergy were susceptible to the idea of Slavic solidarity? Could it ignore the almost 3,000,000 Transylvanian Rumanians and the 700,000 Italians of Trentino, Istria, and the towns along the Dalmatian coast looking toward Rumania and Italy—two states that, after having belonged for thirty years to the Austro-German diplomatic system, had declared early in August 1914 their neutrality in the European war?

It is significant to note that whereas in Hungary, where the electoral law afforded a majority to the Magyar element, the cabinet maintained the parliament in session, the President of the Austrian Council dared not convene the *Reichsrat*, in which universal suffrage assured a non-German majority, and governed by decree. As it became apparent that preparations were being made for a long war, the leaders of the Czech movement—at least those who had succumbed to the democratic concepts of Western Europe —Masaryk, Beneš, Stefanik—and one of the leaders of the national Dalmatian movement, succeeded in fleeing abroad and attempted to make contact with Austria-Hungary's opponents. On the front, from the winter of 1914–1915 on, the loyalty of certain troops was doubtful, particularly of those predominantly Czech. In order to limit the threat of disruption, the governments of Vienna and Budapest had no recourse but to impose obedience by force. When Great Britain and France decided to blockade food and essential raw materials, the economic difficulties were more marked in Germany than in Austria-Hungary. In Austria-Hungary agricultural production was sufficient to satisfy the needs of the population if the crops were normal, and the iron ore deposits were enough to satisfy the needs of the metal industry; only the cotton industry suffered when the importation of raw material was stopped in 1915. But even in peacetime, in good years as well as bad, Germany bought 20 per cent of her cereals and 40 per cent of her fats from abroad; from France, Sweden or Spain she bought 12,500 tons of iron ore; she also had to resort to importing all of her raw cotton, copper, rare metals, rubber, and petroleum. The government, which in 1913 had commissioned a study of "war economy," instituted on August 15, 1914, a bureau of raw materials which, following the suggestions of the great industrialist Walther Rathenau, was to draw up a memorandum of natural resources; to make as many purchases as possible from neutral states and requisitions from occupied countries; to find substitute products and to recover used materials; finally, to allot raw materials among manufacturers. During the autumn of 1914 the industrialists organized themselves into "war societies," which divided up the labor force and assured the fulfillment of armament orders, while at the same time, the Grain Commission rationed the consumption of bread. However, these were still only precautionary measures. The economic situation at the end of 1914 was not serious, and food shortages were not as yet critical. During the year 1915 the European neutral powers contributed to feeding the German population. Also, the first measures taken toward the rationing of bread in February 1915 and of meat in October were moderate. Food shortages were not serious until the winter of 1915–1916. The situation rapidly deteriorated during 1916, when the blockade was more effective.

The prospect of a long war was thus dangerous to the Central Powers, whose resources would diminish the longer the hostilities continued. In order to avoid, or at least to delay, these difficulties, is it possible to count on the effectiveness of a policy of reprisal? The German government considered this method at the beginning of 1915, when it embarked on submarine warfare; it hoped that this obstacle to neutral navigation would cause the United States to demand that Great Britain ease the blockade. But, above all, successful military operations bring relief: the occupation of Belgium and northeastern France during August of 1914, and of Poland during the summer of 1915, gave the German economy important resources in the form of raw materials and even food.

Among the Entente powers, the Belgian army consisted of only six divisions of infantry and was unable to get reinforcements, since Belgium had been invaded. The Serbian army, at the price of a considerable recruiting effort, succeeded in bringing to the front eleven divisions. Although Great Britain, through her naval power, was to play an essential role in the general conduct of the war, she at first played only a modest role in the struggle on the Continent. Her immediately available forces were reduced at the outset of the hostilities to five divisions of infantry; they increased only as quickly as the possibilities of induction and armament permitted: twenty divisions were deployed by May of 1915; thirty-five in October of 1915; seventy by the spring of 1916. The appeal for volunteers was sufficient during two years to furnish the required numbers; not until 1916 was it necessary to resort to obligatory recruitment. During the first two years of the war the success of military operations therefore depended on the French and the Russian armies.

There were notable differences between the three countries that bore the principal burden of the struggle, from the point of view of economic strength as well as from that of morale.

During the years that immediately preceded the conflict, foreign observers had often said that France was a nation that was old, anxious, incapable of a concerted national effort. Their opinion was founded on a series of facts that might seem contradictory: demographic stagnation, resulting in an insufficient proportion of young people in the population; an unwillingness to accept increasing military costs, clearly expressed during the spring elections of 1914; a marked increase in the Socialist electorate, which affirmed its pacifist convictions far more rigorously than did the German Social Democratic party; and a decline of initiative in middle-class business circles. As soon as war was declared, those who had been counting on these weaknesses received a rude surprise. Mobilization was achieved under conditions that the general staff had hardly dared hope for: the pacifist militants expressed no reaction at all, promptly rejoined their units, often enthusiastically. The parliamentary parties, including the Socialists, were unanimous in rallying to the slogan of "sacred union" and in granting to the government virtually unlimited credit. Public opinion manifested its contempt toward young men who were not serving their country. Morale was high.

But the economy was in serious difficulties. The agricultural yield was threatend by the desperate shortage of manpower, for since the beginning of the hostilities France had mobilized more men than any other belligerent; in addition, arable land had decreased to 500,000 hectares by the autumn of 1914. Industrial production was seriously affected by the invasion of the northeastern provinces—namely, through the loss of the coal region of the north and part of the coal region of the

Pas-de-Calais. Obliged to mobilize its economic resources under difficult circumstances, the French government had to rely largely upon imports: Great Britain supplied the coal; the United States filled the food and raw materials gap and provided the means of relieving the matériel and munitions shortage.

Great Britain, where industry still had all the means of production and the major part of its labor force, was at first able to maintain an almost normal rate of economic production. The state contracted for the manufacture of arms without regard for price. The industries that were not supplying the needs of the army were encouraged to keep to their normal schedules: "business as usual" was the order of the day. The sale of manufactured goods abroad, particularly textiles—which, in peacetime, made up 34 per cent of British exports—facilitated the financing of food imports and helped to stabilize the exchange rate. It also assured earnings that enabled part of the exceptional war expenditures to be covered, thus making it less essential to borrow. Obviously this could only be a temporary situation. As the war continued, the value of the pound sterling plummeted, shipping became increasingly difficult, and the government was forced to adopt the methods of a planned economy. In May 1915 the state set up controls on the war industry, on the distribution of raw materials, and on the type of manufacture to be undertaken. In February of 1916 it decided that all merchandise necessary to the war effort could be requisitioned, at a price to be determined by the government. And yet the "conscription" of industry and business was only slowly developed through a series of conversions and compromises. As long as Britain was able to preserve the freedom of her maritime communications and to import food and raw materials, the economic difficulties were not serious enough to affect the smooth operation of the war industry. Not until the spring of 1917 did the shortage of ships oblige the state to take over imports and allotments itself, to direct industrial manufacture by means of producers' associations and to institute rationing for civilian consumption.

The morale of the British people, which had always been especially high during the great crises of its history, was shaken over the Irish question. During the spring of 1914 the antagonism between the Catholics of southern Ireland and the Protestants of Ulster—respectively partisans and adversaries of the Home Rule act—had grown so intense that civil war seemed imminent. Was the intervention of Great Britain in the European war going to bring about a lasting solution? On August 3, 1914, John Redmond, the leader of the Nationalist party in the House of Commons, had declared that during the hostilities the government could count on the loyal support of the Southern Irish; but this declaration was opposed by extreme nationalists, who saw in the European war an opportunity to obtain not only the autonomy promised by the Home Rule Act but also independence. This clandestine resistance ended in the Easter Rebellion of 1916 and the formation of a republican revolutionary government. Although the movement was put down within a few days, the Irish nationalists continued their agitation.

At first the situation in the Russian empire was difficult in quite another way, in regard to both morale and economics.

There was no communication between the members of the court circle and the Russian people. The peasant masses remained passive. The working classes were guided by the influence of the Socialist intellectuals, who for the most part did not admit to following the path of the German and French Socialist parties. They rejected the Entente Cordiale and, advised by Lenin, who had fled to Switzerland, anticipated that a military defeat would pave the way to political and social revolution. The more active members of the bourgeoisie—in particular the members of local assemblies, municipalities, and *Zemstvos* —openly manifested their distrust of governmental and administrative authority which had proved incapable of organizing the life of the country in wartime. The Duma, which in the beginning seemed prepared to support the government, became intransigent when it realized that the cabinet was seeking to shorten the parliamentary sessions and preferred to legislate by decree. At the same time one should not overlook the presence within this "Russian nation" of alien ethnic groups, discontent and uninvolved, who saw in the international crisis the opportunity to overthrow a regime and a domination under which they had suffered. The government was not unaware of the state of mind of these national minorities and, in order to ward off latent threats, took a whole series of measures ranging from the most brutal severity to vague promises of liberal reform. The Jews were expelled from the theater of military operations and deported *en masse* into the interior of the empire; the Finns were placed under strict control which extended even to schools and churches. The Poles, on the other hand, received on August 14, 1914, from the commander in chief of the armed forces, the promise of getting—though only at the end of the war—an administration of their own: a promise that the Minister of the Interior knew he would forget when the moment came. National unity, for which the Czar had made an appeal at the beginning of the hostilities, thus remained an empty formula.

The economic situation was precarious. During peacetime Russia had bought from abroad, especially from Germany, nearly one third of the manufactured goods needed by its population, and depended on imports for all its chemical products and all the mechanical equipment necessary for its industry. Metallurgical production, already insufficient for the manufacturing of armaments, was now partially disrupted, for Germany no longer supplied machinery, and the Polish coal and iron deposits quite near the frontier were soon occupied by the enemy. The critical shortage of war materials that affected all the belligerents by the autumn of 1914 was most severe in Russia. In order to redress this deficiency, it would have been necessary to import by sea from Great Britain, France or the United States. But the closing of the Danish straits—a decision made by the Danish government on the first day of the war—had prevented traffic between the North Sea and the Baltic; the Ottoman straits, the

Bosporus and the Dardanelles, were closed by the Turkish government six weeks after the outbreak of war. The last clear route, navigable in summer only, passed through the Arctic Ocean, terminating at Murmansk and at Arkhangelsk; furthermore, this northern coast was linked to the interior of the empire by a single railroad of inadequate capacity. The mastery of the sea enjoyed by the Entente powers was useless to the Russian empire, which found itself virtually isolated from the rest of the world, and which suffered from this circumstance even more than did Germany. The lack of metallurgic and mechanical industries, further aggravated by administrative disorder, caused, from 1915 on, a crisis in rail transportation. It was impossible to replace either locomotives or rolling stock. The neglect of the railroads during the winter of 1915–1916 hampered the supply of food to large towns. In this agricultural nation, in which available resources exceeded those of peacetime—for exports had come to a halt—the urban populations suffered from shortages and were subject to food rationing. Here was one further reason for the working classes to heed the clandestine propaganda conducted by the opponents of the regime.

The London Pact, signed by the three great Entente powers on September 5, 1914, included a mutual pledge not to sign a separate peace. But this agreement did not indicate the nature of the coalition's war aims. But the adjustment of national policies is difficult.

France wanted to obtain the liberation of Alsace-Lorraine. Beyond this principal aim what could be expected from a total victory? Certain political and diplomatic circles envisaged a Balkanization of Central Europe: the partition of the German empire, which not only would separate Prussia from the southern German states, but would also dismember Prussia herself and give France the opportunity to annex the German territories on the left bank of the Rhine; the destruction of the dual Austro-Hungarian Monarchy by the liberation of nationalities subject to German or Magyar domination. And yet these opinions met both public and parliamentary resistance. Was the dismemberment of the Austro-Hungarian empire desirable? If the Danube region were fragmented into small states, it would become a zone of least resistance, most vulnerable to the designs of the major powers. Germany, even defeated, would find a way of exerting her influence in the area. True, if the German empire were dismembered, this risk would disappear. But this hypothesis is far more than that of the dismemberment of the Austro-Hungarian empire. And even if it were possible, would this dismemberment of Germany endure? With the exception of course of those areas inhabited by national minorities, the strength of patriotic feelings would hardly permit one to believe it. Therefore, only on the question of Alsace-Lorraine was the French public more or less unanimous.

Russia's interest was to guarantee free passage for her merchant fleet at all times in the Bosporus and the Dardanelles: this was a necessity for the economic life of the empire, because the bulk of her wheat exports had to be sent by this sea route. Giving her war fleet access to the Mediterranean would afford Russia a source of strength in her foreign policy. The assurance that its merchant fleet would have free passage at all times through the Bosporous and the Dardanelles was an important objective for the empire. As Prince Troubetskoy said, this question of the straits was the focal point of "all the empire's foreign problems." Was the future of Central Europe therefore of secondary importance? It goes without saying that Russia might well have an interest in dismembering the Austro-Hungarian empire, since for 150 years the latter almost constantly hindered or frustrated the Czar's Balkan policies. But in order to achieve this result, it would be necessary to support nationalist claims. But how could Russia support the Czech or the Yugoslav movements while she refused to satisfy the nationalist protests of Russian Poland? And yet the Czar did not discount the eventual dismemberment of the Dual Monarchy (he said as much to the French ambassador in November of 1914); but this was a mere statement of principle, to which his political actions gave only limited support. The total collapse of Germany would open the way to the founding of new republics; it would be a dangerous example, foreshadowing the end of czarism.

Great Britain entered the war to prevent Germany, her chief

commercial rival, from dominating the Continent and to hold the ports on the Flemish coast that would give the German fleet the means of directly threatening the security of the British Isles. But the moment she engaged in this struggle, she became concerned for her imperial interests and economic zones of influence outside Europe. The principal positive results that might ensue from a victory would be the following: eliminate Germany's presence in the regions of Africa where the latter's proximity might endanger British interests, and in the archipelagoes near Australia; destroy the successes achieved by German policy within the Ottoman empire since the beginning of the construction of the Baghdad railroad. She did not desire the Balkanization of Central Europe, which, she believed, would be a source of permanent trouble in international political relations and a danger to general economic prosperity. She was even so far convinced of the difficulties involved in a victory as to avoid a premature statement in favor of France's claim on Alsace-Lorraine.

Was it possible to reconcile these divergent interests? They might have stumbled on two points: the Polish question, because the reconstruction of an independent Poland had for long had French sympathy; and the question of the Ottoman Straits, where the interests of Great Britain had, for a hundred years, been constantly challenged by Russian policy. But the relative importance of the two problems was very uneven: while sentimental preferences, as demonstrated by the mood of the French public regarding Polish nationalism, were forced to yield to the necessity of maintaining the Franco-Russian alliance, it seemed *a priori* more difficult to get Great Britain to accept the idea that she should allow the Russian war fleet access to the Mediterranean.

Thus during the earliest months of the war the weak points of the two opposing coalitions began to come into focus. What opportunities would these weaknesses suggest to the governments in framing their war policies?

The field of diplomatic action is easily defined. France and Great Britain had to find a way to cripple the Austro-Hungarian monarchy, even if they were not bent on destroying it. They therefore made contact with the leaders of the Czech and Yugoslav nationalist movements, at the same time avoiding making premature alliances. After the isolation of Russia had been achieved by the closing of the Ottoman Straits, Berlin and Vienna hoped that a rift would develop between Russia and Great Britain.

Economic strength was first and foremost in the minds of everyone. British naval domination halted the supply of foodstuffs and raw materials to Germany and the Austro-Hungarian empire. Thus the blockade became an important aspect of the conduct of the war. In order to ensure the effectiveness of this superiority, France and Great Britain did not hesitate to extend the doctrine of "war contraband." Disregarding the legal definition established in 1909 by the London Declaration, they applied it to food supplies, then to cotton; they also decided, on October 29, 1914, to seize from neutral ships all merchandise likely to be used in the manufacturing of war matériel, when being transported toward a neutral port bordering on Germany, unless the shipper could prove that his merchandise was not destined for German manufacturers. The German government retaliated on February 4, 1914, with submarine warfare, directed against enemy, and even neutral, commercial navigation—an even more serious violation of the rules of international law. The Anglo-French proclamation replied by announcing that all merchandise "destined for the enemy," whatever its nature, could be seized. The Central Powers therefore ran the risk of being deprived of all imports by sea, unless these rules could be circumvented, and unless fraud was not both easy and frequent. Needless to say, the exercise of the right of seizure resulted in incessant complaints, and submarine warfare in turn brought vehement protests. Thus the economic war was waged at the expense of the neutrals—despite the fact that in other parts of the world this same war offered them the opportunity of making enormous profits.

The European Neutrals

The neutral European countries, whose attitude could have shifted the balance of military and economic strength, were on the alert. The course of military operations was likely to induce an immediate threat to the territorial integrity of some and to cause damage to the economic interests of others. The clauses of future peace treaties could affect everyone's interests, to the extent that they would modify the balance of power on the Continent. But it was not only a question of protecting their present status: the international situation might well offer countries who had not yet achieved national unity—the case of almost everyone except Norway and Holland—the opportunity to realize their aspirations. The impetus of nationalist emotions was the prime mover; in practice, however, it had vastly different effects.

Denmark, who controlled the entrance to the Baltic, would have had the best reasons to take sides in the war: she could have claimed all the northern part of Schleswig, which, though inhabited by Danes, had been annexed by the Prussians in 1866. But in such a case Denmark would have been subject to attack by the Germans without being able to count upon immediate support from British, Russian, or French troops. It was therefore necessary to sign a declaration of neutrality and not even dare to refuse Germany the right to mine the straits—thereby making a mockery of this neutrality. Furthermore, the major part of the merchandise she imported from the United States, or even from England, was resold by her merchants to Germany.

Sweden could have had designs on Finland. Although the Germans made diplomatic overtures, she was careful not to be drawn into accepting their offer, since she knew perfectly well that possible success against Russia would be temporary. But she sold her iron ore to Germany, transporting it through the Baltic, which English cruisers were unable to enter.

Although the Balkan states were able to furnish the belligerents —particularly the Austro-Hungarians—with foodstuffs, they played only a minor role in the economic struggle. Only Rumania, on account of her oil possessions, was able to furnish important resources for the conduct of military operations. But she herself had just emerged in 1912–1913 from wars in which she had been pitted, first against the Balkan states and Turkey, then against Bulgaria and her neighbors. The Treaty of London, which had

recorded the results of the Turkish defeat, and the Treaty of
Bucharest, which had finalized the defeat of Bulgaria, had left
behind them national and religious hatred, fears and particularly
violent controversies in these regions, where the mixture of populations would not permit the establishment of a linguistic or
sectarian border. The European war, of which the Austro-Hun-
garian-Serbian conflict had been, if not the basic cause, at least
the excuse, would inevitably modify the *status quo*. A Serbian
victory would have permitted the realization of the unification of
the southern Slavs at the expense of Austria-Hungary. An Austro-
Hungarian victory would doubtless have meant the dismemberment—perhaps the disappearance—of the small Serbian state.
In both cases the balance between the Balkan states would have
been upset.

Bulgaria, the loser in 1913, saw the hope of a revenge that
would give her the opportunity to take from Serbia a part of
Macedonia, where Bulgarians formed the relative majority. Greece,
who had upheld the treaty of alliance signed in 1913 with Serbia,
was obviously interested in preventing the success of the Bulgarian
revenge, since she also had possessions in Macedonia. But Turkey,
after having reclaimed Adrianople during the course of the second
Balkan war was not prepared to cede to Greece eastern Thrace
and, especially, the islands in the Aegean Sea.

Rumania was hardly indifferent to these disputes over Balkan
territory, since she had acquired during August 1913, at the expense of Bulgaria, part of the Dobrudja; but national sentiment
was more interested in questions outside of Balkan politics: those
posed by the problems of Rumanian-speaking people subjected
either to Russian domination in Bessarabia or to the sovereignty of
Austria-Hungary in Transylvania, in Bukovina, and in the Banat
of Temesvar. Transylvania was the special object of interest in
this regard, because the Rumanian population, larger in number and
more compact than in Bessarabia, gave evidence of a more
active national awareness. Public opinion, influenced by a group
of politicians, was thus from the outset hostile to the Dual Monarchy. The Austro-Hungarian diplomatic representative felt a
"wave of hatred" rise around him. It appeared impossible to the

Crown Council to uphold the alliance made with the Austro-Hungarian empire. King Carol, a Hohenzollern, still had sufficient authority—thanks to the services he had rendered the state since 1867—to frustrate those advocating intervention on the side of the Entente powers. This bitter dissension brought about a declaration of neutrality on August 3, 1914. But would nationalist Rumanian sentiment pass up the opportunity of obtaining satisfaction?

Of all the neutral European nations, Italy was the country whose future attitude was by far the most important. Despite the treaty of the Triple Alliance, she declared her neutrality on August 3, 1914. As grounds for this decision, she pleaded Austria-Hungary's refusal to honor her demands for compensation, based on Article 7 of the treaty; but she also was aware of possible strategic developments in the Mediterranean. Since Britain was going to enter the war, did she not have to fear that the Italian coastline, and consequently the industrial centers of Genoa and Livorno, would be at the mercy of gunfire from the British fleet?

And yet this neutrality seemed nothing short of being a provisional solution. In the early days of the war the Italian government had indicated her concerns via secret soundings: the European war offered her the opportunity to satisfy national pride by liberating Italian-speaking inhabitants under the domination of the Austro-Hungarians. Total satisfaction? In order to gain the Trentino, western Istria, along with Trieste and Gorizia, and finally the towns along the Dalmatian coast, she would have had to take part in the war and conquer these Austro-Hungarian territories. But if she were to be content with partial satisfaction— the ceding of Trieste—could she not obtain it by negotiation? To avoid seeing Italy enter the conflict, perhaps the Austro-Hungarian government would make the sacrifice.

Also Italian diplomacy was exploring the terrain on both sides: what chance would she have of gaining an "amicable" cession, and what promises would she be able to obtain from the Entente powers, if she were to decide upon armed intervention? The only policy that President of the Council Salandra refused to consider was that of pure inaction: if the government neglected to take advantage of the circumstances at hand in order to satisfy public opinion, the "extremist" parties, he said, would blame the dynasty.

On September 30, 1914, in a report to the King further developing the same theme, he argued that the choice between neutrality and armed intervention was still a difficult one. Of course participation in the war was the only means of realizing national aspirations, but the country was prepared "neither from a moral nor from an economic standpoint" to undergo sacrifices that were not strictly indispensable, and the current rise in national pride was perhaps nothing but a flash in the pan. Also, during the course of a speech given on October 16, Salandra advised the Italian people not to let themselves be carried away by prejudices or by emotion, and to be concerned first and foremost with self-interest. He was therefore in favor of diplomatic bargaining.

This policy was similar to that favored by Giolitti, the leader of the Liberal party and the statesman whose personality dominated the Italian parliament for twelve years. "Why enter the war?" was the question asked when it appeared that Italy could gain appreciable advantages without getting involved in the conflict. The majority of Socialists and the majority of Catholic politicians announced that they were in favor of neutrality: the former as pacifists, and the latter following the instructions of the Holy See; both desired a conciliatory approach toward Austria-Hungary, the only major power whose government was devoted to the cause of Catholicism. And yet armed intervention had its supporters in each of these political groups. The right wing of the Liberal party, which refused to stand behind Giolitti, Abbé Murri's Christian Democrats, Bissolati's Reformist Socialists, supported by certain trade-union elements, and finally a small number of Socialists, inspired by Benito Mussolini and the Freemasons, also supported the movement. But these "interventionists," who came from very different persuasions, and whose only common ground was their desire to find a lasting solution to their irredentist claims, were in the minority in parliament, where the influence of Giolitti dominated and was supported, even in the autumn of 1914, by only a modest proportion of public opinion. It was hardly surprising, therefore, bearing in mind these conditions, that the government was inclined toward neutrality. Furthermore, this neutrality would have to be "purchased." Italy's future attitude depended above all on the advantages she might derive from negotiation, which the Austro-Hungarian government, on the insistence of Germany, ended by accepting in principle in January of 1915.

The concerns and interests of the neutrals opened a whole field of action in the diplomacy of the belligerents, proliferating efforts and promises, correlated to the military, naval, or economic strength that each of these countries could muster. It is true that rival diplomatic activities were subordinate to the "war map," since, before undertaking any commitment, the neutrals weighed the chances of victory of one or the other ally. They were also subordinate to the map of nationalities, sometimes on account of geographical conditions that dominated economic life. Therefore diplomacy was conducted within fairly narrow confines. A bait would be proffered to a neutral government by pointing out the territorial advantage guaranteed if it were to participate in a victorious war; influence would be exerted on the press to create a current in public opinion capable of swaying that government's decision. More often than not, these negotiations with neutral governments involved delicate diplomatic conversations between members of rival coalitions who had difficulty in agreeing among themselves over the advantages they might have to offer.

Indeed, the Scandinavian states, absolutely determined to remain neutral, solicited attention from the belligerents only when they were able to play a role in the "economic war." It was to Germany's advantage to respect this neutrality, for she could thus benefit from gaps in the blockade, and the Allies thought they would be able to close these gaps by diplomatic means. The two Iberian countries were too far from military operations for their presence at the conference table to be solicited at the outbreak of the war: the British government thought it was hardly worth accepting a meeting suggested by Portugal, her old ally. Interest was therefore centered around the Balkan states. The role played by Bulgaria and Greece might be important when it came to deciding the nature of operations undertaken against Serbia by the Austro-Hungarian army. The attitude of Turkey and Rumania might influence the operations on the Russian front. But this interest also centered around Italy, the only major neutral power whose intervention would impose on Austria-Hungary the burdens and dangers of war on two fronts. Diplomatic maneuvers remained intimately linked to the strategy of a war of coalition.

World-Wide Prospects

The European conflict opened new prospects throughout the world, not only because economic warfare endangered the interests of the largest neutral power, the United States, but also because the struggle being waged between the European powers had paralyzed their expansion in other continents.

The economic, financial, and demographic conditions will suffice to explain the decline of this influence. It became practically impossible to export manufactured goods from France, because the whole of her industry was mobilized for war purposes; the same was true in Germany on account of the blockade; only England's export market remained active, though somewhat curtailed, because her textile industry continued to work for foreign markets. The export of capital was suspended, for the belligerents were obliged to channel all their resources to finance the war. The mobilization of all men of active age almost completely eliminated emigration.

But it was not only the material nature of European expansion that was seriously restricted. White solidarity in black Africa, where in the past the whites had, despite rivalries among themselves, more often than not been united against the natives, was destroyed. The European colonies turned into a theater of operations, and the countries at war used native troops not only in colonial warfare but also in the battles of Europe. The religious missionaries were hardly aloof from national rivalries. In southeastern Asia—where European expansion had met with resistance from great ancient civilizations and, failing for the most part to penetrate the collective mentality, had imposed itself only through superior technology and maintained itself by force— European prestige, on account of this internal strife, was profoundly damaged. Finally, in Islam, Turkish propaganda advanced the slogan of a "holy war" against the Christians, in the hope of being able to provoke trouble in French North Africa, in Egypt and among Indian Muslims. This jolt to European influence offered possibilities to major powers in competition with Europe, just as it did to the peoples subject to colonial domination.

In America the immediate result of the European war was renewed interest in the possible success of the idea of Pan-Americanism. High circles in Washington were of the opinion that solidarity among nations of the New World should be achieved under the aegis of the United States government and to the advantage of its political, economic, and financial influence. During preceding years this design of domination had met with considerable success in Central America. However, in South America and in Mexico it met with serious resistance from both the public and political circles. Economic and financial conditions gave a focus to this resistance: the fact of European predominance in commerce and capital investments in all of South America; the presence in Mexico of British interests which, although largely exceeded by United States commercial interests, had nevertheless managed to retain enough power to counteract the policies of American business. Since the European countries were now engaged in a conflict absorbing all their strength, the field was left open to the United States. That the Panama Canal was incorporated on August 15, 1914, at the precise moment when the war broke out, was a coincidence of symbolic significance.

But the attitude of the United States toward the European war was far more important. If America decided to throw its strength onto the balance of power, it could, after the delay required for the creation of an army, play a decisive role. And yet this prospect was foreign to the ideas, sentiments, and traditions of the American people. Doubtless an important segment of the public, particularly in New England, would express its support for Great

Britain, and the violation of Belgian neutrality was certainly vehemently condemned by the majority of Americans. But why abandon the policy of isolation? Why renounce the precepts of Washington and Jefferson, who recommended keeping the United States out of European affairs? Abandonment of a line of conduct that had appeared wise for more than a century, and that had contributed to the development of American prosperity, would have to be considered necessary by both the public and the government. To begin with, United States political interests did not seem to be affected by the conflict between the great European powers. Also, the American public's first reaction was virtually to manifest a sense of affliction and "painful astonishment." The war was a trial for the whole of humanity because it unleashed violent instincts and threatened to shake the very foundations of contemporary civilization. This was also the opinion of President Wilson himself, who was convinced that the conflict would undo several centuries of civilization. The United States therefore wanted a speedy conclusion to the hostilities and sought an opportunity of promoting the re-establishment of peace. When on September 8, 1914, the President ordered a day of prayer for peace, he was responding to the current of public opinion.

And yet, even if these pacifist convictions suffice to explain the feelings of the average American, they were not the only motives behind government policy. The President, Secretary of State William Jennings Bryan, and Colonel House, personal adviser to Wilson, were convinced that a speedy peace, which would be a compromise peace, would be in the interests of the United States.

The main reason for this conviction was the fear of dissension among the American public. "The people of the United States are drawn from many nations, and chiefly from the nations now at war," wrote Wilson in his address on August 18, 1914. "It is natural and inevitable that there should be the utmost variety of sympathy and desire among them with regard to the issues and circumstances of the conflict. Some will wish one nation, others another, to succeed in the momentous struggle. It will be easy to excite passion . . ." Thus, the address recommended to all citizens that they should exhibit not only a "moral neutrality" but also impartiality, and that they not manifest a preference for one side or the other. In the same spirit the Secretary of State, with the full backing of Wilson, announced on August 15 that if the American banks offered loans to those countries at war, they would violate "the true spirit of neutrality." Bryan, who looked upon financial assistance as "the worst of all contrabands, because it commands everything else," commented in a letter to the President on the meaning of this advice: he said that if foreign loans were to be authorized, Americans would be subscribing to them according to their sympathies; thus, there would be groups of people among the population with a "pecuniary interest" in the victory of one or another of the belligerents; this would increase dissension among Americans; furthermore, the banks, in order to support the interests of the foreign country to whom they would have offered loans, would not fail to try to exert an influence on the press. How precarious, therefore, would be the neutrality of the United States!

This speedy peace would be all the more desirable in that the European conflict could in the long run affect United States interests in the world market. What would be the consequences if war were to end with the total victory of one of the coalitions? "If the Allies win," wrote Colonel House to the President on August 22, 1914, "it means largely the domination of Russia on the continent of Europe; and if Germany wins, it means the unspeakable tyranny of militarism for years to come." Such was the reaction of a liberal who feared above all the triumph of an authoritarian political regime. But was there not also reason to fear that Japan, at the expense of United States interests, would be able to profit from this European war to acquire a dominant position in the Far East?

Economic concerns did not seem to have any importance in these first reactions manifested by public opinion or by the United States government. And yet did not the United States command great resources of raw materials and foodstuffs which were necessary to the countries at war? Could she not consequently become the great provider of war matériel? Did not the European conflict offer the opportunity of prosperity to American producers and merchants? In fact, during the first three months of the war, these consequences were not yet evident. At that time the Europeans were convinced that the war would be a short one, and relied on their reserves. Further, since the British and French merchant fleets were involved in troop transportation, and the German merchant fleet had been immobilized by the blockade, there were insufficient means of maritime transport to maintain an active flow of commerce across the Atlantic. American exports to Europe, even raw cotton, were therefore very much reduced. The United States Congress, in order to appease the producers, decided that the government should buy and store five million bales of cotton, to be paid for out of the federal budget. At the same time European capitalists, who had made short-term investments in the United States, withdrew their funds; these withdrawals caused a devaluation of the dollar and of the pound sterling. Therefore, the first effect of the European war on the United States was economic and financial. Moreover, the majority of the general public and even leading economic circles did not as yet see the material advantages that American production might gain from the war. The banks therefore willingly accepted Bryan's suggestions.

However, by October of 1914, when it became evident that a long war was in sight, the economic factors of United States foreign policy were rapidly transformed. The belligerents—in fact only Great Britain and France, since Germany was paralyzed by the blockade—began to buy arms and munitions, raw materials (particularly cotton and copper, petroleum and foodstuffs) on the American market; and the rate of these purchases was to augment from month to month. In order to permit the Europeans to increase these purchases, and in order to avoid seeing them place part of their orders in other markets—Canada, Australia or Argentina—the major American banks deemed it necessary to extend them credit, because they would soon be unable to pay cash. These suggestions went contrary to Bryan's advice; however, they were urged on the President by Under Secretary of State Lansing. On October 24, 1914, Woodrow Wilson authorized

Lansing to inform the banks that the government saw no objection to extending bank credit to the belligerents in order to allow the settlement of commercial debts. This decision, which was to be completed and enlarged upon in 1915, marks a special step in United States policy toward the war in Europe. In the interest of economic prosperity those in power had permitted a financial tie to be in fact established with the countries at war.

At the same time the role of supplier that the United States assumed in the European war gave a whole new importance to the question of freedom of the seas. The citizens of the United States now had a direct interest in participating in the controversies and difficulties that the exercise of the blockade and the practice of submarine warfare caused the neutrals. They were now more or less exclusively tied to Great Britain and France both economically and financially. How could this practical situation fail to have political consequences? As soon as the United States became the supplier and the creditor of one of the coalitions at war, her neutrality could no longer remain impartial.

Japan found herself in a different situation, for the European war, whatever its outcome, offered nothing but profitable opportunities.

In her attempts at economic and political expansion on the Asian continent, she had found herself up against positions acquired by the great European powers. True, she succeeded in being treated by these powers as an equal: the international banking consortium—formed in 1913 in order to supply the young Chinese republic with the primary necessities for "modernizing" the administration, for equipping industries and for developing railroads—had granted a share to Japanese interests. But within this system Japan found herself surrounded by Europeans who were watching over her activities. During the course of the negotiations preliminary to the formation of the consortium, the "Westerners" had clearly demonstrated this to be their design.

These great European powers were now at odds with each other; they were temporarily unable to exploit the Chinese market. Here was an excellent opportunity for Japanese political and economic influence. Even between 1902 and 1905, Anglo-Russian antagonism in the Far East contributed to the first great Japanese successes. Needless to say, the European conflict offered even more favorable opportunities for territorial expansion. And the nascent Japanese industry, during this period when European competition was paralyzed, would doubtless have the opportunity to develop its exports to China and to acquire the upper hand in the exploitation of coal and iron ore deposits. From the moment the European war started, Tokyo was clearly aware of these possibilities. The Black Dragon Society, which comprised the most active partisans of political expansion, published a manifesto to the nation: "This is the most propitious moment for Japan to resolve the Chinese question. A more favorable occasion might not present itself for another thousand years."

The immediate goal was to gain possession of the "leased territory" owned by Germany since 1898 in the Bay of Kiao-Chou: Japan could acquire the naval base of Tsing-Tao and the rights or interests that the treaty of March 6, 1898, gave to the Germans in the Chinese province of Shantung. On August 8, 1914, the Japanese government, by invoking the Anglo-Japanese treaty of alliance signed in 1902 and renewed in 1911, offered Great Britain limited military and naval collaboration. Actually the Anglo-Japanese alliance stipulated only the common defense of holdings in the Far East and in India. Germany did not directly threaten either these interests or these rights. But the Japanese government had no other diplomatic excuse to give for intervening in the conflict between the European powers. The British cabinet thought it a mere pretext and preferred to turn down the offer: it considered Japanese intervention useless, and even annoying as being likely to provoke discontent in the United States, whose consequences would have to be borne by the Entente powers. But how was Japan to be prevented from carrying out her plans?

Thus these were the possibilities that were beginning to emerge by the autumn of 1914 and that were to influence the development of international relations during the course of the war. In this development, the political and economic aspects were closely and constantly linked with naval or military operations. One should therefore bear in mind the "war map" and the problems of strategy when examining the foreign policy decisions whose consequences in turn modified the balance of power.

The War in Europe
(August, 1914 – February, 1917)

After the failure of the German plan of operations in the autumn of 1914, the war remained European for thirty months. The colonial operations in Africa, the Japanese attack on the German naval base at Tsing-Tao, and the attempted Turkish assault on the Suez canal were merely incidents.

Despite the enormous efforts and sacrifices of the belligerent armies, from Gorlice to Verdun, from the Dardanelles and Salonika to the Somme, from Gorizia to Tarnopol, a "military decision" remained out of reach. The great neutral power, the United States, whose intervention could have weighed decisively on the balance of power, limited itself to being the supplier to one of the great coalitions. It was a role of considerable importance, since without these supplies Great Britain and France would not have been able to sustain their efforts. But this economic assistance did not seem sufficient even in the long run to give the two Western powers the means to win.

The longer the war continued, the more serious were the consequences for European interests in the other continents. In Latin America as well as in the Far East and the Ottoman empire, positions of long standing were threatened or overthrown.

These are the two aspects that the study of international relations must consider.

The New European Belligerents

The Germans held the initiative in military operations for eighteen months. Thus, the 1915 campaign was distinguished by the effort of the German army, assisted by that of Austria-Hungary, to defeat the Russian forces, which Britain and France were no longer able to support directly after Turkey's entry into the war. This offensive was conducted for five months, during which it could not be stopped by either the diversionary attempts of Russia's allies—the French offensives on Artois and Champagne and the Anglo-French attack on the Dardanelles—or by the entry of Italy into the war. The military results were considerable: the Russian army was obliged to abandon not only the part of Galicia it occupied in 1914 but the Lithuanian and Polish territories of the empire as well, losing thereby in dead, wounded, and prisoners more than 1,700,000 men—that is, almost half of its troops—and leaving a large part of its artillery in enemy hands. The Russian forces were unable to regain the offensive for months. However, no political advantage was obtained. The Czar remained faithful to his promises of alliance, despite three German attempts to enter into secret discussions. Having gained the cooperation of Bulgaria in order to settle the Serbian question within three weeks, the German high command resumed its efforts on the French front. In February 1916 the great offensive before Verdun began, which, according to Falkenhayn, would "bleed the French army white." He was able neither to take Verdun (although this was not his principal objective) nor to inflict on the French troops losses greater than his own.

Starting in July 1916, the Entente forces regained the initiative. For the first time they put into execution almost simultaneously a common plan of operations: the French offensive on the Somme, the Italian offensive on the Carso and the great effort of the Russian general, Brusilov. Their success was only partial, even though, in August, Rumania offered her assistance to what seemed the winning side. At the end of 1916, the outstanding aspect of the situation was the equilibrium of the opposing forces. Five times, however, in all the stages of this struggle, the intervention of new states acted to modify the respective strengths of the two coalitions. Why did these states yield to the entreaties of the belligerent powers?

Turkey was the first of these nations to come into line. The government of "Young Turks" headed by Enver Pasha had signed a secret treaty of alliance with Germany against Russia on August 2, 1914. On August 11, it had authorized the German cruisers *Goeben* and *Breslau,* pursued by the British fleet, to pass through the Dardanelles, which remained closed to English ships. On September 26 it had closed the straits to commercial navigation, which amounted to preventing the forwarding of war matériel anxiously awaited by the Russian armies. It had, however, put off its actual entry into the war. On November 1, 1914, it decided upon that step after three months of delay; it was convinced, no doubt, that the Ottoman empire had everything to fear from a Russian victory. Although in the past Great Britain had protected this empire from Russian ambitions, she would surely be obliged in this case to allow Russia freedom of action, lest the coalition be disrupted. On the other hand, a German victory would offer no threat to Ottoman interests, as Germany had not only contributed to the consolidation of the empire by constructing the Baghdad railway, but also had assumed a position in the world as protector of Islam.

Did not the Entente powers, however, seek to exploit the hesitation of the Ottoman government?

Actually the diplomacy of the Entente powers seemed rather halfhearted in this area. Only the British cabinet, fearing an attack on the Suez Canal, wished to obtain a promise of Turkish neutrality. In exchange for this promise, it would have agreed to a guarantee of Turkish territorial integrity, not only for the period of the war in Europe but for the future as well. Russian government circles were reluctant to accept such an agreement, because

they were unwilling to give up hope of one day gaining free access
to the sea, and the European war might offer the opportunity to
fulfill this hope. At the end of August, however, when the Russian
armies met defeat at Tannenberg in eastern Prussia, the Czar's
government agreed to align itself with British policy. With a German victory likely at that time, however, the Ottoman government
backed down. Ten days later the outcome of the battle of the Marne
and the failure of the Austro-Hungarian offensive in Galicia led
certain members of the Ottoman government to have doubts
about German victory. But Enver Pasha, convinced of Germany's
power, remained faithful to the commitments of his treaty of alliance. In cooperation with the German mission, he decided to present his colleagues with a *fait accompli* as a means of overcoming
their resistance. He ordered the bombardment of Odessa and
Sebastopol by the Ottoman fleet, whose two principal ships, the
Goeben and the *Breslau,* were former German cruisers now under
the Ottoman flag. This was a case in which the personal role of
a statesman was the deciding factor.

The intervention of Italy presents more difficult questions for
the historical interpreter. In October of 1914 the government of
Salandra had seemed inclined to follow the policy proposed by
Giolitti—that is, one of "purchased" neutrality. It had therefore
attempted to enter into negotiations with Austria-Hungary to obtain the peaceful relinquishment of Trentino and, in January of
1914, was anticipating success in this effort. But the government
circles of the Dual Monarchy were afraid that by yielding to the
claims of Italy they would be encouraging others, especially the
claims of Rumania over Transylvania. As soon as Austria-Hungary
backed down, the Italian government made contact with the
Entente powers at the beginning of March 1915, trying to find
out what advantages would be promised if Italy decided to enter
the war. Informed of these preliminary negotiations by the Italians
themselves, Vienna agreed to enter into discussions.

For one month Italian diplomats bargained with both sides.
What was the outcome by the middle of April 1915? If Italy
decided to enter into the war against Austria-Hungary, she would

gain not only those territories of the Dual Monarchy inhabited by Italian-speaking peoples but also the Upper Adige valley inhabited by Germans, that part of Istria with a Slavic population, and half of the Dalmatian coast. She might also occupy the port of Vallona and the islet of Sasseno off the coast of Albania, thus commanding the northern entrance of the Otrante Channel. Finally, if the Ottoman empire were broken up, she would receive the region of Adalia, upon which she had fixed her sights in the beginning of 1914; and, should the German colonies be divided up, some "compensations" might be added to the territories of Libya or Eritrea. She was able to obtain these promises easily enough, since the Entente occupied enemy territories. Only the question of the Dalmatian coast gave rise to some resistance on the part of Russia, who was concerned about the protection of Serbian interests. The fulfillment of these pledges, however, would of course depend upon an effective contribution to victory.

If, on the other hand, Italy were to deal with Austria-Hungary, she might obtain, as the price of her neutrality, the Trentino and the Italian Veneto along with Gorizia, the establishment of Trieste as an autonomous territory within the framework of the Dual Monarchy, and freedom of action in Albania and in the Dodecanese in the Aegean. She would not, however, get the Brenner border region, or the Slavic regions of Istria, or the Dalmatian shoreline, whose towns were largely inhabited by Italians, or the prospect of territorial expansion into Anatolia or in the colonial area.

The greatest difference between the two solutions concerned the Adriatic. If Italy possessed neither Trieste nor Istria nor the Dalmatian coast, she would be unable to gain a dominant position in that sea.

The Italian government therefore concluded that a "purchased" neutrality would not suffice to fulfill Italy's national aspirations as she saw them. On April 26, 1915, the government signed the Treaty of London in secret with the Entente powers: in this it committed itself to go to war against Austria-Hungary in one month's time, in consideration of the promises that had been made to it. However, when on May 3 the government denounced the Treaty of

the Triple Alliance, a vigorous opposition was set up by the "neu-
tralists." Why go to war at the very moment when Austria-Hungary
was prepared to give almost complete satisfaction to the claims
of Italian irredentism? At Montecitorio, citadel of neutralism, the
parliamentary majority expressed its continued adherence to
Giolitti's policy, provoking on May 13 the resignation of Salandra.
The reaction in Rome, Milan, Turin, and Florence was violent,
both in the press and in the streets, with cries not only of "Viva
la guerra!" but also of "War of revolution!" The King, himself a
partisan of the policy of intervention, pointed to this wave of
opinion when refusing Salandra's resignation. Parliament thereupon yielded, voting the credits needed for the mobilization of the
armed forces.

What was the significance of these spirited moments? In abandoning the policy of "purchased" neutrality at the very moment
when it seemed about to bear fruit, and in opting for participation in the war, Salandra and his Minister of Foreign Affairs,
Sonnino, were motivated by their Adriatic strategy. This design
could be fulfilled only by armed intervention. But was this hegemony in the Adriatic worth the sacrifices and risks of war, a war
that even the most ardent supporters of armed intervention were
aware would require a considerable effort? It is therefore per-
missible to conclude that the decision of the Italian government
was influenced by another factor: would Austria-Hungary, once
victorious, keep the promises she had made at the hour of her
life-or-death struggle?

What is surprising is the support given to these political calculations by a wave of public opinion. Since the irredentist claims
could apparently be satisfied by an agreement with Austria-
Hungary, why did "the people" demand an action that went
beyond the traditional aims of Italian national sentiment and involved not only great risks but immediate consequences whose
price these people were to pay on the battlefield?

This outburst—which was not really a mass movement, since
the rural population played almost no part in it—found its principal supporters not only among the young intellectuals, professors, and petty officials, but also among large segments of the

working class. In Milan, for example, when the "official" Socialist party and the Central Trade Union attempted to oppose the policy of intervention by ordering a general strike, their appeal went unanswered. What motive impelled these advocates of war? First, there was the desire to "resolve the national problem" and to achieve Italian unity. This was the argument that the "interventionist" journalists invoked in a manifesto published on May 14. But they were also caught up in a movement of great passion, by the "furious and magnificent" accents of Mussolini's articles in the *Popolo d'Italia* where he denounced the "flabbiness" of the middle class, which wished to play the "comedy of being a great power" without taking the risks, and begged his countrymen not to "act like feeble old men." He preached that it was their duty to "make history." They were caught up also in the conviction that Italy must not, as D'Annunzio told them, consent to be merely a "museum, an inn, a summer resort," and in the desire to show the world that the Italian nation was still capable of great sacrifice. It was this spirited awakening of the collective consciousness that swept away the vacillations of the parliament.

The intervention of Bulgaria came about through an entirely different set of circumstances. The government at Sofia, even if given the opportunity to be paid for its neutrality, was not inclined to follow this path. When on May 23, 1915—three days after the Italian vote for war credits—the anxious Austro-Hungarian government offered to let Bulgaria, in return for remaining neutral, acquire Serbian Macedonia at the end of the war, King Ferdinand refused this proposition that seemed to him illusory: if the Serbian government, discouraged by the Entente's promises to Italy, indicated its readiness to conclude a separate peace with the Central Powers, Austro-Hungarian diplomacy would quickly forget its commitments to Bulgaria. Given the situation of the Balkan peninsula, the only real hope that Bulgaria might have to fulfill its national aspirations was to take part in the general conflict.

There was little doubt about which camp she would join. The Entente powers in May of 1915 could give but one firm promise: If Bulgaria went to war against Turkey, she would recover

Adrianople and the part of Thrace that she had conquered in 1912 and then lost in 1913. Other possibilities were offered only under certain conditions: part of Greek Macedonia with Cavalla if Greece obtained compensatory territory in Asia Minor after the war; a part of Serbian Macedonia if Serbia received "equitable compensations" at the expense of Austro-Hungarian territories in Bosnia-Herzegovina and Dalmatia. No doubt Great Britain and France would have gone further by promising *all* of Serbian Macedonia, but they were unable to overcome the resistance of Belgrade. The Central Powers, on the other hand, had more tempting bait, since they could offer the immediate occupation of all of Serbian Macedonia and would even obtain from Turkey a broad correction of the Thracian frontier in Bulgaria's favor. Thus Austro-German diplomacy was warmly received at Sofia. The chief obstacle encountered in Bulgarian parliamentary circles was offered in the name of Pan-Slavic solidarity—a solidarity with which the sovereign, a Coburg, was unable to feel any sympathy. The heads of the political opposition—Stamboliski, Guechov, and Danev —who remained in close contact with the czarist legation, refused to consider a break with Russia which had in 1878 been responsible for the creation of Bulgaria. But this opposition was not based solely upon religious and cultural affinities; it laid stress also on Russia's might and on the risk that Bulgaria would run in opposing her.

The pace of military operations put an end to this hesitation. The summer campaign of 1915 on the eastern front seemed to forebode a complete defeat of the Russian army. King Ferdinand's government had therefore nothing to fear in the way of Russian reprisals. On September 6, 1915, as German armies encircled Vilno, the King came to terms with the Central Powers. On September 21, as they reached the Berezina, he gave the mobilization order. Bulgarian policy was dictated here more as a function of the "war map" than by the personal calculation of the King.

The position of Greece was in large part determined by circumstances of domestic politics tied to dynastic interests. It was King Constantine's understanding that foreign relations were his own concern and not that of his ministers. He deemed it imprudent for the Greek state to embark upon a course of "expansionism," and, as brother-in-law of Kaiser Wilhelm and an alumnus of the Prussian War Academy, was convinced of the eventual triumph of the German empire. The President of the Council, Venizelos, was of Cretan origin and, as such, had been and remained a partisan of Greece's "grand concept": that is, to oppose resolutely any Bulgarian claims upon Cavalla, to extend Greek territory at the expense of the Ottoman empire into the Aegean area and Asia Minor, to participate in the control of the Dardanelles, perhaps even to reconstitute a Greek empire extending to Constantinople. These were the aims he more or less pursued, or at least envisioned. He hoped to realize them with the cooperation of Great Britain and perhaps of France, although certainly not of Russia. He was not displeased by the differences between his personal views and those of the King, since he hoped to force the monarch to yield to the will of his ministers and to practice parliamentary democracy, and felt that these questions of foreign politics would offer a favorable ground on which to seek national support. This conflict of ideas and personalities was marked by bold moves and sudden changes of direction.

At the beginning of March 1915, when Great Britain and France were seeking to force the Dardanelles in order to regain contact with Russia, Venizelos proposed that Greece offer military assistance. The King, however, refused to approve this offer and forced the President of the Council to resign. By the end of September, Venizelos was returned to power. With the mobilization of Bulgaria, he declared himself prepared to come to the aid of Serbia, provided that France and Great Britain send an expeditionary force into the Balkans. On October 2 he secretly authorized the debarkation of this expeditionary force at Salonika, although Greece was still neutral. On October 5 he finally gained parliamentary approval for Greece's entry into war against Bulgaria. At this point, however, he was forced once more by the King to step down. The accomplished fact could nonetheless not be denied. King Constantine did not dare oppose this violation of Greek neutrality, although he made no secret of the fact that he would

gladly have done so if he had had the power. The security of
Anglo-French forces was thus endangered, since the territory of
neutral Greece could harbor an enemy force directed against
them. General Sarrail, commander of the expeditionary force,
persistently emphasized this danger and insisted that the King
of Greece be deposed.

In the Autumn of 1916 the Western powers in fact gave their
support to a Greek "National" government formed by Venizelos
at Salonika. In order to avert any hostile actions, France and
Great Britain set up a blockade against Greece, gained control
of her communications and attempted to secure the disarmament
of the Greek army. In December the French command contemplated forcing the King to abdicate and forming a republican
"Venizelist" government. This was the solution that prevailed in
June of 1917, when the French government had obtained, not
without difficulty, the consent of Great Britain and sent Jonnart
to Athens as high commissioner. The latter proceeded to act without awaiting the explicit assent of Russia and Italy.

In this case—as in that of Bulgaria—strategy was the determining factor. In an attempt to rescue Serbia, threatened by
Bulgarian attack, and to maintain a "bridgehead" that might
eventually prove useful, France and Great Britain decided to
open a Balkan theater of operations and to establish supply bases
for their troops on Greek territory. In so doing, they were obliged
to make a mockery of Greek neutrality and to put into power
the politician who would offer them the guarantees they required.
In these political maneuverings, the feelings of the Greek people
played no appreciable role.

Rumania's entry into the war was, on the other hand, a decision
made freely by a government whose head, Bratianu, dominated
the parliament. Since the death of King Carol in October 1914
and the accession of his nephew Ferdinand, he controlled the
Crown as well.

The conditions then necessary for national unification determined the orientation of Rumanian policy. An Austro-Hungarian
defeat could lead to the "liberation" of the Rumanian populations

of Transylvania, Bukovina, and Banat—some three million persons —whereas a Russian defeat could allow at the most the liberation of the Bessarabian Rumanians. The Rumanian state thus seemed destined to play a role on the side of the Entente. To forestall this eventuality, the Austro-Hungarian government could have, of course, contemplated "buying" Rumanian neutrality by ceding territory in Bukovina and the Banat of Temesvar as well as by declaring an autonomous status for the Transylvanian Rumanians. Germany insisted vigorously upon these concessions several times, but the authorities in Vienna, and especially in Budapest, refused to take such a course. The President of the Hungarian Council, Stefan Tisza, whose strong personality dominated the foreign policy of the Dual Monarchy, was absolutely opposed to such dealings with Rumania. Should Rumania go to war on the side of the Central Powers, he was prepared at the most to cede the southern portion of Bukovina—but nothing more.

This left the way entirely open to the Entente. Nothing could be easier than to promise the Rumanians the annexation of vast Austro-Hungarian territories—in the future. Nonetheless, the negotiations stalled for eighteen months. Was Rumanian public opinion the cause of this delay? Actually the military situation was at the bottom of it. The Rumanian government did not wish to enter the European conflict until the armies of the Entente seemed assured of victory. This is why it ignored the most pressing entreaties during the summer of 1915, a critical period for the Russian armies. In the summer of 1916, however, it appeared disposed to open serious negotiations, just when the German army found itself undergoing a "battle of attrition" on the Somme, and Austria-Hungary was caught up in a great Russian offensive in Galicia and Bukovina and on the Isonzo front with the Italians. The negotiations were delayed once again by disagreements between the French and Russian general staffs: the French wished to set the Rumanians against Bulgaria, and the Russians wished to set them against Austria-Hungary. In the end Bratianu made the decision: he set aside the French plan, since he wished above all to settle the Transylvania question by armed force.

The treaty of alliance and military convention signed on August 17, 1916, accorded full satisfaction to all Rumanian claims. When on August 27 the chief minister brought his policy before the Crown Council for approval, he used as his decisive argument the general military situation: "A war of attrition reverses the odds in favor of those who have the strongest reserves."

However, in its anxiety to obtain the most favorable conditions on paper, the Rumanian government waited too long to choose sides: it had let go by the most difficult hour, militarily, for the Central Powers. Since the middle of August the Italian and Russian offensives ceased, while the French offensive on the Somme had run out of steam. The German high command, to which Hindenburg and Ludendorff had recently been summoned, was able to pick up from the other theaters of operations the reinforcements needed by the Austro-Hungarians and Bulgarians. In November of 1916 these German divisions forced through the Carpathian passes and decided the fate of Rumania. In two months she was almost entirely overrun by the enemy.

In all these cases, the diplomacy of the belligerent powers was of only secondary importance. They simply exploited, in a more or less shrewd manner, circumstances whose causes were essentially beyond their power to manipulate. The governments of those states that decided to intervene acted almost always from political motives: a desire to fulfill national aspirations by liberating populations under foreign domination, or a desire to reinforce the might or the prestige of the state and to prevent any modification of the balance of power that might detract from it. In evaluating these motives, should one attribute the predominant role to the leadership of an individual or to "public opinion"? The peasant masses of the Balkans were passive. Only the cultured and the urban bourgeoisie expressed an opinion. Neither in Turkey nor in Bulgaria nor in Greece did this segment of the population voice its opinion. It was the government, rather, that used propaganda to form a public opinion that would support its position. In Rumania the expression of national feeling among the people seemed more spontaneous, although it would be difficult to assess its real influence. Excepting in Italy, where a wave of popular opinion on the part of the urban population gave a decided impetus to the course of events, the calculations of the politicians were the moving force.

By the end of 1916 none of these interventions had brought any decisive military results. Turkey's entry into the war hindered Russia's efforts by cutting off the route through which she most easily received war matériel. She was unable, however, to compel Russia to cease fighting and could not even prevent the Czar's armies from undertaking a new offensive in the summer of 1915. The Bulgarian government's decision resulted in the total occupation of Serbian territory, but the Serbian army, reconstituted at Corfu, found its place once more on Balkan battlefields alongside the English and French troops of the eastern army. The Rumanian army's campaign, which had engendered high hopes among the Entente powers, ended in disaster. The pressure applied on Greece to force its participation had in actuality only the limited goal of safeguarding the rear of the eastern army. Even though the Italian intervention more seriously modified the balance of power and eased the situation of the Russian armies during the summer of 1915, it resulted in but a single victory, the taking of Gorizia, which in the end was of little consequence.

However, the commitments the great opposing powers made to these newcomers in order to persuade them to enter the war crippled future diplomatic action, because they set up new obstacles to the search for a compromise peace with one of the enemy states. The Central Powers, who were contemplating the possibility of a separate peace with Russia, were impeded in their attempts by the decision they had taken in the Balkans in order to bring Turkey and Bulgaria into their camp. Fulfillment of the promises the Entente Powers gave to Italy and Rumania presupposed the total defeat and dismantling of Austria-Hungary, which limited the area of possible negotiations. The commitments undertaken by both coalitions had this same effect as far as war aims were concerned. In March of 1915, France and Great Britain yielded to the urgent entreaties of their ally Russia and agreed that after their common victory Russia might annex Constantinople, eastern

Thrace, the European shore of the Bosporus and the Dardanelles, as well as "part of the Asian shore." In March 1916 they set up a plan for dividing up the Asian territories of the Ottoman empire. In February 1917, France allowed Russia to fix her western borders where she would on the conditions that the coal-bearing Saar Valley become French and that the German territories on the left bank of the Rhine be detached from the empire and become an "autonomous and neutralized" state. Germany and Austria-Hungary, whose armies had occupied all of Poland since the autumn of 1915, announced in November of 1916 that they would re-establish an independent Polish state at the end of the war. This proclamation was issued in the hope of encouraging a flood of volunteers in occupied Poland. This hope soon faded, but once more the promise limited the prospects of negotiating a separate peace with Russia. Furthermore, Germany, by asserting her right to ascendancy over occupied Belgium, closed the door upon any attempts to establish secret diplomatic contacts with Great Britain.

The political program of both camps remained annexationist, in spite of the stalemate that seemed to prevail on the battlefield and the seeming inability of either coalition to seize the advantage.

The Decline of European Influence in the World

As the war went on, the possibilities it gave rise to in the relations between the continents were more sharply defined. In China, in western Asia, in Latin America, the political, economic, and even intellectual positions long held by the Europeans were tottering. In the Far East the Japanese threatened to compete with European interests. Japan had at first acted solely against German interests. The Japanese government had declared war on August 23, 1914. On November 7 it had obtained the surrender of Tsing-Tao and occupied the leased territory of Kiao-Chou. It did not intend to take part in the conflict between the great European powers, and it had at no point envisaged sending an expeditionary force to Europe, despite the fact that the French press and even the French Foreign Minister were anticipating its arrival. The

Japanese attitude toward the European war had been clearly and publicly enunciated on November 19, 1914, by the Japanese Minister of Foreign Affairs, Baron Kato. "If we have been obliged to fight against Germany, it is because we wish to maintain peace in the Orient. What necessity is there to send Japanese troops to Europe, if we have no direct interest there relating to the security of our country and peace in the Orient?" In Japanese government circles, however, this "peace" in the Far East meant an eastern Asia subordinated to Japanese hegemony. China's political as well as economic independence was thus threatened even more crucially than by European expansion between 1895 and 1913. At the same time the positions held by the Entente powers were equally threatened, for although Japan was theoretically their ally, at war against Germany, she was basically their rival.

The extent of Japan's ambitions became clear in January of 1915 when the head of the Chinese government, General Yuan Chi-kai—nominally president of the republic but in effect dictator since autumn of 1913—received a Japanese diplomatic note which formulated twenty-one demands. The Japanese government declared itself willing to restore to China, at the end of the European war, the formerly German-leased territory that it had taken over— on condition that it received another leased territory at some other point on the coast. This restitution would take place, however, only upon the prior fulfillment of a whole series of conditions. Japan claimed economic advantages, assuring her a "sphere of influence," in three Chinese provinces: Feng-tien, or southern Manchuria; Shantung; and Honan, the region directly to the north of Hankow, the commercial center of China's interior. In southern Manchuria, where she already possessed the main railroad line and most of its branches and also leased the territory of Port Arthur, these concessions were to last for ninety-nine years instead of twenty-five. Furthermore, Japanese subjects, including Koreans, would be permitted to acquire land and thus effect its colonization. In Shantung, Japan would inherit the advantages accorded to Germany in March 1898—railway and mining concessions—besides the leased territory. She would receive as well the right to construct and exploit new railroads. In Honan the deposits of iron ore at

Han-Yeh-Ping, in which Japanese capital already had an interest, were to be exploited by a Sino-Japanese corporation. Furthermore, the Chinese government was to promise never again to transfer or concede any part whatsoever of its coastline to a third power without the consent of Japan. This precaution taken against the European states was in line with a priority accorded to the Japanese in Fukien, opposite Formosa. Finally came the demands contained in the "fifth group" of the note. The Chinese government must permit the collaboration of "Japanese advisers" in its political and financial services as well as in the army, the presence of Japanese officials in the upper echelons of the police, and the opening of Japanese schools. In short, a set of requirements that seemed designed to institute an embryonic protectorate. The Japanese government, in its instructions to its ambassador at Peking, did, however, allow that the application of the "fifth group" might be deferred.

Yuan Chi-kai argued earnestly, supported by a wave of public opinion, but what could he do? Not only was he unprepared to offer effective armed resistance, but he also feared the consequences that such a conflict might inflict upon his political regime. The Japanese government threatened to support the Chinese political refugees living on its soil who were struggling against Yuan's dictatorship.

The effectiveness of Chinese resistance would depend basically on the support that the great powers might offer. The Chinese government placed its only hope in these powers.

The German government, although in a state of war with Japan, seemed prepared to encourage the Japanese demands. If the Japanese authorities concerned themselves deeply in Chinese affairs, would this not more certainly guarantee that they would not send an expeditionary force to Europe? The Entente powers were also distracted by their immediate preoccupations and did not maintain a coherent attitude (Mr. Mario Toscano's studies have well demonstrated this). The French government, engaged in a struggle for its existence, scarcely had the leisure to concern itself with the Far East question. French economic interests, almost entirely concentrated in the south of China, were not, moreover, directly threatened by the "twenty-one demands." The Russian government was more concerned because of its interests in northern Manchuria. It feared above all the possible consequences of the "fifth group." In a note addressed to Tokyo, Great Britain, whose predominance in Chinese economy was directly threatened, protested against the scope of the Japanese demands. The cabinet, however, aware of its impotence, carefully refrained from offering the slightest promise to Yuan; it did not even wish to commit itself to giving financial assistance to China in the event of a Sino-Japanese war. In fact, only the United States would have been in a position to act in any useful way. The tone of the note addressed by the American government to that of Japan on March 13, 1915, was actually quite mild: it demanded that Japan drop the clauses tending to infringe on the "independence, the integrity, and the commerical freedom" of China. It added, however, that the United States had no intention of urging Yuan to resist and was not "jealous of Japan's pre-eminence" in the Far East. It is true that the pressure of American diplomatic communications increased toward the end of April, but they did not assume a menacing tone. At no point could Yuan foresee the possibility of armed assistance from the United States. So that when, on May 7, 1915, he found himself confronted by a Japanese ultimatum, supported by troop movements in Manchuria and a fleet off the coast of central China, he resigned himself to yielding. He was, however, successful in persuading the Japanese to set aside, at least temporarily, the provisions of the "fifth group." The outcome of these events is recorded in the Sino-Japanese agreements of May 24, 1915.

If the Japanese government consented to abandon part of its program, it did so no doubt because it feared that by going too far it would cause the American government to react more energetically. Moreover, it did not have unanimous parliamentary backing for its action. The most energetic partisans of an expansionist policy in China were restrained by the resistance of the Diet whose dominant party, the *Seiyukai,* represented the business community. This group considered it unnecessary and imprudent to attempt to impose on China a sort of military and political control by means of war, while it was possible to obtain without war the economic advantages that would fulfill Japan's needs. Instead of continuing along these lines, would it not be better to content themselves with their already considerable success, rather than risk turning the Chinese leaders against Japan? These objections had been clearly formulated in the course of debate in the Diet, as the delivery of an ultimatum had aroused severe criticism. The cabinet had nonetheless sent the threatening note, although it partially took into account the views of the opposition.

What was the outcome of this Japanese policy? No doubt the agreement of May 24, 1915, opened virtually unlimited prospects. But the coin had two sides. The essential fact was that a national reaction appeared for the first time in Chinese "public opinion"— that is, among the intellectuals, the students, and the merchants of the big cities and free ports. The press, led by the English-language Chinese papers, viewed the signing of the agreement as an "intolerable humiliation." The Chinese chamber of commerce of Peking preached resistance to the spread of Japanese influence, which, if successful, would lead to "national ruin." For several months the merchants' associations boycotted Japanese goods. This was a precise confirmation of those fears voiced by the business group in the Japanese Diet. The Japanese government was therefore uncertain of the future, especially as it was distrustful of the possible reaction of the United States.

As a result Japanese diplomacy wished to assure itself at least of the acquiescence of the European powers. It succeeded easily, thanks to the vicissitudes of the war in Europe. In July of 1916 the Czar's government—much in need of Japanese industry for supplying its troops with arms and ammunition, and having been obliged to transfer its Siberian garrisons to the European theater— agreed to sign a pact with the Tokyo government calling for cooperation in the Far East. The two states, by common agreement, were to take all measures that might become necessary "to safeguard China from the domination of a third power." This precaution was taken by Japan not only against an aggressive return of Germany, which, if victorious in Europe, would wish to recover her territory of Kiao-Chou, but also against the contingency of American intervention in Chinese affairs. In this collaboration with Russia, Japanese public opinion found an important support for its designs on China. In February and March of 1917, Great Britain and France in turn gave evidence of their good will. Hoping to receive the aid of Japanese battleships in broadening the struggle against Germany's submarine warfare, the two Western nations promised the Japanese government that at the peace conference they would support its claims to the German Pacific archipelagoes and to German rights and interests in Shantung. Here was one more precaution taken by the Japanese against American pressure.

In short, forced by the exigencies of the war in Europe, the three Entente powers undertook commitments whose clearest result was to thwart any resistance the United States might offer to Japanese pre-eminence in the Far East.

In the Middle East, where German political activity, so intense before 1914, was now paralyzed, and where American economic or financial interests were insignificant at that time, the Entente powers were making important preparations for the future. Two strategies dictated their political choices: the desire to neutralize the Ottoman government, now an ally of the Central Powers, which was capable of directing a military action either against the Suez Canal and Egypt or against Russia along the Caucasus frontier; and the necessity to establish a route across Persian territory, by which war supplies destined for Russia might be forwarded during the winter months when naval convoys were unable to get to Russia's northern ports of Arkhangelsk and Murmansk.

Their immediate concern was to encourage the revolt of the various "nationalities" against Ottoman domination. While the Russians pursued this policy among the Armenian peoples, the British made use of Arab nationalism, the first signs of which had become apparent as early as 1840, and which had intensified since 1904. Even in 1913 the British High Commissioner in Egypt, Lord Kitchener, had made contact with the heads of this movement. In March of 1915 the British government began to consider the formation of "a Moslem political entity" which would be independent of the Sultan and would be centered upon the holy cities of Islam. The aim of the secret negotiations in July of 1915, with Hussein, Sherif of Mecca, was to determine the extent of this state, which would reach the Persian Gulf to the east, including within its borders Mesopotamia and the Syrian interior, although not the coastal region of Beirut and Alexandretta. The declaration of independence made in July of 1916 was of much greater significance than the hostilities in which Turks and Arabs were engaged around the holy cities. The rupture of Moslem unity was indeed an important advantage to the Entente powers.

In Persia, where Great Britain and Russia had imposed their economic, financial, and political influence since 1907, Turkish entry into the war had encouraged the nationalist opposition that had been trying to resist this European exploitation. In the legislative assembly numerous "democratic" deputies made no secret of their desire to throw in their lot with the Turks and consequently with Germany. To preclude this risk, Russian troops marched on Teheran during the summer of 1915, placing the Shah's government under their direct control. Meanwhile the nationalist leaders fled to the region nearest the Turkish border, where they established a provisional government. For almost two years thereafter, the entire central part of Persia remained exposed to the strikes of the nationalists and their Turkish allies. Only in the spring of 1917 did the concerted action of British and Russian troops assure the domination of the Entente in Persia. It remained for the Russian Revolution to endanger this situation soon afterward.

This policy of the Entente, so suited to immediate necessities, was to give rise to difficulties on the morrow. The impetus the British gave the Arab movement was to be turned against European interests in 1919 and 1920, and Iranian nationalism was to be reinforced by foreign occupation.

The repercussions of the war in Europe were felt the most strongly in Latin America, especially in the areas of economics and finances. All the nations increased their exports as a result of the tremendous rise in orders from European buyers. In Argentina, a great supplier of meat, grains and raw wool to Europe, the volume of exports climbed from 502,000,000 gold pesos in the last normal year before the war to 900,000,000 in 1918-1919. Imports from Europe, however, were rapidly declining because industrial mobilization and the lack of maritime transport rendered Great Britain and France unable to ship sufficient quantities of coal, textiles, metallurgical products, and construction materials and equipment. They also stopped supplying investment capital, although previously its influx, particularly heavy between 1910 and 1913, had given a strong impetus to the economic life of these countries. The United States moved in to occupy in part the place previously held by Europeans in these markets. Her trade with Latin America rose from $814,000,000 in 1913 to $2,332,000,000 in 1919. From 1911 to 1913 Argentina, for example, purchased more than 30 per cent of its imports from Great Britain and only 15 per cent from the United States. In the years 1917 to 1919 the English share dropped to 23 per cent, while the American share reached 35 per cent. Unable to look to the London market, the Argentine government turned to the United States to float its bond issues. This example was followed by Bolivia and the large cities of Colombia and Chile. Nor must we ignore the efforts exerted by New York banks. In 1915 the National City Bank opened agencies in Buenos Aires, Montevideo, Río de Janeiro, São Paulo, Bahía, and Caracas. The Guaranty Trust installed itself in Argentina, and the Mercantile Bank set up branches in Peru and Venezuela.

In Central America the United States was not satisfied merely to take advantage of opportunities that might enhance her economic and financial influence but utilized this influence to exert political pressure.

In 1913, at the time of the Mexican civil war, Great Britain had pledged her support to President Huerta, who favored British petroleum interests, whereas the United States supported the insurrectionist government of Carranza. President Wilson's policy of armed intervention succeeded in bringing about the resignation of Huerta in July of 1914. As soon as Carranza took power in September of 1914, however, he was beset by insurrections. The principal leader of these rebellious movements, General Villa, criticized the President for his complacency toward the presence of foreign economic and financial interests, namely those of United States citizens. This new civil war paralyzed the exploitation of mineral and petroleum deposits. To put an end to it, President Wilson sent

off an expeditionary force under General Pershing in the spring
of 1916, with orders to "capture Villa." Carranza himself protested,
since he would have lost all authority over the Mexicans if he had
accepted this armed intervention. Although the expeditionary force
remained on Mexican soil for one year, the pressure exerted by the
American government was fruitless, because it basically went
against the national sentiment of the Mexican people. How could
this situation be resolved? In Congress, Senator Falk, spokesman
for the great oil interests, demanded the "complete occupation" of
Mexico. This would, however, have entailed a war—a dangerous
risk at the very time when the United States had to watch over
events in Europe.

Between 1910 and 1914 the great New York banks had invested
large amounts of capital in the republic of Haiti, following the
methods of dollar diplomacy. The Europeans also were owed considerable sums, however, since the Haitian loans had all been floated
in Paris, London or Berlin. President Wilson had already considered establishing a "sphere of influence" in June 1914, in order
to bar the way to a possible British or German move against the
island republic. The war in Europe encouraged this policy. The
projected financial convention formulated by Washington provided
for United States control over tariff policy and the collection of
customs duties. The Haitian government resigned itself to accepting
the convention in September 1916. Meanwhile, taking advantage
of revolutionary incidents on the island, the United States sent a
landing force to occupy the capital. The convention of September
16, 1915, included, in addition to the terms of the original agreement, stipulations relative to the economic development and political control of the republic. The exploitation of natural resources
was to be directed by American engineers, and the police were to
be staffed by American officers. The convention conferred on the
United States the right of intervention with a view toward "maintaining the independence" of the Haitian republic and to ensure
the existence of a government capable of "protecting the lives,
property, and individual liberty" of its citizens and of foreigners
residing there. In short, a quasi protectorate was established.

Although he had declared in October 1913 that a foreign policy based chiefly upon the protection of "material interests" was a dangerous one, Woodrow Wilson continued nonetheless to practice dollar diplomacy in the Caribbean, which the United States dominated politically and strategically, and from which it intended to eliminate European financial influence.

This was, however, only one aspect of the question, and undoubtedly not the most important. Of greater consequence was the surge of vitality that the European war imparted to the entire economic life of the United States. Exports increased in volume from $329,000,000 in 1914 to $2,716,000,000 in 1915 and to $4,272,000,000 in 1916. The surplus in balance of payments, which had been $435,000,000 in 1914, reached $1,042,000,000 in 1915 and $2,674,000,000 in 1916. The influx of orders brought about a considerable increase in industrial production and an enlargement of the area given over to the cultivation of cereals, as well as an increase in prices. The production of wheat, for example, climbed from 763,000,000 bushels in 1914 to 1,025,000,000 in 1915, with the price increasing from 89 cents to $1.66. The production of steel nearly doubled between 1914 and 1917, while that of petroleum increased by 27 per cent. National income valued at $33,200,000,000 in 1914 rose to $45,400,000,000 in 1916: an increase of about $12,000,000,000 in two years, whereas in the course of the four years preceding the war the increase did not exceed $5,000,000,000. The effects of this unprecedented boom were felt not only in the metallurgical industries (the sale of war matériel represented only 28 per cent of exports destined for Great Britain and France), but in the production of raw materials and agricultural products as well.

Thus began the decline of Europe's role in the world. Economic circles in both Tokyo and New York were aware of the significance of this decline. In Europe, where attention was focused on the vicissitudes of war—even among the remaining neutrals—it passed almost unnoticed.

At the end of 1916 the military efforts of the two clashing coalitions began to weaken. At the same time their economic difficulties were growing more acute. The shortage of food and raw materials was felt the most in Germany, although the conquest of Rumania brought some hope of alleviation. However, it was also felt by the urban populations in Russia and even in France and Great Britain. These latter, despite the undoubted advantage of being able to import by sea, could not fully exploit this advantage because of the exchange imbalance and the lack of tonnage available for transatlantic transport. Shortages everywhere accentuated a price rise, already rendered inevitable by inflation. Also, the average rise in salaries in every country remained decidedly less than the rise in prices.

Here was a situation that the proletariat could have exploited to foment social protests, and that could undermine the slogan of "sacred union." The Socialist International Bureau had, in August 1914, proven itself incapable of enforcing the doctrine of the International. Since the spring of 1915 the bureau's passivity had stirred up in all the belligerent states criticism and activity among small groups of socialists who were determined to place class solidarity above patriotic duty. These groups had coordinated their actions during the course of two conferences held in Switzerland, at Zimmerwald in September 1915 and at Kienthal in April 1916. The "International Commission" formed at Berne under the presidency of a Swiss, but dominated by the Russian revolutionary émigrés, especially Lenin, had appealed to the "proletarians of Europe" to remind the working class of its duty toward itself: refuse to place yourselves "at the service of the propertied classes." "Turn your arms not against your brothers but against the internal enemy." Force the governments in this way to conclude a peace "without annexations or war indemnities." This revolutionary doctrine did not, it is true, find a sufficiently large following in proletarian circles to cause serious concern to the various governments. It might, however, have found a favorable reception among populations who were growing ever more anxious owing to the apparent futility of their efforts and sacrifices and of their sufferings both moral and material—and to the prospect of having to renew these efforts and to bear these sufferings for an indefinite time.

During these uncertain hours a peace offer was made publicly for the first time. The timing was only coincidental. When on December 12, 1916, the German and Austro-Hungarian governments sent a note that proposed negotiations but neglected to state the basis for such talks, it was not with the intention of recognizing the war weariness of the people or of opening the way to a compromise. They wished simply to improve their moral stature in the eyes of the neutral nations and, above all, of the United States. But this Austro-German initiative suddenly acquired some importance when, a week later, it was taken up by none other than President Wilson. The belligerents were invited by the greatest of the neutral powers to make public their war aims.

The Entente powers decided to publish their reply. In a laboriously drafted note of January 10, 1917, in which vague formulas did not always succeed in disguising diverging viewpoints, they not only demanded the evacuation of invaded territories and the reparation of damages, but also announced their intentions to liberate the non-Turkish nationalities from Ottoman rule and to redraw the map of Central Europe by freeing from foreign domination the population of Alsace-Lorraine, the Italians, the Rumanians, the Czechs, the Slovaks, and the Yugoslavs, and by re-establishing a Polish state, whose future status was, moreover, not defined. Needless to say, they made no reference to the secret agreements they had reached on the partition of the remnants of the Ottoman Empire.

The German goverment refused to state publicly its conditions for peace but deemed it sufficient to make them known to the President of the United States. It would agree to the evacuation of Belgium, on the condition of securing rather far-reaching "guarantees": occupation of the fortresses of Liège and Namur, control of the railways, and the denial to Belgium of the right to maintain an army. It demanded also that France cede the Lorraine iron-ore basin: and, above all, it wanted to extend its borders to the east, beyond Polish territory, which would also be included within the Austro-German system.

Thus none of the belligerent governments took up the American suggestion. This probably did not mean that the governments were unaware of their people's fatigue. But this war weariness did not yet seem to have reached the point when it was likely seriously to impede the war effort. In spite of accumulated disappointments, the general staffs in both camps still hoped to obtain decisive results during the coming months. The Entente was able, thanks to the manpower reserves of Russia and to the institution of obligatory military service in Great Britain, to raise the number of its infantry divisions. Thus, starting in February and March of 1917, it was capable of undertaking collective offensives, whose plans had been outlined at the inter-Allied meeting at Chantilly in November 1916. The Central Powers were aware that they could not anticipate a victory "on land," though they believed they could win by means of submarine warfare: backed by powerful armaments (the German submarine fleet, which had comprised 30 ships in 1915, now had 154) and waged ruthlessly, this warfare would enable them to paralyze the transport of food and materials to England, where the population would be thrown into partial unemployment and then famine. The experts maintained that within six months the British would be powerless and would sue for peace.

Even with the increasing war weariness, the governments were losing their sense of reality. This state of affairs silenced the objections of those in Paris who doubted the effectiveness of the new offensive, or of those in Berlin who contested the peremptory assertions of the military and naval technicians.

The United States Enters the War

At the hour when morale was sinking in all the belligerent countries, at the very moment when the internal crisis in Russia attained a revolutionary momentum resulting in the fall of the regime on March 15, 1917, the entire complexion of the war was transformed by the intervention of the United States. In January 1917, President Wilson—who had been re-elected several weeks previously after a campaign in which he had taken for his theme the maintenance of American neutrality—stated in a message to the Senate his desire to see the war in Europe terminate in a "peace without victory." He had told his confidant, Colonel House, that the American people did not want to go to war at any price, and that the intervention of the United States would be "a crime against civilization." Then, early in February 1917, he broke off relations with Germany. At the beginning of April he requested that Congress pass a declaration of war, which was approved by the great majority of representatives and senators and was welcomed enthusiastically by public opinion. What were the causes, immediate or deeply rooted, that led to this intervention? What was its significance, not only for the European war, but for international relations in the entire world?

The Causes of Intervention

It is easy to describe the change in attitude in the United States toward the war in March of 1917, both in government circles and in public opinion.

On January 31, 1917, one week after his "neutralist" declarations to the Senate, President Wilson received a note from the German government declaring the coasts of the British Isles and of France to be "in a state of blockade," and announcing that in the North Sea, the English Channel, and the western Mediterranean "neutral ships would circulate at their own risk and peril." Thus submarine warfare, begun in 1915, but in fact suspended since May 1916 in order not to offend American feelings, was to be resumed. It would be waged "unrestrictedly."

President Wilson responded by breaking diplomatic relations, hoping that this gesture would suffice to bring Germany around. He told his advisers that he would take every opportunity to avoid war. Only if the German threat were followed by "willful and unjust acts" would he bring himself to defend the freedom of the seas by arms. It would thus seem that his intention was to wait until an American ship was torpedoed by a German submarine under conditions in which Germany was clearly to blame.

He soon, however, found himself obliged to go beyond simple diplomatic pressure and to adopt a position of "armed neutrality." He was impelled to this by economic circumstances. The first reaction of American shippers to the risks imposed by the declaration of unrestricted submarine warfare was to discontinue traffic in the blockade zone. This decision largely paralyzed exportation to England and France and resulted in congestion in American ports, which became overloaded with merchandise that merchant ships had stopped removing. To remedy this situation and to encourage the shippers to resume navigation, it seemed necessary to provide merchant ships with the means of defending themselves against submarine attack, thus posing the question of the arming of the American merchant fleet. On February 26 the President pointed out the necessity of this measure. On March 12 the merchant fleet were authorized by a presidential decision to carry guns.

From then on, gun battles between one of these armed ships and a German submarine could break out at any time in the Atlantic. To avert that risk, the German government would have to give the order not to attack American ships. But this would be tantamount to abandoning submarine warfare: an "unthinkable possibility," declared Kaiser Wilhelm. "If Wilson wants war, let him make war, and let him have one." On March 19 the steamship *Vigilentia* was sunk with all hands. On March 20 the President decided upon armed intervention and called a special session of Congress, which two weeks later declared war.

If one were to judge solely from these simple facts, the United States shift from neutrality to intervention was a direct result of the German strategy of unrestricted submarine warfare. President Wilson determined his course of action upon being notified of the German declaration. He had hoped to leave room for a possible withdrawal on the part of Germany, however slight this likelihood might be; but when her threats were translated into action, he came to an inevitable conclusion. This seems to be a reasonable interpretation of the events. But is it entirely satisfactory? It fails to consider basic factors that guided the President's actions. What role must be accorded to the pressures of vested interests or to the currents of public opinion? To attempt to answer these essential questions one must look considerably beyond the final crisis. How did the interests or the sentiments of the American public develop during 1915 and 1916, and how did the government put its neutrality into practice?

The role the United States had filled as supplier to Great Britain and France since October 1914 had been a source of great prosperity to industry, agriculture, and the export trade. However, the question of foreign trade relations was linked to that of freedom of the seas and the financing of exports, and thus to the very concept of neutrality.

The blockade imposed by Great Britain and France deprived the American export trade of the additional profits it might have realized by supplying Germany as well as the Entente. The submarine warfare waged by Germany in reprisal struck even more directly at the interests of these exporters and, apart from material damages, inflicted loss of human life. Although the champion of the rights of neutrals, the United States did not respond in the same way in both cases. She limited her protests against the blockade merely to legalistic harangues, which the British ambassador advised his government not to take "too seriously." Her protest against German torpedoing, especially when the ships involved carried American passengers (147 victims in the sinking of the *Lusitania* in May 1915), took on a threatening tone, although these threats were still verbal.

Was United States neutrality impartial in relation to the question of freedom of the seas? No, said the German government, since American policy was stricter toward the Central Powers than toward Britain and France. This gave the United States the perfect opportunity to reply that the measures she took in response would be in proportion to the severity of damages inflicted by each side. Indeed, the United States might have exerted more serious pressure on Britain and France by threatening them with an embargo on exports. Such an embargo would have deprived American industry and business of the exceptional profits that the war in Europe was yielding. Washington therefore refrained from resorting to this measure; at the same time it demanded that Germany partially curtail its submarine warfare. It had, in fact, obtained satisfaction, since the German note of May 4, 1916, had promised that submarines would not sink merchant ships without giving previous warning and would spare the passengers and crew.

The German government broke this promise on January 31, 1917, by deciding to resume "unrestricted" submarine warfare. A blow to American interests, no doubt, but even more to the prestige of the United States.

The question of the financing of exports produced other consequences no less important. To pay for their purchases, Britain and France needed the financial cooperation of their supplier. The American government had at first considered that granting credits to belligerents would be incompatible with "a true spirit of neutrality." In October 1914 it had nonetheless abandoned this doctrine, realizing that if the Europeans were obliged to pay cash, they would soon have to discontinue their orders. The banks therefore received authorization, first informally, then officially, to extend credit to foreign governments for the settlement of commercial debts. Eighty-five per cent of the British and French orders were addressed to the Morgan Bank, the principal agent for these transactions, which in turn allotted them to manufacturers and at the same time extended the credits necessary for payment. As collateral for these credits, the British and the French governments deposited with the bank American securities that their respective countrymen had held until then. But this method of financing was soon inadequate, since the Entente powers found it increasingly difficult to put up the collateral. Then, in October 1915, President Wilson authorized the financing on the American market of an Anglo-French loan of $500,000,000.

In all, the Entente powers received, in the form of lines of credit or of loans, $1,929,000,000 between November 1914 and November 1916, whereas Germany received at the most $5,000,000. One more "distortion" of neutrality, said the Germans. Actually this financial assistance was simply the consequence of the economic situation. How was the boom to be maintained without granting bank credits to the belligerents and without the authorization to finance foreign loans on American markets? It was, said the First National Bank of Chicago, a case of business necessity.

Thus the neutrality of the United States did not in fact prevent her from forming financial bonds with one of the belligerent coalitions and from furnishing the Entente powers with the resources that would allow them to circumvent the economic difficulties Germany was experiencing.

Were the advantages accorded to the countries of Western Europe conferred out of a sentimental preference?

Such a preference was clearly evident among the majority of intellectuals and political figures, especially in New England and New York and in eastern business circles, whose contacts with Europe had always been frequent. The greatest concentration of banking and commercial institutions was in this region. Anglo-American kinship, an awareness of the solidarity uniting the New and the Old Worlds, fear of German hegemony on the Continent, distrust of Prussian militarism, the desire to see liberal and democratic principles kept safe—these were the motives behind this course of action. These sympathies worked only to the benefit of Great Britain and France, however, and not to that of autocratic Russia.

There was stubborn resistance to these preferences on the part of a small but vocal minority. These were the German-Americans—four million of them at least—concentrated mostly in the Great Lakes region; the Irish—more than four million—who would have considered a British victory disastrous; the recent immigrants from Eastern Europe, Jews or Poles who had been victims of Russian nationalism and the czarist regime; and finally certain Catholic groups.

All the same, even if United States intervention in the European war had its active partisans and its determined opponents, the great mass of the population, in the Midwest, in the South, and in the West, retained the suspicion and reserve toward these "European quarrels" which the founders of the American republic had recommended. "Undoubtedly," noted the British ambassador in April 1915, "the great mass of people has no desire to be involved in the European war." And Colonel House wrote, "Ninety per cent of all Americans are opposed to armed intervention."

Opinion in government circles was not unanimous. Secretary of State Bryan, an ardent pacifist, resigned in May 1915, convinced that the United States should in no event take part in the war. Lansing, who replaced him, favored the policy of credit, which amounted to forming a link with the Entente powers. He adopted this attitude because it answered the immediate needs of economic prosperity. In formulating his foreign economic policy, the President yielded reluctantly to the suggestions of Lansing, which in turn corresponded to the wishes of business and industry. He was no less convinced that in spite of the material benefits, the United States ought to seek an end to the conflict. This is why he sent Colonel House to Europe on two occasions, in the hope that the latter's conversations with the belligerent governments might open the way to American mediation. Would this contemplated arbitration be impartial? At first this appeared to be the case. In March of 1916, on the other hand, the Wilsonian proposals (the restoration of Alsace-Lorraine to France, the acquisition of an outlet to the sea by Russia) corresponded with the war aims of the Entente, while according territorial advantages to Germany only outside of Europe. There is therefore reason to suppose the President of the United States became personally more favorable to the cause of the Entente, insofar as the results of the 1915 campaign excluded the likelihood of a Russian victory. He did not, however, lose sight of the danger to which a policy of intervention would expose the American nation—especially with the large proportion of Germans in the population.

In short, during the first two years of the war in Europe, nothing indicated that the United States, in spite of the essential role it played in the economic war, would be likely to relinquish its political neutrality. But was not the community of material interest established with Great Britain and France in the nature of a preparation for such a relinquishment?

In the second half of 1916 these internal contradictions began to be felt in the American body politic and appeared in the fluctuations of public opinion and in the attitude of governing circles. Foreign economic policy seemed reopened to debate. Britain gave the signal for this reappraisal when in July of 1916 she prohibited her subjects from doing business with eighty-five American firms suspected of supplying Germany through European neutrals. Was not the publication of this blacklist, whose apparent aim was to reinforce the blockade, in reality a means of keeping American exports from certain markets which Britain meant to keep for herself after the war? The press demanded, in return, restrictions on goods furnished to the British, and Congress passed a law authorizing the President to make this reprisal. But Wilson, although he privately declared that he was "growing impatient," chose not to apply this law, since an embargo on exports to Britain would entail heavy losses to industry and a drop in farm prices. A few weeks later, however, the Federal Reserve Board, with the assent of the President, took an action that in effect would limit these exports. In a policy statement published on November 28, 1916, it recommended that the banks neither invest in treasury bonds of foreign countries nor extend credit to these countries—namely Great Britain and France—except against "real guarantees." This meant, in short, a return to the system practiced prior to October 1916, and struck a blow at the credit of the Entente. This statement had the immediate effect of drying up American participation in the British and French loans. From that point on, Great Britain and France would have to make gold shipments in payment for their purchases. It was obvious that they would not be able to keep up their orders for very long. Thereupon Lloyd George decided to put a halt to any new contracts in the United States. "An unpleasant surprise," said the British ambassador in Washington. But even beyond the economic and financial consequences, London and Paris were concerned over the ulterior political motives of the American President. It was probable, they surmised, that Wilson was thinking of proposing himself as mediator in the European conflict, and that he expected to persuade the western powers to accept a compromise peace by means of these economic and financial pressures.

The motives behind the American decision were in fact as much economic as political. On one hand, the growth of American exports was becoming excessive, according to the Federal Reserve Board, causing a rise in the cost of living and, consequently, social unrest. On the other hand, foreign credit policy was giving rise to serious objections, as credits were being accorded unilaterally to the Entente powers. "A creditor is liable to become so inextricably involved with his debtor as to become unable to disassociate himself." Such were the arguments confronting Woodrow Wilson.

The President seemed not displeased by these arguments, in view of the state of public opinion, which favored his emphasis on neutrality.

The occasion of the presidential elections allowed the American public to express itself on United States policy. It would be erroneous to assume that such a consultation of public opinion gives an accurate indication of the electorate's attitude on foreign policy, since the voter's choice is most often determined by internal political questions. The elections of 1916, in which Wilson was re-elected by a slim majority, were no exception. It is significant to note that the campaigning President emphatically declared himself, as did his Republican opponent, Hughes, to be in favor of the maintenance of neutrality: "keep the United States out of the war" was the slogan of both parties, since it corresponded to the wish of the electorate. The sole important difference between the candidates' statements concerned economic relations with the belligerents. Wilson maintained that even while adhering to neutrality, he had brought the country an unprecedented prosperity through his foreign economic policies. Hughes criticized the incumbent for not having defended American rights as firmly in the case of England as in that of Germany, but he hastened to add that if he were elected, he would not prohibit the sale of war materials to the belligerents—that is to Britain and France. The electorate's choice between these two viewpoints was unclear. The German-Americans themselves were divided, because, although they had confidence in Hughes, they distrusted the interventionist left wing of the Republican party under the domination of former President Theodore Roosevelt. The eastern industrial states, although themselves beneficiaries of the Wilson economic policy, voted against him, because they did not forgive him for having weakened tariff protection in 1913. The western farmers, however, who had realized great profits in the past two years, gave their votes to the man who had been responsible for these profits. Can a meaningful interpretation be drawn from an analysis of these electoral results? The only certain fact was the approval given by the great majority of citizens to the maintenance of neutrality. This attitude did not preclude a show of "moral disapproval" vis-à-vis Germany.

Can we not determine a correlation between these "neutralist" sentiments and the government-ordered break in economic and financial relations with the belligerents?

The practical effect of these tendencies was, however, uncertain, since both the Republican and the Democratic camps announced their intentions to protect the security of maritime communications necessary to the export trade. This security was almost assured since the virtual suspension in May 1916 of German submarine warfare against the neutrals. But the German government reserved its right to resume it in case the United States did not demand that Great Britain relax the blockade. But in fact the blockade was intensified without a hint of reprisal on the part of the American government. Wilson, moreover, while adopting the slogan of neutrality which his party strategists considered indispensable, doubted that he could really keep the country out of war. Does this mean that he wished for war, or even that he was resigned to it? He could not have felt this way, since directly after his re-election he began preparations for a "peace initiative." And the failure of this initiative in December 1916 was to confirm him in his neutralism.

It was at this point that, at the insistence of its general staff, the German government decided to resume submarine warfare and to wage it "unrestrictedly." This convinced President Wilson that the intervention of the United States was inevitable. If he hesitated two more months, it was because he wished above all to be able to count upon the support of public opinion, which was not yet "ripe." How and why was the American public converted to the idea of taking part in the war?

Economic interests and the feeling of national honor and prestige of the United States are interrelated. When, in February 1917, American ports were overloaded with cargo that American merchant ships were no longer removing, the ensuing "economic congestion" rapidly affected the centers of production, since exporters ceased purchasing raw materials or food. The midwestern farmers and southern cotton planters felt the direct effect of "unrestricted" submarine warfare on their material interests. Whom could they blame, if not Germany? Previously indifferent to the vicissitudes of the struggle between European powers, these segments of the population came to understand that it was not easy to stay "out of the war." It is at this point that the incident of the "Zimmerman telegram" occurred. The British Intelligence Service had intercepted and decoded a message addressed to the German diplomatic representative in Mexico from the German Secretary of State for Foreign Affairs. He was instructed to offer Mexico an alliance with Germany if the United States entered the war; to suggest the possibility of Mexico's regaining territories annexed to the Union in 1848; and to advise the Mexican President to contact the Japanese government. The telegram was communicated to President Wilson who released it to the press on March 1. That Germany should seek the cooperation of Mexico, where in the previous year the United States had sent an expeditionary force to protect her economic and financial interests; and that she should consider seeking the support of Japan, rival of the United States in the Far East and the Pacific—were these not proofs that Germany was determined to stop at nothing? The resulting wave of indignation was most violent on the Pacific and the Gulf coasts, but it was reflected in the press almost everywhere in the United States.

Thus, within two weeks, those segments of the population that had previously been the most devoted to "neutrality" became aware of the German danger. The government therefore felt freer to prepare for the intervention it now considered inevitable.

Had it not been for the German decision to resume unrestricted submarine warfare, the United States would not have gone to war in the spring of 1917. Even the German ambassador was convinced of this fact.

Later the opponents of Wilson's policies tried to dismiss this argument, setting up a contradictory theory which attempted to attribute the intervention of the United States to the workings of American economic and financial interests. They said that the reversal of public opinion in February and March of 1917 in favor of intervention had been induced by a press campaign. The press, in turn, was in the hands of the great financial institutions. The banks, and especially the Morgan Bank, which had extended credits to Britain and France or had underwritten the French and English loans, were deeply committed. The defeat of the Entente could mean a disaster for them. They were interested in directing public opinion against Germany at a time when the success of her submarine warfare severely threatened the transportation of goods and supplies to the British Isles, and when Russia's military operations were being impeded by revolution. President Wilson, although personally independent of the banking interests, was indirectly subject to their influence. He yielded to them all the more willingly since his personal sympathies led him to uphold the democratic countries. How valid is this interpretation which, though based on simple hypotheses, is tainted with a decided political viewpoint? If it were accurate, it would be difficult to explain why the midwestern and the southern press kept its peace, until the disclosure of the Zimmerman telegram brought about its sudden change of attitude.

But if financial interests seem not to have played a predominant role, can the same be said for economic interests? There is no doubt that the United States practiced a unilateral policy in her foreign economic relations during 1915 and 1916, which benefited one of the coalitions. And there can be no doubt that the German press justified the resumption of submarine warfare at the beginning of 1917 on the basis of this fact. Must one conclude, however, that the German decision to employ unrestricted submarine warfare was a response to this American policy, and that Germany wished to force the United States to choose between real economic neutrality and war? In the deliberations of the German authorities leading to the decision to wage unrestricted submarine warfare, no one seems to have mentioned such an argument. Their sole design was to cut off Britain's supply lines and to force in this fashion a "decision" that could no longer be expected from the operations of the land war.

The Effects of Intervention

In his message to Congress on April 2, 1917, President Wilson announced that the United States would intervene in the war "with all its power and all its resources." This declaration was hardly unnecessary, since in official American circles, advocates of intervention had often considered that the participation of the United States in the hostilities would not extend to the battlefields of Europe: it would be limited, on the one hand, to broadening economic and financial assistance which the Entente powers already enjoyed during the period of neutrality, and, on the other hand, to the commitment of naval and air forces. This concept of restricted participation seemed so well established that the French ambassador in Washington never questioned it. Hence the French government showed no impatience at Washington's stalling during February and March of 1917. Since an active American role was hardly anticipated in military operations—the brunt of which was now being borne by the French army—the advantages expected from American intervention seemed to be reduced to financial facilities and moral support—which would be highly appreciated no doubt but would be insufficient to decide the outcome of the war. Not until March 20—ten days before the entry into the war—was there a change in outlook. President Wilson decided, with the consent of his cabinet, that participation in the European conflict would be total and that the American nation would send a great army to the front.

How can we measure the real impact of this American intervention on the outcome of the war, beyond its contribution to morale?

The immediate benefit—and it was an important one—was to frustrate the strategy of German submarine warfare. In April of 1917 the submarines sank, by torpedo or by gunfire, 874,000 tons of shipping, including neutral ships engaged in supplying England. These results exceeded by 30 per cent the forecasts of the German naval general staff. At that rate Great Britain could have been brought to her knees "within six months," especially since neutral shippers, given the gravity of the risks involved, preferred to keep their ships in port. In London the First Sea Lord, Admiral Jellicoe, hid his anxiety from neither the cabinet nor from the commander of the American naval forces. The entry of the United States into the war at this juncture threw out all the German calculations because of the appreciable increase of merchant tonnage now available for supplying the British Isles. The American merchant fleet was placed entirely at the disposal of the inter-Allied transport organization. Most of the Latin American nations, which, following the example of the United States, had entered the war—although not all intended to take part—confiscated German merchant ships that had sought refuge in their ports since 1914, and placed them at the disposal of the United States or the Allies. Finally, the neutral European countries were warned that they would be deprived of American goods as long as their ships refused to sail. There were certainly other reasons for the failure of submarine warfare, both technical and tactical; however, the danger of England's capitulation was immediately averted by the increase in tonnage available.

The Entente was soon to receive further considerable advantages, both economic and financial. The effectiveness of the blockade was increased, since the participation of the United States in the war made it possible to fill gaps in the system and exert increased surveillance over the European neutrals. The constant difficulties the British, French, and Italian governments had been suffering in financing their purchases in the United States disappeared, since the American Treasury received authorization to make advances on a nation-to-nation basis of up to a total of ten billion dollars.

The military implications were not so immediate, although they were no less decisive. Compulsory military service, made law on May 18, 1917, would furnish reserves of manpower larger than those of any of the belligerents, with the exception of Russia. Undoubtedly this great American army, which would have to be created from the ground up, could not be deployed before the spring of 1918. But from that moment on, the balance of military power was to shift rapidly in favor of the Entente powers. The Americans could deploy one million soldiers in 1918, two million in 1919. These troops would moreover be assured of receiving from American industry all the material resources required. The outcome could scarcely be in doubt.

Upon breaking diplomatic relations with the United States, and with her subsequent entry into the war, the Central Powers were faced with a choice. They could have sought to conclude a general peace—which would have been a compromise peace—before the American army appeared on the battlefield. In so doing, they would be acting in accordance with the wishes of a large part of the populace, which in all the countries at war was showing signs of war weariness and increased interest in the propaganda of international socialism. They could, on the other hand, attempt to obtain a decisive victory before American troops entered the conflict. But how could they achieve these military results which until that point had eluded them?

They found their chance in Russia's internal crisis. The Provisional Government formed on March 17, after the abdication of the Czar, had announced in a communiqué from its Minister of Foreign Affairs, Milyukov, its intention of continuing the struggle, "until the end and without faltering," within the framework of the war aims fixed by the Allied governments. But although he had the support of the liberal bourgeoisie, he was at odds with the socialists—Bolshevik or not—all advocates of a peace without annexations. These socialist tenets corresponded to the deep feelings of the peasant masses who were prepared to "forget the war." Their sole concern was with the agrarian reform that the downfall of the czarist regime seemed to promise. The Russian army was disorganized and threatened with "dissolution." This was the single factor, from a military standpoint, which might have eased the threat posed to Germany and Austria-Hungary by the intervention of the United States. Accordingly, the German government offered Lenin all its facilities to speed from Switzerland to Russia across German territory, in order to take up the leadership of the pacifist movement. On May 4, 1917, Lenin issued an appeal to the people in an attempt to overthrow the Provisional Government. He was unsuccessful, but he did manage to obtain the resignation of Milyukov and his replacement by Terechenko, an advocate of peace "without annexations." The new minister stated that although he wanted general peace, he of course rejected any notion of a separate peace. Clearly, he hoped that the prospect of a "democratic" peace might produce a surge in the nation's morale. Russia's commitment to the obligations of the alliance was nonetheless compromised, since the government realized that it was powerless before the apathy of the people.

A general peace or a separate peace between Russia and the Central Powers? This was the subject of the multifarious and entangled proceedings during the spring and summer of 1917. Is it possible to grasp the over-all direction of these tangled maneuvers, many of which were intended only to test the enemy's disposition or will to resist, or to sow mistrust within the opposing coalition? It was logical that the Austro-Hungarian government be the first to consider peace, since, if defeated, the Dual Monarchy would be threatened with dismemberment by the action of nationalities contained within it. The Emperor Charles, who had succeeded his uncle, Franz-Joseph, in November 1916, felt that the intervention of the United States would assure an Entente victory, and desired a rapid peace. On what terms? The offer which he formulated in writing on March 24, 1917—that is, the moment that the entry of the United States into the war became a certainty—and which was transmitted to Paris by his brother-in-law, Prince Sixtus of Bourbon-Parma, was a personal initiative. The Emperor proposed, without the knowledge of his ministers, not only a return to the *status quo ante*, but the concession to Serbia of access to the Adriatic and the restitution to France of Alsace-Lorraine. He promised that if the offer were accepted, he would urge these solutions upon his allies "by all possible means." He was thus proposing a general peace, a peace in which he would bring his influence to bear forcefully on the decision of Germany or Bulgaria.

When, however, after an initial contact had been made, the Emperor Charles reiterated his offer on May 8, this time with the knowledge of his Minister of Foreign Affairs, the terms were much more vague. The Austro-Hungarian note allowed for the possibility of an exchange of territories with Italy (whereas the Emperor's letter made no reference to the Italian question) but did not expressly repeat the previous offers. Why? Obviously because the Austro-Hungarian government had been convinced in the interim that German leadership rejected absolutely the idea of relinquishing Alsace-Lorraine. Bethmann-Hollweg had indicated on March 27 that he would consider at most restoring to France a part of southwestern Alsace, on condition of receiving in exchange the iron mines of Briey!

Did the Emperor Charles, in renewing the conversations with France and Great Britain, decide to disregard German resistance? In his desire to bring the preliminaries to a successful conclusion,

Prince Sixtus stated as much to Paris and London. He even went so far as to tamper with the documents. The French translation of the Austro-Hungarian note, which he read to the President of the Republic without giving the latter the original, included a passage in which allusion was made to a possible "separate peace" between Austria-Hungary, France, and Great Britain. This passage, however, had been inserted by the prince. The French and the British governments, in deciding not to reply to this offer, were of course unaware of this subterfuge. But they noted that the conditions set forth by the Emperor made no mention of Russia and Rumania. In fact, the Emperor was planning for Austria-Hungary and Germany to be compensated with territories taken from Russia and Rumania for concessions they would make elsewhere. Could this Austro-Hungarian offer be taken seriously? How can one believe that peace would have been possible if France and Great Britain had trusted the Emperor? The basic misunderstanding would have become clear as soon as negotiations had begun.

While the German government refused to concern itself with the preoccupations of Austria-Hungary, it did not rule out the possibility of a negotiated peace. On April 23, 1917, the Chancellor came to an agreement with the general staff on this subject. The government once more took up a scheme that it had discussed with Vienna concerning Alsace-Lorraine: namely, the exchange of the Thann-Altkirch region for that of Briey. It refused to grant real independence to Belgium which was to have imposed upon her a "political and economic" alliance with the German empire as well as a military control exercised by the presence of garrisons at Liège and Zeebrugge. It planned to demand that Russia relinquish Courland, Lithuania, and Poland, to be compensated by a small cession of Rumanian territory. Thus, even on the morrow of the United States entry into the war, the German government and general staff remained "annexationist." At the Kreuznach conference they imposed their views upon the Austro-Hungarian government as well. It is true that on July 19 the Social Democratic and Catholic Center majority in the Reichstag declared itself in favor of "a peace of lasting reconciliation between peoples" and condemned "territorial conquest gained by force." But both the military leaders and the Chancellor ignored this resolution. In order to understand the orientation of German diplomacy during the summer of 1917, one must examine the spirit of its program.

When Baron von Lancken attempted in June to entice Aristide Briand, who was at that point no longer a member of the French government, to an exchange of views in Switzerland, the German diplomat was authorized by his government to offer "the southwest angle of Alsace" and perhaps "several French-speaking centers in Lorraine." Briand, on the other hand, in accepting the proposed interview, thought he would be able to obtain the restitution of Alsace-Lorraine. However, the two negotiators would soon have perceived that they were at cross purposes. Alexandre Ribot, President of the French Council, canceled the proposed talks, fearing that to accept them would indicate a lack of resolve on the part of France. However, one cannot call this a "lost opportunity." Ribot's negative decision only spared Briand a disappointment.

The opportunity seemed more promising when the Austro-Hungarian government asked the Pope, through the intermediary of the German Catholic deputy, Erzberger, to take the initiative in issuing an appeal to the belligerents; this resulted in the publication of a note by the Holy See on August 9, 1917, which proposed the restoration of Belgian independence, suggested the settlement of the Alsace-Lorraine and Italian irredentist questions by "reasonable compromise," but made no mention of Eastern Europe. Great Britain let it be clearly understood that, as far as she was concerned, the Belgian question was the essential factor in a peace negotiation, without making the slightest allusion to French and Italian claims. The German government did not fail to recognize the importance of this offer. By promising to restore Belgium to full independence, it might hope to open the way to a preliminary peace talk, in which France and Italy, fearing a British defection, would be obliged to participate. Consequently Richard von Kühlmann was prepared to give up Belgium if need be. But on September 11, 1917, at the Crown Council convened at the château of Bellevue, the general staffs opposed this position, stating that Germany must at least retain "control over Liège and the Flemish coast." The Emperor was called upon to arbitrate this dispute. Kaiser Wilhelm was prepared to give up the Flemish coast but wished to retain the right to occupy Liège: in other words, he refused to allow the restoration of Belgian independence. The Holy See's note remained unanswered.

In short, the German government did not see fit to relinquish its war aims in the West despite the threat resulting from the American decision to intervene. It desired to retain its dominant influence in Belgium and to acquire the iron ore of Lorraine.

As for Russia, no mention was made of her in the peace offers that the Central Powers tendered to Britain and France. In the Austro-German colloquies, however, this question came to the foreground when the Russian Mensheviks proposed the convening of an international socialist conference at Stockholm, thereby giving a wider circulation to the pacifist doctrine. At the beginning of June, a Swiss Socialist deputy, Grimm, undertook to make known to the Russian Provisional Government the territorial claims of the Central Powers—namely, Poland, Courland, and Lithuania. He was unable to start any formal negotiations but did leave with the impression that peace was indispensable to Russia "politically, militarily, and economically." Can we not suppose, said the Austro-Hungarian Minister for Foreign Affairs, Czernin, in speaking to the Germans, that the Russian Provisional Government would agree to negotiations if the Central Powers moderated their demands? Thus the prospect of a separate peace with Russia remained the chief concern of the Austro-German alliance during the course of that summer of 1917. It was this prospect that determined the state of mind of German ruling circles. Why should they make sacrifices in the West when they could count on the defection of Russia?

American intervention, therefore, did not produce all the political results that it might have, because of the Russian revolution.

In order better to understand the effects of this intervention, however, one must consider not only the events in Europe: the participation of the United States in the European war put a new light on affairs in the Far East.

United States diplomacy had displayed its opposition to Japanese policy in China in 1915. In January 1917, just as France and Britain had resigned themselves to making concessions to the Japanese government, the American government declared that it did not recognize the "special interests" of Japan in Shantung, but it went no further than this statement of intention. The decision of the United States to enter the European conflict would lead her to build up her navy and to create an army that, once the war was over, would give her the means to take some sort of action in the Far East and in the Pacific. It would also assure the American government an important, perhaps dominant, role in the peace conference that would deal with the disposition of German interests in China. There was therefore nothing surprising in the strengthening of American policy in eastern Asia. There were two complementary aspects to this diplomatic activity: an effort to enhance the international position of China and an attempt to put a check on Japan and to limit her ambitions.

The Chinese government had yielded to the Japanese demands in May 1915 because it found itself alone against Japan. Would not the most effective diplomatic means to redress the situation be to allow China a seat at the peace conference, where the Sino-Japanese dispute would be submitted to the arbitration of the great powers? Let China declare war on Germany—at least nominally, as had Japan—and this result would be achieved. The entry of the Chinese republic into the war thus became the first goal of American policy. It remained only to convince the Chinese government. The President of the Republic, Li Yüan-hung, and the Prime Minister, Tuan Chi-jui, were in basic disagreement on this question, as on so many others. Tuan, who was in close contact with the generals governing the northern provinces, wished to enter the war, thinking thereby to find the opportunity to develop his armed forces with the aid of American credits and to assure the military leadership the upper hand in political life. Li declared himself in favor of neutrality precisely to upset this calculation. He was supported by the majority in the parliament, the press, and the chambers of commerce. In short, the question of possible intervention was dominated by internal Chinese politics—that is, by the conflict between the liberal idea of Young China and the autocratic traditions of the militarists.

The question was settled by a *coup d'état*. Tuan, whose policy was condemned by the legislature, organized a military revolt among the generals, forced the President to dissolve the parliament, and installed himself in Peking as dictator. On August 14, 1917, the Chinese government declared war on Germany. Although this was indeed the outcome it sought, American diplomacy was not satisfied with it, since the immediate result was the threat of secession. In Canton, Sun Yat-sen, father of the Chinese revolution of 1911, formed a rival government to the one in Peking. Once more China was thrown into civil war, this time with the Tuan government seeking financial aid from the Japanese. Hope of consolidating China seemed farther away than ever.

The Japanese government took advantage of these circumstances. It attempted to avert the opposition of the United States and to obtain commitments that it could use to its advantage at the future peace conference, and that it would not fail to utilize in the interim to intimidate the Chinese government. The American government accepted an offer for preliminary talks because it wished to avoid difficulties in the Far East as long as the war in Europe continued. On both sides, the negotiations were considered only as a temporary expedient. The limited results of these negotiations were contained in the Lansing-Ishii agreement of November 2, 1917. The Japanese government promised to respect the independence and territorial integrity of China as well as the commercial advantages accorded to the various powers by treaty; but it obtained recognition from the United States of the "special interests" of which Japan might avail herself in China "particularly in the areas contiguous to her possessions." It was a perfect specimen of a vague diplomatic agreement which could be interpreted in any number of ways the moment it had been signed. Furthermore, it constituted a mere postponement of the Japanese-American dispute on Chinese affairs.

It must be noted, however, that the United States clearly indicated its desire to contain Japanese ambitions. The entry of the United States into the war against Germany therefore marked a turning point in her Asian policy, even though this policy would for a time remain subject to the requirements of the hostilities in Europe.

The United States government intended to fulfill this new role in international relations without entering into written agreements with the Entente powers, which it considered not as allies but as "associates." Even though it had received a general briefing on French and English war aims in April 1917, it preserved its freedom of action in this area. It did not subscribe to the pact of September 5, 1914, thus retaining its right to withdraw from the conflict whenever it wished. It thus had substantial means of applying pressure. Moreover, the ideas it considered to be the only valid ones were quite different from those that prevailed in France or even in Great Britain. President Wilson wished for a peace that would offer the "national minorities" of Europe and the Near East better standards of living—an improvement that would not necessarily imply independence. He desired a peace that would destroy "German militarism" and the "Prussian military clique," without necessarily seeking to crush Germany politically or economically, in the hope that, once the defeat of the militarists was assured, the "liberal" movement would triumph in that country. He expected that the peace would be a lasting one, due to the reorganizing of international relations. It was not his intention to coerce his "associates" to his personal viewpoint by diplomatic pressure during the course of the hostilities, since he did not wish to provoke discord. He did indeed, however, count on being able to "impose" his vision of the world once the war was over.

Wilson outlined his program for peace in his message of January 8, 1918, without waiting for the end of the war, in order to make an impression on public opinion, to undermine the morale of the enemy, and also to weaken the resistance of the French and English "nationalists." In his "Fourteen Points," the general principles —condemnation of "secret diplomacy," lowering of "economic barriers," reduction of armaments—were formulated in terms vague enough or reserved enough not to cause irritation. Three ideas, however, were essential: the wish to ensure absolute freedom of the seas; the desire to establish the settlement of territorial disputes based on the principle of nationalities, from Alsace-Lorraine to Poland, from the Adriatic and Macedonia to the Ottoman empire; the establishment of a league of nations which would offer all states, large and small, "mutual guarantees of political independence and territorial integrity." Nevertheless, the message took care to allay impatience in some quarters. It avoided, for example, promising complete independence to nationalities of Austria-Hungary, suggesting only that they might expect "the greatest latitude in autonomous development"; for the President still hoped to persuade the Emperor Charles to embrace the idea of a separate peace. Wilson's cautious approach in this case was not reflected in the stance he adopted with respect to the intentions of his "associates." In the beginning of February 1918 he expressly reminded the French and British governments that he did not feel himself obliged to "subscribe to the war aims of the Allies."

The Collapse

Even as the possibility of peace negotiations was being contemplated or even discussed openly during the summer of 1917 in response to wavering public opinion and social unrest, even as the governments of the belligerent states in Europe seemed more or less sincerely disposed to go along with these endeavors, the indecisiveness of the Austro-German leadership was coming to an end. In the autumn the governments of the Central Powers reaffirmed their resolve to pursue the war until victory and rejected any compromise plan. In Berlin on October 9, Kühlmann, who had two months previously advocated a negotiated peace, declared that Germany would "never" make the slightest concession over Alsace-Lorraine. In Vienna, Czernin confirmed Austria-Hungary's agreement, notwithstanding the personal views of the Emperor Charles. Parliamentary circles appeared inclined to allow these governmental positions to develop without weakening them by criticism.

Why this at least apparent renewal of firmness on the part of Austria-Hungary? The failure of the attempted peace endeavors does not offer sufficient explanation. The direct cause must be sought in the increasingly precarious situation of the Russian Provisional Government and in the disintegration of the Russian armed forces. The Central Powers now had a chance of dismembering the opposing coalition.

They found no difficulty in achieving this goal, which in fact soon came about of its own accord. As soon as Lenin seized power in November of 1917, he announced that he would conclude a peace. Four months later the Russian defection was a fact. The Central Powers could now hope to snatch a military victory in France before the arrival of the American troops. They nonetheless failed in the spring of 1918 when they attempted what they hoped would be a decisive action. The fourth German offensive was broken in Champagne on July 15, at the very hour when twenty-seven American divisions were preparing to enter the lines. From that point on, the balance of military power was upset in favor of the Allies, whose margin of superiority increased month by month. German arms could no longer achieve a victory. In two weeks the execution of the offensive plans established by Foch on July 24, 1918, sufficed to convince the leaders of the Central Powers of imminent defeat.

On August 8, after the battle of Montdidier, Ludendorff saw the war as lost. "I see," said Kaiser Wilhelm on August 10, "that we must declare ourselves bankrupt. We are at the end of our strength. The war must come to an end." By prolonging the war for three months, Berlin and Vienna's only hope was to tire the adversary and gain a compromise peace. The effort was in vain.

Thus, only the military factors were decisive. It is, however, necessary at this point to determine the part played in the series of collapses—the defection of Russia, the Austro-Hungarian armistice, finally the German armistice—by economic and social conditions, by political calculations, by weakened morale, or by individual errors.

Russia and the Separate Peace

The certainty of Russia's remaining in the war became questionable when the policy of adherence to the Allied war aims advocated by the Minister of Foreign Affairs was blocked by the Petrograd Soviet on May 4, 1917.

As a whole, public opinion heeded the peace slogans launched by Lenin and the Bolsheviks: peace "without annexations or war indemnities," but, above all, immediate peace, which would be the necessary preface to a political and social reconstruction. The Bolshevik leaders were resolved to conclude such a peace separately if Russia's allies refused to follow her.

The army had been disorganized by the defection of a good number of officers who refused to serve the republican regime. It was further ravaged by the desertion of the peasants, whose only concern was to be present in their villages on the day of the division of the lands. "We must expect it to collapse as soon as it makes a move," said the French commander in chief to the War Commission, with reference to the Russian army. This forecast was confirmed on July 1, 1917, when the attempted offensive ordered by Minister of War Kerensky came to a halt on the very first day because the reserves refused to go into the lines. General Busilov saw "no means of forcing them to fight any more."

Finally, uncertainty of what lay ahead brought commerce to a halt in the cities; and this economic crisis was aggravated by a monetary crisis which caused the peasants to refuse to sell their produce, thus increasing the difficulty of providing food for the urban centers. In the countryside the prospect of agrarian reform, announced but then postponed until the meeting of a constituent assembly, gave rise to disorders that the authorities were powerless to suppress.

In short, the country was in complete chaos. The situation was understandable if one remembers that most of the population had never understood the reasons for the war, and that the administration, long before the fall of czarism, proved incapable of organizing the feeding of the urban centers. These were the underlying forces that paved the way and finally brought about the separate peace.

What resistance did they encounter? The Provisional Government, reshuffled after Milyukov's resignation, was in fact dominated by Kerensky, a "revolutionary socialist," a representative of *Russian* socialism, hostile to the internationalist slogans of the Bolsheviks. Kerensky declared himself to be a resolute opponent of a separate peace. His authority, however, was precarious.

In his relations with Russia's allies he accepted the program of peace "without annexations or war indemnities" and at the same time proclaimed his continued support of the alliance. Thus, he found himself in disagreement with the western powers on the Alsace-Lorraine question and on Italian irredentism. This disagreement became obvious when on May 28 the Provisional Government adopted a project suggested by the Dutch socialists for the convening at Stockholm of an international socialist conference at which the question of peace "without annexations" would be discussed in the presence of the Germans. The French, British, and American governments would not allow their socialist delegates to take part in the conference. Kerensky continued nonetheless to declare that he would not renege on Russia's commitment to the alliance. The Russian people considered this position a false one, notwithstanding its moral and legal basis. How could the mass of the people be expected to consent to continuing the war out of mere fidelity to commitments made by an overthrown government, and be dedicated to furthering French and Italian claims? Thus, the theory of honoring alliances received only slight response. It was upheld mostly by those members of the intelligentsia and the industrial bourgeoisie who had sponsored expansionist policies before 1914, and who had grown up amid a background of nationalist traditions. It might also have been upheld by the members of the bureaucracy who came from similar backgrounds, but whose interests had been linked to the czarist regime; but they were by and large opponents of the Provisional Government.

In internal politics this government was threatened from both sides by attempted *coups d'état:* one took place in July—a strike by the Bolsheviks; another in September—a plot led by the commander in chief of the army. It mastered one with the aid of Cossack troops, and the other with the assistance of its Bolshevik opponents. But these remarkable feats could not be repeated. In October of 1917 anarchy mounted. The government was aware of it but hoped to remain in control of the situation for six more weeks until December 6, when elections to the Constituent Assembly were to take place, the outcome of which would, it was hoped, consolidate the government's power. But the Bolsheviks were intent upon depriving it of this reprieve. "We must not wait for the convening of the Constituent Assembly," said Lenin, addressing the

Central Committee of his party, "since the Assembly will not be on our side."

The Bolshevik thrust was fully prepared for the great day, without the government's being able to count on the assistance of moderate elements, which were convinced of the former's ineptitude. In fact, the outcome of the crisis depended on the support that either the government or the Soviet would receive from the army. When the Petrograd garrison placed itself under the orders of the Soviet on November 3, the government appealed to the cadets of the military schools and tried to assemble a concentration of cavalry regiments drawn from the front. The Minister of War, General Verkhovsky, doubted the effectiveness of these measures, however. What must be done, he said, is to deprive Leninist propaganda of its appeal, the most attractive element of which was the promise of an immediate peace. Could they not explain the situation to the Allies and at the same time request them to release Russia from her commitments? If France and Great Britain refused this authorization to conclude a separate peace, then the Provisional Government would continue the war and "resign itself to its fate." But Kerensky would not hear of this suggestion. He intended to resist the Bolshevik onslaught without making concessions to the programs of his opponents.

Due to the "neutral" stance adopted by the top military leaders, the revolution of November (October 25, 1917) brought about the downfall of the government. "The political struggle taking place in Petrograd should not involve the army," said General Cheremisov, commander at Pskov. In fact, only the Cossack cavalry corps came to Kerensky's aid—and not until November 7 at that. His counteroffensive collapsed five days later.

The first decision of the new government was to announce that it would make peace without annexations. But the decree concerning the question of nationalities, dated November 15, granted to the peoples of Russia the right to determine their own fate and even to form independent states. Since the territories occupied by the Central Powers were mostly inhabited by peoples unrelated ethnically—Poles, Balts, Ruthenians—this decree implied the definite relinquishment of these territories.

The sole causes of this Russian defection were internal. Economic crisis, administrative disorder, collapse of morale, all worked to the benefit of the promoters of a social and political revolution; as did the clearsightedness of the Bolshevik leaders who, in order to ensure the success of this revolutionary movement, announced their intention to put an end to the war—a war that most of the population had abandoned six months previously. The other belligerents, friend or foe, played virtually a passive role in these proceedings. Of course, the German government had facilitated the return of Lenin in April 1917; but it hardly seems possible that it would have desired the success of the Bolshevik Revolution. The ensuing paralysis of the Russian armed forces was, as far as Germany was concerned, a sufficient result. Russia's allies made virtually no attempt to help Kerensky consolidate his government. President Wilson merely noted the "gradual disintegration of the regime," "the increasing anarchy," but sent no instruction to his agents. The English and the French governments were no more active. The sole undertaking that the Allies attempted in common, on October 9, was intended to remind Kerensky— as if he could be unaware of it!—of the necessity of re-establishing discipline in the army, and to maintain order "in the rear." If the Provisional Government proved equal to this, it could count upon the "entire support" of the United States, France, and Great Britain. But nothing more was promised than moral support and some financial assistance. Only on November 6 did the American ambassador advise his government to offer Kerensky two divisions to be sent into Russian territory to bolster the morale of the Russian people. The following day the Provisional Government was swept out of power by a Bolshevik *coup d'état*. The Allies, however, remained spectators, aware that the Russian army, ravaged by desertions, was no longer an effective fighting force, that the large majority of the Russian people wanted immediate peace "at any price," and that there was no way of keeping Russia in the war.

It did, however, take four months to achieve this "immediate" peace. On November 21, 1917, several days after having put down Kerensky's counteroffensive, the Council of People's Commissars decided to enter into preliminary discussions with the Central Powers. On the twenty-seventh, having broken the resistance of the commander in chief, General Dukhonin, the council called upon Russia's allies to join in the discussions: otherwise, Russia would act alone. On December 15 the armistice was signed without serious difficulties. But the drawing up of the peace treaty at the Brest-Litovsk conference involved prolonged and heated debate which continued until March 3, 1918.

In those bitter negotiations the conflict seemed to lie in the interpretation of the "free, self-determination of peoples" and basically in knowing whether the Central Powers would or would not annex the major part of the territories occupied by their troops. The Soviet delegation would agree to allow the populations of these territories to decide their lot by plebiscite. But it insisted that the voting be "free," and consequently that it take place after the removal of the occupying troops. The Germans and the Austro-Hungarians refused evacuation prior to the elections, which would deprive them of the means of exerting pressure on the voters, through whom they fully expected to achieve their end. Each side was perfectly aware of the other's aims and sought only to achieve propaganda advantages in prolonging the negotiations.

The Soviet delegation wanted to force the Austro-Germans to show their hand by inducing them to declare openly that they would not agree to a peace "without annexations"; it hoped that this revelation, duly noted by the working classes of Germany and Austria-Hungary, would provoke resistance to the policies of these governments and general staffs. The great strikes at the war plants in Berlin and the general strike announced in Vienna in January led it to believe that such resistance could be effective. This hope of revolutionary contagion explains the actions of Soviet diplomacy.

Needless to say, the Austro-German delegates replied by pointing out the contrast between the principle expounded by the Soviet government and the armed struggle it was carrying on against the separatist movements in the Ukraine, the Caucasus, and Siberia, thus making a mockery of the right of "free self-determination of the peoples."

The Soviets had basically gained from the armistice the one

result they required immediately: namely, the possibility of deploying their armed forces on the "fronts" created by the civil war. They could thus defer signing the peace treaty without any inconvenience. On the other hand, the Austro-Germans were growing impatient. They needed to clarify their relations with Soviet Russia in order to be able to devote all of their strength to the great offensive they were preparing to launch on the French front before the American forces came into the lines. Moreover, they would need to procure in Russia the cattle and grain urgently needed to overcome the food crisis, which was becoming serious, especially in Austria-Hungary.

Given these conditions, what was the policy of each government?

Germany and Austria-Hungary had to determine precisely the extent of the annexations they planned upon, and to agree on the methods they would employ to achieve them. In December 1917 the two governments had decided that Courland, Lithuania, and the Polish territories would be detached from Russia and divided between the two central empires, with Germany claiming the Baltic countries and Austria-Hungary taking Russian Poland, after a "rectification of the border" in favor of her ally. Were they to persist in this program under Russian resistance?

In Austria-Hungary the government was so eager to obtain a rapid peace that it would gladly have accepted the Russian formula of plebiscite after evacuation. In Germany all of the political parties, with the exception of the Socialists, supported the annexation policy of the government and the general staff. The Austro-Hungarian Minister of Foreign Affairs, Czernin, did not dare undertake a separate peace negotiation and therefore followed the path outlined by his ally. He was nonetheless seeking a solution that would fulfill the immediate needs of his country—namely, to provide food. The opportunity arose in connection with Ukrainian separatism. On January 10, 1918, the National Assembly at Kiev, which six weeks previously had refused to recognize the Bolshevik government, brought a declaration of independence to the Brest-Litovsk conference. The recognition of this independence and the conclusion of a separate peace treaty with the republic of the Ukraine would assure Austria-Hungary of a means of obtaining the resources of a region particularly rich in agricultural produce. It was of little concern to the Austro-Hungarians that this peace treaty with the Ukraine promised future dangers and would tend to dangerous involvement of the Central Powers in the vicissitudes of the Russian civil war. "Austria," declared Czernin to his German allies, "is like a man who jumps out of the window because his house is on fire." It was imperative to acquire a million tons of grain in the coming months.

On February 9, 1918, the treaty was signed. But the Ukrainian government no longer had any real authority, since Bolshevik troops had begun to invade the independent republic and were to occupy Kiev that very day. The Soviet delegation at Brest-Litovsk was thus in a position to declare the peace treaty invalid. In order to obtain the deliveries promised, the Central Powers had only one possibility: to grant military assistance to the Ukrainian government to reconquer its territory. The Austro-German troops were thus in effect going to reopen hostilities against the Bolsheviks.

The German Foreign Minister, Kühlman, believed that this measure would suffice. The Soviet Russians would be unable to respond to these localized hostilities by breaking off the armistice, since they had no resources whatever for resuming the war. The attitude of the Russian delegation confirmed this prediction. Trotsky refused to pursue the peace discussions but refrained from denouncing the armistice. However, German Supreme Headquarters were determined to bring the matter to a close by forcing the Soviet government into complete submission. Otherwise, it was explained, it would be necessary to maintain an eastern front at a time when all available resources were required to obtain a decision on the western front. It would not suffice merely to force a signature from the Russians to accomplish this. Kaiser Wilhelm agreed with the military. The resumption of hostilities on February 18, 1918, encountered no resistance. A simple "military march" in the direction of Petrograd was enough to bring back a Russian delegation to Brest-Litovsk, which declared that it was yielding to force, and which signed the peace treaty without even wishing to examine the text.

By this Treaty of Brest-Litovsk, Russia relinquished its territories in Poland, Courland, and Lithuania, leaving to the Central Powers the problem of determining their eventual status. She promised to withdraw entirely from Livonia and Estonia, albeit without renouncing sovereignty over those regions. She recognized the independence of the Ukraine and of Finland. The ceded regions were those that had the highest yield of wheat and sugar beets, where two thirds of the coal resources were to be found, and half the steel works. The Soviet government agreed in Articles 5 and 7 not to hamper German purchases in Russia by imposing excessive tariffs.

Two days later the Rumanian government, which could not save, without the support of Russian troops, the small portion of national territory it had been able to spare from invasion, signed the peace preliminaries at Buftea. By the Treaty of Bucharest on May 7, it ceded the Dobrudja to Bulgaria and surrendered its economic independence in favor of the Central Powers.

The war was over on the entire eastern front, confirming apparently the opinion of the German Supreme Headquarters.

The Soviet government was divided over its course of action until the last minute before it resigned itself to capitulation.

Lenin had indicated his position at the beginning of January. As he was convinced that the Bolshevik regime, threatened by civil war, would not be able to survive if it had to face a resumption of hostilities against the Central Powers, his sole aim in the Brest-Litovsk negotiations was to draw out the proceedings in the hope that a social or a political crisis would meanwhile erupt in Berlin or Vienna. If, however, the Central Powers were to denounce the armistice, then the Soviets would have to yield without any attempt at resistance. Was it not the safety of the Russian Revolution that "mattered the most to the world"?

This attitude was bitterly criticized by the new army commander in chief Krylenko and by Bukharin, who would have offered a "violent resistance . . . to the rapacious appetites of the German bourgeoisie." The local soviets, with the exception of the Petrograd Soviet, supported this firm stance.

An apparent compromise between these two extremes was suggested by Trotsky, Commissar for Foreign Affairs. It consisted of rejecting German peace conditions but declaring the armistice to be still in force, with the expectation that the German government would tolerate such a situation for fear of arousing public discontent. Should this expectation be in vain, or should the German army reopen hostilities, then capitulation would be necessary.

Trotsky's resolution was approved by Stalin and Kamenev and adopted by the Central Committee of the Bolshevik party on January 22 by a vote of nine to seven. The end result was basically the same as that of Lenin's plan. The only difference was in the attitude to be taken if Germany were to denounce the armistice. Immediate capitulation, said Lenin. Capitulation, said Trotsky as well, but only after having undergone a new test of strength, in order to demonstrate that the Bolshevik government was not "in league" with Germany.

This therefore was the policy adopted after the signing of the Ukrainian peace treaty. On February 10, at Brest-Litovsk, Trotsky declared that although Soviet Russia was breaking off the peace talks, she was "withdrawing" from the European war, and that she would demobilize her armed forces in order to offer further proof of this intention. This tactic was unsuccessful, however, since the German army did resume hostilities. Lenin immediately caused the Central Committee to address a request for peace to Germany: even though Bukharin upheld once more the theory of "revolutionary war," and Trotsky suggested waiting to see how the enemy offensive developed. After five days of anxious waiting, the Central Committee was notified of the German conditions. They were even more stringent than might have been predicted from the tenor of the Brest-Litovsk discussions. Lenin subsequently obtained a vote in favor of peace by a small majority. The army, he said, would not, could not fight any further. If it still counted "a hundred thousand good troops," it would be possible to attempt resistance. But in its present state, it could only continue its retreat all the way to the Urals, and Russia would finally have to accept even worse peace conditions. But the major argument that he presented to the Central Committee on February 18, and that he was to repeat before the All-Russian Congress of Soviets on the occasion of the ratification of the peace treaty, was once again that of the "safety of the revolution." If Russia made peace, even having thereby to relinquish "a few provinces," the revolution would be safe. If she continued the war, the "collapse of the revolution" would be inevitable. Such a peace was no doubt "an incredible humiliation for the Soviet regime," but it did enable this regime to avoid a "complete débacle." This was essential. We must, concluded Lenin, "hold on to our positions and await the rising of the international proletariat."

The lengthiness and difficulty of the negotiations between Russia and Germany offered Russia's allies and associates the opportunity for diplomatic action. Did the latter attempt to restrain the Soviet government and to avoid the separate peace?

When the Council of People's Commissars called upon the Western powers to participate in the armistice talks at the end of November 1917, an international conference had previously been convened in Paris to study problems of military and political cooperation. The United States representative, Colonel House, had suggested the "reappraisal" of war aims in the light of the Russian program—namely, peace without annexations. But the French government would not hear of a peace based on the *status quo ante,* and had been supported by Italy and Great Britain. The American proposition therefore was tabled. Lloyd George put forward another suggestion: the Allies, while refusing to be associated with the negotiations undertaken by the Bolsheviks, could release Russia from the obligations she had contracted in the pact of September 5, 1914, and thereby authorize her to conclude a separate peace. They would have nothing to lose by agreeing to this suggestion, which would enable them to continue diplomatic relations with Russia, for there was no way of forcing the Soviets to respect commitments made by the czarist government. There was even a possible advantage to be gained, since Russian resentment would be directed against Germany alone when the latter came to demand the cession of territories. In short, Lloyd George's main objective was to avoid a Russo-German alliance. Neither Clemenceau nor Sonnino accepted this solution, since they did not wish to deal with the Council of People's Commissars as a "regular" government qualified to speak for the Russian nation. Contact had not, however, been completely broken off, and the Soviet general staff had a clause inserted in the armistice convention by which the Germans agreed not to transport troops from their eastern front to the French front until the Russo-German peace was signed. This clause seemed likely to remain a dead letter for lack of a means of enforcement. But it seemed to stand as an indication of good will in the relations between Russia and France.

In January of 1918, when it became apparent that there was a conflict between the German and the Russian viewpoints, and that there was a possibility of the talks breaking down, President Wilson, at the request of the American ambassador to Russia, took steps prompted by Colonel House's suggestion. The message he addressed to the American Senate on January 8 outlined what he felt should be the basis for a general peace, which was not merely an effort to "reappraise" war aims, a partial disavowal of the secret agreements concluded between the Allies before April 1917, or an appeal to the principle of nationalities; rather, it was also meant to encourage the Soviet government in its resistance to the German demands. The Central Powers, declared Wilson, were "imperialistic," whereas the Russians exhibited "loyalty" and "largeness of view." The United States added to the conditions of a future peace "the evacuation of all Russian territory," on the assumption that Russia should have "an unhampered and unembarrassed opportunity for the independent determination of her own political development and national policy. . . ." It offered to give the new Russia "assistance also of every kind that she may need." But when the French and the British governments made simultaneous declarations relative to their war aims, they avoided any allusion to the Russian question.

Two weeks later, however, the French ambassador offered the Soviet government assistance in reorganizing its armed forces, in addition to financial aid. On February 19, when Germany had just reopened hostilities, he promised Russia "the military and financial support of France." Lenin and Trotsky—who for three days waited in vain for a German response to their offer of capitulation—thought it prudent not to reject the French offer. Despite the opposition of Bukharin, who advocated armed resistance to Germany but opposed any compromise with a "bourgeois" government, the party's Central Committee gave Lenin and Trotsky full powers "to accept the aid of the French imperialist brigands against the German brigands." On February 22 the French move was endorsed by the Allied ambassadors, though they promised no other effective assistance than technical aid in the destruction of the railways in order to halt the advance of enemy troops. On the evening of February 23, however, the Soviet government received the German reply and decided to yield. The Allied offer was thus made in vain.

The offer was renewed, however, on March 5, in the hope of encouraging the All-Russian Congress of Soviets to refuse ratification of the Brest-Litovsk treaty. The proposal hinted at Japanese military assistance. When Trotsky demanded details on what other help might be received, the American reply noted that the United States was "unfortunately" not in a position to give any "direct and effective aid."

Could these vague and last-minute offers of assistance have been of any practical use to Russia? Even if it had received the promise of armed support, the Soviet regime would have been swept out by the German troops long before the arrival of outside help. From the moment that it decided to "save the revolution," it had no other choice than to conclude peace.

From the moment it was signed, this separate peace with Russia seemed to open to Germany the hope of a decisive victory in the French campaign. The effects of this peace should be examined.

It decidedly eased the food shortages in Germany and especially in Austria-Hungary. It facilitated the use of aviation as well as the organization of military transport, thanks to Rumanian petroleum. On the other hand, it helped to provoke internal difficulties in the two Central empires. Communist propaganda infiltrated Germany, while the national minorities in Austria-Hungary became more actively discontented, reflecting the Brest-Litovsk debates on the right of "free self-determination of peoples."

On the military front, however, it yielded few of the results that might logically have been expected. In fact, the German high command drew little advantage from the Brest-Litovsk peace during the series of offensives waged on the French front between March 15 and July 15. During these four months it left behind sixty divisions—about one million men—in the territories of the former Russian empire. If it had launched ten or twenty of these divisions into battle during the critical moments on March 25, April 9, or May 27, it would greatly have increased its chances of wresting a decisive victory from the Allies. Why, then, did it consider it necessary to maintain an "eastern front" despite the signing of peace with Russia? In the Ukraine it had been obliged to maintain large forces without which the peasants would not have delivered grain and cattle. It had of its own free will left large garrisons in Livonia and Estonia in order to back up a political measure. Finally, it had judged it indispensable to maintain at least a curtain of troops to limit the risks of Bolshevik "contagion" spreading into Germany. But, above all, the German high command feared that the Soviet government might change its policy. The execution of this treaty, whose conditions had been imposed by force, gave rise to some difficulties, particularly in the Baltic countries. On June 9, 1918, the Germans decided that it would be advisable to reopen hostilities and overthrow the Bolshevik government. The separate peace had thus been disappointing.

This same question—the maintenance of an eastern front—was the major concern of Britain and France in examining the consequences of the Treaty of Brest-Litovsk. (Of course they did not suspect Ludendorff's intentions.) How could they prevent the German chief of staff from bringing back the troops now available to the battlefields of Picardy or Champagne? Clemenceau and Lloyd George thought of forming an expeditionary force in Siberia in cooperation with the Japanese, who had hitherto refused to participate in any European military operations, but who gladly agreed to act in a region where they might obtain considerable advantages. Wilson, despite his mistrust for Japanese expansion, finally agreed.

Would this Allied expedition be organized with the consent of the Soviet government, or without it, or even perhaps against it?

In the event of the second of these three possibilities, the Soviet government would no doubt be forced into seeking an alliance with Germany. In the event of the first, there was the risk that the German army might intervene in the Russian civil war on the side of the "Whites." In April 1918, Lenin seemed inclined to accept a collaboration with the Entente and the United States, declaring that he was prepared to discuss the means of mounting a Siberian expedition. Trotsky, reticent at first, finally agreed to the idea of negotiations, on condition that "Japan's price for assistance" be clearly determined in advance. Certain of the members of the diplomatic or military missions that the Allied powers still maintained in Russia—the Frenchman Sadoul, the American Robbins, the Englishman Lockhart—were in favor of these negotiations and were certain of Soviet acquiescence. However, these men were minor officials; the heads of the missions were distrustful or hostile to the idea, especially since such negotiations would imply *de facto* recognition of the Soviet regime. "Inadmissible," said the French ambassador, Joseph Noulens.

When in May the Bolsheviks began their struggle at Chelyabinsk with the Czech Legion, which consisted of former prisoners freed from Russian camps, and the Allied embassies took these legionnaires under their protection, the incident turned to the advantage of the anti-Soviet forces. The instructions of the French government on June 20 said that the Czech Legion should be the nucleus around which the "Siberian and Cossack partisans of the re-establishment of order" were to group themselves. On August 5, 1918, the "Allied"—in reality Japanese—expedition began in Siberia. Although it was intended to tie down the German forces still stationed in Russia, it became an act of intervention in the Russian civil war.

It is hardly surprising that the Soviet government turned to Germany, and that after its defeat of August 8 on the French front, the German government felt it necessary to consolidate the peace of Brest-Litovsk. This would permit the massive transfer of manpower, hitherto maintained on the former eastern front, to the western lines. On August 27, 1918, a new German-Russian agreement was signed, whose secret articles provided for a collaboration.

Germany was to give assistance to the Soviet government against the "White" army in southern Russia and against the small Anglo-French expeditionary force that had landed in northern Russia. Russia, for her part, was to renounce the sovereignty she had theoretically retained over Livonia and Estonia. Actually the principal result was the transfer of 500,000 German soldiers to the French front within a period of three months. But these reinforcements, whose intervention might have been decisive in the spring offensive, came too late to assure the success of the defensive. By now the Allied forces were growing at the rate of 250,000 men per month, due to the American contribution.

In short, relations with the Soviet government were not conducted in a realistic manner by either camp. The German government and general staff, determined upon large territorial annexations, did not perceive the advantages of a conciliatory peace which would have permitted them to transfer their military effort to the French front more rapidly. The Western powers did not see the necessity of seeking agreement with the Soviet government. Perhaps this was because they considered the Bolsheviks solely responsible for a separate peace which basically corresponded to the wishes of the major part of the Russian population. Above all, by "recognizing" this government, they would have relinquished an argument that they planned to use in upholding the nullification of the Treaty of Brest-Litovsk. The United States seemed to have a clearer understanding but was unable to defend its viewpoint. At no stage was the Russian question accorded its full importance.

The Dismemberment of Austria-Hungary

The predominant causes for the collapse of Russia were social. Undoubtedly the military defeats of 1915 had prepared the way for this crisis, but by the end of 1916 the military situation seemed to be stabilized. The state of mind of the peasant population, the success of extremist socialist propaganda among the working class and the intelligentsia, and the indifference of part of the bourgeoisie were factors contributing to the events of 1917. In the case of the Danubian monarchy, the causes were of an entirely different nature.

In 1914 the Austro-Hungarian government had wanted a European war because it felt that only a military victory would check the forces that threatened the disintegration of the state. It had waged this war with all the energy at its disposal as long as the Emperor Franz-Joseph was alive, until November of 1916, without daring to count on the support of a major part of the population. Symptoms of a crisis were apparent from the beginning of 1917 on. This was no doubt in part the result of the death of Franz-Joseph. The new Emperor Charles, nervous, quiet, and whimsical, did not have that simple, somewhat naïve confidence in the destinies of the monarchy that his uncle had retained during sixty-eight years of a reign marked by numerous trials. But the more serious threats were linked to the economic situation and the attitude of the national minorities. Austria, which suffered from a shortage of food, could not depend on the agricultural resources of Hungary, since the "economic compromise," in effect since 1867, allowed the minister in Budapest to prohibit the exportation of grain and cattle, even if they were intended for the non-Hungarian territories of the Dual Monarchy. Encouraged in December 1916 by the declaration in which the Entente powers had declared their "war aims," the protests of the national minorities were given a new impulse in March 1917, when the fall of the czarist regime opened up prospects favoring Polish nationalist claims.

What role can we attribute to each of these causes in the development of the Austro-Hungarian crisis of 1917-1918?

The shortage of food became more serious in the Austrian half of the Dual Monarchy in the autumn of 1917. The daily bread ration fell to 165 grams a day and was not always fully distributed. The weekly rations were 200 grams of meat and 40 to 60 grams of fats. These difficulties in the provision of food were the immediate cause of the social unrest which took on a threatening aspect by the middle of January 1918. Trade-union leaders issued orders for a general strike as a warning; and in order to force the peasants to make deliveries of produce, the government withdrew from the front thirty battalions which were to call on the farms. The Emperor foresaw a revolutionary upheaval if the food crisis was not averted, and he sought means to overcome it. The meager stocks still at his disposal would be exhausted before the end of March. Collapse would thus be inevitable. This was the threat that obliged Austria-Hungary to consider the Ukrainian peace as the only means of salvation. The government realized that this peace might lead to future dangers, but as Czernin put it, "A possible death is preferable to a certain death." At least through this Ukrainian treaty, and subsequently through the Rumanian one, the government was able to obtain some relief and to avert immediate dangers. Thus economic difficulties did not play the decisive role in the crisis that foundered the Dual Monarchy in October of 1918.

The nationalist movements had a very different impact. There was a direct correlation between the development of the minorities' protests, the international situation, and the internal political situation. This was because the Emperor Charles convened the Austrian parliament, whose activity had been suspended since the beginning of the war, and thereby gave the national groups an opportunity to restate their demands publicly.

The Czech protests had been weakened up until the end of 1916 by the divergent tendencies between the "external" resistance groups. One of these, under the leadership of Masaryk and Beneš, sought support from Great Britain and France, while the other looked toward czarist Russia. These conflicting views were reconciled in March 1917, after the fall of the Czar, when the congress of the Czechoslovak League held at Kiev adopted the program of the National Council, that is, of Masaryk and Beneš. Unity was not yet achieved, however, between these émigrés and the Czech nationalists who had remained in the country. The former demanded independence, while the latter would have been satisfied with autonomy. The declaration read in the *Reichsrat* by the Czech deputies on May 30, 1917, confined itself to demanding that the Dual Monarchy be transformed into a confederation of states, which would include Bohemia. It was not until January 6, 1918, that the National Council at Prague rallied to the program of the émigré leadership. "Our nation demands its independence. She wishes to form a sovereign and democratic state incorporating its historic lands with its Slovak branch."

The Yugoslav nationalist movement, though deeply shaken by the Italian intervention in May 1915 and almost crippled at the end of 1915 by the Serbian defeat, picked up momentum at the beginning of 1917. The mistrust that existed between the Orthodox Serbs and the Catholic Croats, sustained by czarist policy which favored Orthodox interests, began to fade after the Russian revolution of March. The pact signed by Trumbic and Pacic at Corfu on July 20, 1917, amounted to a compromise. Their common goal would thenceforth be the establishment of a Yugoslav state whose ruling dynasty would be Serb but whose Croatian population would have the right to an autonomous status. The Serbs and the Croats wished to include the Slovenes in this state, but the promoter of the Slovenian national movement, Koroseč, was hesitant at first. Not until March 2, 1918, did he put in his claim for independence and declare himself to be in favor of the Yugoslav state.

In short, the leaders of the two national movements did not adopt a program for the dismemberment of the Dual Monarchy until the right of "free self-determination of peoples" became the central topic of discussion at the Brest-Litovsk debates. But was this coincidence truly significant? Other explanations must be sought in the policies of the Austrian and Hungarian governments as well as in the diplomatic activities of Austria-Hungary's opponents.

As for the governments, which in the time of Franz-Joseph had simply refused to consider the demands of the nationalities, they had adopted a more flexible outlook since the accession of Charles. In Austria the head of the Emperor's cabinet, Polzer-Hoditz, established a reform plan that might have satisfied the minority groups if they had confined themselves to demands of autonomous status. Except for the Italian irredentists, this was generally the case. The Emperor, however, was unable to find Austrian statesmen willing to put this plan into effect; and when he contemplated naming a new prime minister, Joseph Redlich, he was obliged to back down in the face of German protest. Charles considered reforming the Hungarian electoral laws to give a voice to the national minorities. He had been able to force the retirement of Stefan Tisza, President of the Council, who had violently opposed any measure of this kind, but he did not find more effective support in the new president, Esterhazy. Thus the policy advocated by the reformers found a cool reception. The resignation in November 1917 of Polzer-Hoditz marked the end of these endeavors. Thereupon the militants of the nationalist movements proceeded to demand independence, having lost any hope of gaining autonomous status.

As for the policy of the Allies, the Entente powers naturally had to consider exploiting these nationalist movements to their advantage. Two paths were open to them: to encourage the protests of the "minorities" with a view toward provoking the disintegration of the Dual Monarchy; or to take advantage of the uneasiness of the Austro-Hungarian government so as to push it toward making a separate peace. There was, however, no concerted action on the part of the Allies until the end of 1916. True, in their collective declaration of January 10, 1917, they announced their intention to "liberate" the nationalities of Austria-Hungary, but only in the vaguest terms. It could hardly have been otherwise, since Italian interests in the Adriatic were in direct opposition to those of the Yugoslavs, and since the czarist regime intended to preserve its freedom of action on the Polish question.

However, even though the first Russian revolution removed the chief obstacle to the vigorous pursuit of a policy favoring the nationalities, Britain and France still did not subscribe to this course of action. On the contrary, they sought to obtain a separate peace. Even after the failure of Prince Sixtus' negotiations, they continued in this effort. In the last months of 1917—by means of contacts established in August by Count Armand, a secret service agent, and in December by the South African statesman, General Smuts—the French and the British governments promised that Austria-Hungary would keep all of her territories if she would consent to a separate peace. They asked only that the national minorities enjoy an *autonomous* status within the framework of a confederation. In January of 1918, President Wilson, in his Fourteen Points, went only so far as to say that the nationalities of Austria-Hungary should be given "the freest opportunity of autonomous development." The British Prime Minister, too, spoke only of autonomous government; and the French Minister for Foreign Affairs, when alluding to "a settlement of the Austrian question according to the rights of nationalities," refrained from specifying what these rights might include. "The break-up of Austria-Hungary is not one of our war aims," declared Lloyd George. President Wilson's "experts" advised him to "inflame these national movements and then to refuse the extreme and logical consequence of this discontent, which would be the dismemberment of the Austro-Hungarian Empire." The failure of this policy became evident only in February of 1918, when the Emperor Charles, petitioned by a personal envoy to President Wilson, finally answered flatly that the demands of the national minorities could not be satisfied.

The émigré leaders, who gave the impetus to the nationalist movements, had been aware of and deplored these attempted negotiations. As soon as these negotiations had proved unsuccessful, they felt free to demand independence. They henceforth received the support of France and Great Britain who, unable to secure a separate peace, proceeded to include the destruction of Austria-Hungary among their essential war aims. The Italian government, whose authority had been badly shaken in October 1917 by the disaster of Caporetto, abandoned the intransigent attitude toward the Yugoslav question it had maintained since 1915. It yielded in April 1918 to the pressure of those journalists—Salvemini and Mussolini—who had been demanding a policy of "entente" with the "oppressed minorities" of Austria-Hungary. On May 29, Wilson finally made up his mind to encourage publicly "the national aspirations of the Czechs and the Yugoslavs." It is quite likely that he considered this to be a mere expedient, a means of hastening the victory. Nonetheless he was in effect subscribing to the policy advocated by Clemenceau several days previously: "Seek to destroy Austria-Hungary by supporting its nationalities."

To what extent did the personality of the Emperor contribute to the collapse of the Dual Monarchy and the internal crisis which became increasingly apparent during June and July of 1918? The Emperor Charles distrusted Germany. According to his confidants, he went so far as to say that an "overwhelming military success" on the part of Germany would mean the ruin of Austria-Hungary. From April 1917 on he was aware that the intervention of the United States would mean the defeat of the Central Powers. He thus sought to bring about peace, even if it meant resorting to a separate peace. "To march to the bitter end with Germany out of sheer nobility would be suicide." This policy, however, was supported by neither his ministers nor his generals. Could he impose it on them? He had shown some interest in the reform plans of Polzer-Hoditz and had contemplated "reconstructing" Austria-Hungary by transforming the Dual Monarchy into a confederation of states. Because of the opposition he encountered, however, he had dismissed the head of his cabinet and ignored the offers of President Wilson. He was discredited in April of 1918 when Clemenceau published the letter in which he had declared himself in favor of France's "just claims" to Alsace-Lorraine. Thus he found himself obliged to make his excuses to the German emperor and to accept a twelve-year renewal of the Austro-German alliance to save his very throne. How could he, therefore, maintain sufficient authority to design a solution to the nationality problem? The Hungarian government persisted in refusing any suggestion whatsoever for granting autonomy, and the President of the Austrian Council declared that the German population was and should remain the backbone of Austria.

Although these internal difficulties took a distinct turn for the worse during June and July 1918, it was not until August, with the definite prospect of military defeat, that events began to take a really critical turn. At the end of September, with the collapse of the Bulgarian army, the leaders of the minority groups made revolutionary declarations, demanding independence during a session of the Austrian parliament. On October 18 the Emperor decided to announce the transformation of Austria into a federal state. He did not, however, extend this promise to Hungary, finding himself in direct conflict with the militant Magyar leaders. Too late, replied Wilson, autonomy was now insufficient to satisfy the aspirations of these peoples. This reply "shattered the framework of the monarchy." On October 24 the Emperor, resigned to the formation of separate national states, formed new ministries in Vienna and Budapest. He attempted only to provide for a vague link of confederation in the form of a common executive council. That very day the Italian army launched the offensive that was to break the front on the Piave and to demolish the Austro-Hungarian army. Thereupon, while the Emperor called for an armistice, the "national councils" organized themselves into independent governments. The proclamation of the Czechoslovakian republic and the secession of the Yugoslavs occurred on October 29, followed by the formation of a German state of Austria on October 30. The destruction of the Dual Monarchy was a *fait accompli* even before the imperial government signed the armistice of Villa Giusti on November 3. It was accomplished by the "will of the peoples" or at least by their political leaders. The peace conference would scarcely do more than to record the results obtained.

This upheaval of the nationalities was thus the deep-seated cause of the collapse of the Austro-Hungarian empire. There is no doubt that the minorities' discontent was increased by economic difficulties, and that the demand for independence did not take on a revolutionary aspect until prospects of a military defeat were assured. But the final battle, which precipitated the armistice and spelled the failure of the measures intended to preserve a "Danubian confederation," was fought by an army ravaged by desertion and demoralized by the spectacle of political confusion, by an army part of which was hostile to the existence of the Austro-Hungarian empire, part of which was certainly aware that the days of the Dual Monarchy were numbered. It is perhaps true that the nationalist movements would have ended in autonomy and not independence if not for the defeat on the Piave. But this defeat was in large part the consequence of the nationalist movements.

The Defeat of Germany

The collapse of the German empire occurred under totally different conditions. There was no sign of imminent disaster until the beginning of August 1918. At first the notion of an immediate peace or of a "public peace offer" was ruled out. Germany wished to negotiate for a compromise that would permit her to preserve the advantages gained by the Treaty of Brest-Litovsk, and that would force her only to evacuate Belgian, French, and Italian territories. But six weeks later, on September 29, the decision was made to address, without further delay, a request for an armistice and peace to the President of the United States. This was tantamount to an admission of defeat. The terms of the armistice, replied the President, would be such that "a renewal of hostilities on the part of Germany [would be] impossible." The peace, he added, would be based on his Fourteen Points of January 8, 1918, meaning that Germany must not only relinquish the territories she had annexed, but give up Alsace-Lorraine and cede the Polish territories as well. The negotiations could be conducted only with "veritable representatives of the German people" and not with "those who have hitherto been the masters of German policy." On October 27 the imperial government decided to accept Wilson's proposal unconditionally. "The war, as such, is over," said Payer, the Vice-Chancellor. The German delegation at Rethondes received the order to sign the armistice, even if it were unable to obtain a single alleviation of the conditions imposed by the Allies. The only question remaining was a political one: would the imperial regime survive? On November 3 it was toppled by the mass of the German people who blamed the dynasty for defeat and who saw in the person of Kaiser Wilhelm the obstacle to peace.

What role can be attributed to military, diplomatic, or political factors in this collapse?

After the failure of the German offensive of July 15, 1918, Foch felt that the moment had arrived to resume the initiative because of the numerical superiority afforded by the deployment of the American troops, while Ludendorff hoped to be able to hold his defensive positions, thereby maintaining a favorable "war map." The battle of Montdidier on August 8 demonstrated that the Allied high command was now capable of successfully conducting a front-breaking operation. Ludendorff knew from this moment that he was beaten. He admitted to his collaborators that his calculations had been upset, and he announced that the conduct of operations would henceforth be a "mere game of chance." He was no doubt less blunt when he addressed the Chancellor. He still hoped, he said, to maintain his forces "on French soil" and to succeed in "tiring out the enemy." These were hardly words meant to give comfort to civilians. Actually the German Supreme Headquarters awaited anxiously the general offensive that Foch was preparing to launch. "The Wilhelmstrasse is already frightened enough; it would be catastrophic if it were to learn the real nature of the military situation."

The military situation deteriorated further on other fronts. On September 14, even though the Italian army had not yet begun its final offensive, the Austro-Hungarian government declared it was unable to continue the fighting ("This is the end for us," said the Minister for Foreign Affairs), and publicly requested peace negotiations. On September 15 the Bulgarian front was broken by the Franco-Serbian offensive. On the nineteenth the British drove through the Turkish front in Palestine. The German high command was desperate. On September 25, on hearing a report—false in fact—that a serious epidemic had broken out in the French army, Ludendorff admitted to his entourage that he was clutching at this hope "like a drowning man at a straw." The following day, just as Foch's great offensive was beginning, saw the collapse of Bulgaria. The signing of the Bulgarian truce three days later now threatened the southern border of Austria-Hungary.

On September 29 at Spa, Hindenburg and Ludendorff told the Emperor that their troops could no longer continue the struggle. On September 30 they urged that the new Chancellor, Prince Max of Baden, immediately request armistice and peace, since the army was threatened with "disaster." How soon was this likely to occur? Twenty-four hours, said Ludendorff. One week, said Hindenburg. Thus, the Supreme Headquarters took the initiative in imposing its decision on a reticent government. It may have exaggerated its fears (it would later deny so) in order to overcome the government's resistance. However, the Supreme Headquarters was sincere in its anxiety. It was hardly to their advantage to show panic or to leave themselves open to criticism for not having recognized the

danger in time. Undoubtedly the generals told the Emperor that
the request for an armistice did not necessarily imply capitulation,
and that the troops might well resume the struggle after a period of
respite in case the enemy wished to annex German territory. They
did, however, give the impression by their urgency that they were
hard pressed.

The high command did indeed change its tone some time afterward. When the war cabinet examined the conditions posed by
Wilson's second note on October 17, Ludendorff declared that
breaking the front was "possible" but not "likely," and that if the
defensive battle could be prolonged another month, the arrival of
winter would put the army out of commission until the following
spring. The demands of Wilson must therefore not be accepted, he
said. Germany should agree to the truce only if its clauses allowed
her to resume the war. Capitulation was "unacceptable." Why—
after having given the impression at the end of September that
disaster was imminent—did the German high command now seem
relatively confident? Undoubtedly it found some comfort in the
dispatches. Under the repeated blows of the Allied offensive, the
German front wavered, retreated, but did not break. And yet
Ludendorff had good reason to fear a new attack on the bend
of the river Aisne, which would threaten the hinge of this front.
He wanted to gain still more time in the hope that a split might
develop among the Allies. France and Great Britain wished to impose very severe conditions on Germany, whereas the United States
might take an opposite stand if the German army were to hold
out a while longer. Such was the hope expressed by Ludendorff
on October 23.

This illusion was quickly dispelled on the following day by the
publication of the third American note. Ludendorff, however,
persisted in declaring on October 25 that the conditions imposed
were unacceptable, but gave no other argument than that of
"military honor." The government saw through this façade and
dismissed Ludendorff who, having requested the truce, sought to
be released from responsibility. It then accepted the President's
conditions unconditionally on October 27. Thus, it was indeed a
military defeat that brought about the capitulation. The govern-

ment was convinced that any attempt at resistance would be useless.

Any diplomatic moves during the three months following the
battle of August 8, in which the German armies were thrown back
from St. Quentin to Mezières, were of little importance. The German efforts to make secret contact with the enemy apparently went
unanswered. The attempt made by the Austro-Hungarian government received an immediate and unanimous refusal. It was too late
to negotiate.

The only question worthy of examination in this area is the
conduct of the German leaders at the point when they had scored
cumulative successes in both the East and the West but still could
not score a military "decision." They were obliged to decide
whether to rely on the military effort and pursue the offensive on
the Anglo-French front to its conclusion, hoping thereby to bring
about the capitulation of the enemy before the massive intervention
of the American army, or to exploit the successes already gained in
order to effect a favorable diplomatic solution. This would amount
to offering a compromise peace which the enemy, shaken by their
recent military setbacks, might be tempted to consider. Hindenburg
and Ludendorff excluded the possibility of negotiations that would
involve the complete restoration of independence to Belgium as a
prior condition. The Minister for Foreign Affairs, Kühlmann, on
the other hand, thought it prudent to resort to diplomatic means.
The conflict broke out in a meeting of the Reichstag on June 24,
when the minister expressed his skepticism regarding the military
successes: "One can hardly be expected to believe that a final
solution will be reached by military decisions alone, without
diplomatic negotiations." Supreme Headquarters protested against
language likely to shake the morale of the army on the eve of
the new campaign to be launched in Champagne. It demanded and
obtained the resignation of the dissenting minister and caused the
Chancellor to declare that Belguim must remain "under German
influence."

In short, the general staff thought it could dictate the peace
and avoid negotiation at a time when the British Minister for For-

eign Affairs had declared his intention not "to close the door on any peace effort, provided that it rested on a solid basis." It preferred instead to play its last card between the mountain of Reims and the Argonne, and it suffered total defeat.

Finally, did the interior political crisis have any real impact on the causes of the defeat?

The first symptoms of sinking morale began to appear in April 1917 among the working class. The great strike that broke out in the war plants coincided with the success of the first Russian revolution and its slogan of peace "without annexations," and with a considerable worsening in the food situation. The Social Democratic party took advantage of this social unrest to demand that the government seek a compromise peace, and to press for a political reform—the establishment of universal suffrage in Prussia—which had been requested in vain several times before 1914. It had succeeded in obtaining the support of the Catholic Center party for this program. But the "peace resolution," passed by the Reichstag on July 19, 1917, and openly fought by the Supreme Headquarters, was nothing more than a useless gesture; and this frustration that the military leaders inflicted on the parliamentary majority was barely noticed by the working classes.

At the beginning of 1918, however, the social and political malaise reappeared. There was a one-week strike in the metallurgical industry based on a purely political slogan—namely, peace "without annexations" and electoral reform—as well as a conflict over the Brest-Litovsk negotiations between the president of the Emperor's civilian cabinet and the Minister of Foreign Affairs, on the one hand, and the Supreme Headquarters, on the other. The high command in effect dictated the decisions of the government: it opposed making any concessions to the striking metallurgists and maintained an "annexationist" policy on the Polish question. "Germany," said the former Chancellor Bethmann-Hollweg, "is subjected to the dictatorship of the Supreme Headquarters." The resignation of Kühlmann five months later clearly proved that there was some truth in these words.

Such authoritarian methods, however, have to be supported by victories. As long as the 1918 campaign was marked by dazzling successes, the political role of the great army leaders had been tolerated by the public and even by the Reichstag. This ceased to be true as soon as military setbacks began to appear. National morale experienced severe depression after the hopes raised in May and June. The public manifested its distaste for governmental methods and even for the ruling dynasty. In September 1918 the heads of the political parties demanded that new men be appointed to power who would govern in accordance with the majority in the Reichstag. Several days later, when the army leaders declared it necessary to put an end to the hostilities, they were prepared to recognize that, in order to revive the country's morale, the responsibility for national destinies would have to be restored to a parliamentary government. Furthermore, this would be a way of transferring to others the responsibility of a painful liquidation. In short, the announcement of the reforms—parliamentary regime and Prussian electoral reform—sufficed momentarily to silence political agitation. In the Reichstag the new constitution was passed without the institution of the empire being called into question. The crisis of the regime was precipitated by the American note delivered on the following day. By declaring that peace could not be negotiated with the former "masters" of Germany, Wilson intended to have it known that the presence of the Emperor would be an obstacle to peace. He was entirely successful in this move. On October 31 a majority of Kaiser Wilhelm's ministers demanded his abdication. This was the wish expressed by the leaders of the Socialist party and by the trade-union leaders. It was equally sought after by part of the business middle class, especially in financial circles. The Emperor's refusal opened the way, on November 3, to the revolutionary movement. He would not resign himself to abdication until forced into it on November 9. The republic was proclaimed in Berlin under pressure from the workers. The bridges of the Rhine were on the point of falling into the hands of revolutionaries, and the army officer corps declared it impossible to deploy troops from the front for a civil war. The revolution was therefore accomplished without bloodshed.

What was the most important cause of the German collapse? This question has inspired arguments strongly influenced by various political points of view. Was Germany beaten on the battlefield? At the time of the armistice the opinion of German military circles left very little doubt that this was the case. But since operations came to a halt before any disaster occurred, a portion of the public were still under the impression that the defeat was not total. Had she succumbed to the consequences of an economic crisis provoked by the blockade? This was the thesis suggested by the English Prime Minister Lloyd George. Had she been forced to surrender on account of revolutionary activities which paralyzed the resistance of the army and gave the soldiers "a stab in the back"? Ludendorff naturally sought to authorize this version, which also appealed to the German far right. The interpreter of history is obliged to make his choice between these theses.

The blockade did not bring about a shortage of armaments. The German army had a sufficient quantity of munitions in 1918 and even an excess of artillery. It did lack tanks, but only because the general staff was late in recognizing the value of these new devices. On the other hand, food shortages did provoke serious difficulties in 1917 and at the beginning of 1918, which were at the root of the social unrest in the big cities. These sufferings were, however, relieved after the truces of Brest-Litovsk and of Bucharest. Even though in September 1918 the food supply was low, bread and potato rations were higher than they had been six months previously. At no time during the ministerial debates concerning the acceptance or refusal of American conditions was the food-supply crisis cited as a reason for terminating the war. It is true that the food situation sometimes had an influence on the decisions of the high command. In March 1918 the necessity to bring in grain and meat supplies had obliged twenty divisions to be deployed for the occupation of the Ukraine. In October, when the army was in extreme difficulty, Ludendorff declared to the war cabinet that the troops would have to be left where they were, because Germany could not afford to give up such an important source of food supply. In short, the blockade served to undermine the morale of the people and on occasion influenced the actions of the high command; the economic difficulties resulting from it, however, do not seem so grave as to necessitate the plea for a truce.

The theory of the "stab in the back" was especially provocative of Communist propaganda and led to the formation, in early November, of "workers' and soldiers' councils" inspired by the Soviet example in the principal cities of the Rhineland. During the ensuing political debate these incontrovertible facts were given an importance far in excess of their due. Actually the revolutionary events do not appear to have interfered with the defensive. The mutiny of the sailors at Kiel on November 3 undoubtedly prevented the fleet from attempting to leave the port, but even the Admiralty looked upon this attempt as being a mere "face-saving" gesture. The threat against the bridges of the Rhine on November 8 and 9 was not carried out. Furthermore, it should be noted that the decision to accept President Wilson's conditions was made by the German government on October 17, before the first revolutionary troubles. It is nonetheless true that the public had already given signs of unrest, but only since September, when the military situation had begun to appear critical not only to the experienced eye but also to the average person. This decline in the country's morale was purely the result of defeat.

Therefore, it is the military explanation for the German collapse that must be re-examined. The fate of the armed forces alone was the decisive factor. Ludendorff himself had conceded on August 8, 1918, that the war was lost. Did he not tell the government on September 29 that the army was on the verge of "disaster"? Admittedly, he later declared that it would be possible to prolong the defense, perhaps until the spring of 1919. But what would have been the outcome of such a course of action? According to Ludendorff's calculations, the German army might have been able to muster another 600,000 men for this 1919 campaign, but this would have meant enlisting defense workers, which would have brought to a complete halt the manufacture of armaments. In the course of the winter, however, the number of American troops would have increased by one million. What is there to be gained in an attempt to postpone the surrender? said the Chancellor to the war cabinet on October 17. Ludendorff added, "Our situation could not be any worse, so what do we have to lose?" But Prince Max of Baden suggested the possibility of the threat of an invasion of German territory. This dialogue cut short the debate. The war cabinet still did not take into account the immediate threats: the offensive that Foch was preparing to launch in Lorraine in November, and the offensive that could be undertaken in the direction of Bavaria due to the collapse of Austria-Hungary. How could the German high command ward off these fresh assaults? On November 5, Gröner, who had replaced Ludendorff, declared that it was high time they surrendered.

Conclusion to Book I

At the time of the capitulations of Turkey at Moudros on October 30, 1918, of Austria-Hungary at Villa Giusti on November 3, and of Germany at Rethondes on November 11, the solidarity among the victorious powers was already faltering. France, who had borne the heaviest burden in the military operations, and who had demanded a greater effort of her people than had her allies, felt that she had earned their gratitude. But Great Britain, whose naval pre-eminence had enabled the Allies to blockade the enemy, considered her part in the final victory to have been no less important than that of France. Italy, for her part, had grounds for saying that the enemy had been routed on her battlefront. Although the United States had offered only limited participation in the struggle, she knew that her role had been decisive, even in the area of military operations, since she had provided material means, paralyzed German submarine warfare, and shifted the balance of power just in time for the summer offensives of 1918. The inevitable conflicts of interest found their expression in these differences of opinion.

There was, however, no bitterness when it came to the formulation of the military and naval clauses of the armistices. True, the British and the Americans had been of the opinion that the French conditions were too severe. Was it really necessary to deprive

Germany of the major part of her heavy artillery and to impose the occupation of "bridgeheads" on the right bank of the Rhine? They ultimately yielded on the insistence of Marshal Foch. However, the Allies did come to agree over one essential point: they decided to exact such conditions as to make the resumption of hostilities impossible; but they did not contemplate pursuing the war with the sole aim of signing the armistice "in Berlin" and giving the German people a visible proof of its defeat.

The discussion of the political clauses was more difficult, with Lloyd George and Clemenceau contesting the American viewpoint. Why blindly accept the American President's Fourteen Points when they so readily lent themselves to difficulties of interpretation and to unpleasant surprises? Colonel House, the President's personal representative, did not hesitate to announce to the heads of the Allied governments on October 29 that their refusal might possibly lead the United States to negotiate a "separate peace" with Germany. Woodrow Wilson confirmed this threat, specifying the points upon which he would not yield.

I could not agree to take part in negotiations of a peace which would not include freedom of the seas, since we have committed ourselves to combat not only Prussian militarism, but also all militarism, wherever and however it might manifest itself. Neither could I participate in a settlement which would not incorporate a League of Nations, because with a peace of this sort any guarantee of security would disappear within a few years. Each nation would have to resort once more to arming itself, and the result would be disaster. I trust that I shall not be forced to take this step.

The following day, House notified the Allies that if they had any more objections, the President would ask the Senate if it was suitable for the United States to continue the war "for the benefit of the Allies." Great Britain, France, and Italy thereupon agreed to accept the Fourteen Points as the basis of the peace, with two reservations. "I consider that we have won a . . . diplomatic victory," said Colonel House. It was also, however, an omen of future discord.

For the near future the United States had, owing to its strong financial position, at its disposal considerable means for exerting pressure. On November 21, 1918, the American government announced that the system of aid established for war needs would come to an end, and that the Treasury was no longer authorized to "offer advances for reconstruction or other post-war needs." This decision did, however, provide for the possibility of furnishing "limited" credits to "certain Allied governments." It was obvious that this favor would be granted only under certain conditions.

BOOK

II

THE PEACE SETTLEMENT

Introduction to Book II

The collapse of Germany, the break up of the Austro-Hungarian empire, the paralysis of Russia, where the Soviet government was in the midst of a civil war, left the victors with complete freedom of action in drawing up peace treaties. The work at hand was immense, not only because the hostilities had extended to the Far East, the Middle East, and over a large part of Central Africa, but because they brought about profound changes within political institutions, within economic and social life, even within the mentality of the people, and because they had shifted the balance of power between continents.

The governments of the major powers who had played the decisive role in the victory therefore had to settle territorial, economic, and financial questions that arose, particularly in Europe, out of their relations with the conquered countries. But at the same time France, Great Britain, and Italy had to rebuild their own economies and safeguard interests they had possessed on the other continents before the war. The United States, which had not committed all its strength, and Japan, who had deliberately economized hers, had no such problems.

The study of the peace settlement laid down by the treaties of Versailles, Saint-Germain, Trianon, and Neuilly, and the study of the reactions of public opinion regarding the settlement should not neglect the over-all picture—namely, the blows aimed at European interests all over the world.

5

The Decline of Europe

What was Europe's material and moral condition after a war that had ravaged part of the continent for more than four years?

The European Crisis

The war cost the European countries a total of eight and a half million men from two generations: France, Germany, and Russia were the countries most heavily affected. On account of their losses and their permanently disabled, all the former belligerents suffered a manpower shortage. All over Europe the means of production were inadequate. Agriculture yield had diminished, because of lack of chemical fertilizers; sometimes in zones where the fighting had lasted longest, and where the soil was riddled with shells, it was not immediately possible to resume cultivation. Industrial activity was paralyzed because of worn-out machinery, the depleted stocks of raw material, and the complete lack of coal—production of which had diminished by 30 per cent. Rail transport was disorganized, and Europe's merchant fleet, which in 1914 constituted 85 per cent of the world's tonnage, was reduced to 70 per cent. Naturally this crisis was particularly serious in those territories— French and Belgian, Polish, Rumanian, and Serbian—that were

subjected to invasion and devastation; this was also the case of
Russia owing to the revolution and the civil war. Germany, on the
other hand, had retained 90 per cent of her industrial equipment,
of which 10 per cent was in the territories that the peace treaty
was to take away from her through the application of Wilsonian
principles. But she lost virtually all her merchant fleet and her investments abroad; having been forced by the blockade into a policy
of depletion, she had exhausted her stock of raw materials. Great
Britain, whose mines and factories were intact, had lost her important foreign markets and part of her importation facilities
abroad. Her merchant fleet had sustained heavy losses, and she had
contracted a foreign debt that tended to lower the exchange rate,
since the United States had stopped its financial assistance: the
pound, which was worth $4.76 in December of 1918, dropped in
value from month to month; and this depreciation gravely compromised the role of the London financial market in international
commercial transactions.

The dominant feature of the crisis was underproduction. In
order to obtain raw materials and to build up industry, Europe was
forced to call upon the resources of other continents. But she also
suffered a financial crisis that severely curtailed her purchases. The
national debt had risen considerably in every country; it had risen
to six times the 1913 figure in Italy, seven times in France, ten times
in Great Britain, twenty times in Germany. Of course these burdens, which weighed heavily on the administration of public
finances, were not necessarily a sign of impoverishment in a nation.
But foreign debt was a liability to the economies of France, Great
Britain, Italy, and Belgium. All the belligerent countries had to
resort to inflation—some more than others—in order to pay off
the exceptional war expenses; this measure decreased the possibilities of importing. The gold reserves of the central banks were so
depleted that there was no question of turning to them in order to
pay for purchases. The debts that were owed to Europe from
abroad before the war were for the large part paid up.

Compared with this exhausted Europe, the great non-European
countries were prosperous, for the war had given them the oppor-

tunity to increase their industrial production, to change the nature of their agricultural production, and to improve their balance of payments.

The South American countries, which, prior to 1914, were within the European economic sphere of influence—they purchased manufactured goods from Europe and sold there raw material or foodstuffs—had built textile factories and created a heavy metal industry, while at the same time they increased wheat, meat, or cane-sugar exports to European countries. The profits realized by these producers enabled South Americans to amass their own capital, which gave these countries their first hopes of economic independence.

Japan had sold to China, India, and Indochina manufactured goods that Europe could not produce; she had exported to belligerent states—particularly to Russia—war matériel and ammunition. The volume of her industrial production had almost increased by 500 per cent; her balance of payments, which prior to 1914 had been unfavorable, now showed a sizable surplus. Various enterprises, particularly the metal industry, had realized considerable profits: several companies distributed dividends of 20 per cent in 1918, and four among them even issued dividends of 50 per cent.

The United States rapidly increased her economic and financial power: coal production rose from 513,000,000 tons in 1913 to 685,000,000 tons in 1918; steel production doubled; the tonnage of the merchant fleet, which had quadrupled, reached 85 per cent of that of the British merchant fleet, whereas in 1913 it was only 23 per cent. Between 1914 and 1918, exports exceeded imports by nine and a half billion dollars—a sum equal to the entire export surplus of the preceding hundred and twenty-five years. Master of nearly half of the world's gold supply, the United States, while buying up American stocks belonging to foreign capitalists, was also lending ten billion dollars to belligerent countries and had become the great exporter of capital, particularly to South America.

While the governments were discussing the clauses of the treaties and when the parliaments were called upon to ratify them, public opinion in Europe was more preoccupied with difficult, immediate material problems than with international questions. This point must not be forgotten in a study of the peace settlement.

While seriously affected by underproduction, Europe was suffering a moral crisis. She began to have doubts about the principles that had governed the forms of social and political life before 1914.

There was a threat to liberal and democratic institutions. It did not come to light, it is true, immediately after the signing of the armistice in 1918. The victory of the United States, Great Britain, France, and Italy was a victory for the great powers whose political regimes were based upon liberalism, universal suffrage, and the exercise of legislative power by a parliamentary assembly. These institutions had proved their strength, flexibility, and effectiveness during the war; and the small countries, to which the war had given birth, or which it had transformed, did not hesitate to adopt, in 1919, a type of regime that had already proved its worth. But it was a precarious victory—precarious primarily because of the change brought about in the public mentality by the exigencies of wartime. The respect for the rights of the individual, which had been one of the basic principles of liberalism, had been undermined by unusual circumstances; the press had been watched over, and propaganda had been effectively used to influence public opinion. The restriction of freedom outlived the conditions that had imposed it, and public reaction was no longer the same as before the war.

These doubts were aggravated by the influence of new ideas stemming from opposite viewpoints, which sapped the foundations of liberal democracy.

The state, according to Lenin, is and could only be, an instrument of restraint and domination. In the past this instrument, through police and armed force, had served the interests and the designs of the bourgeoisie. The goal of the Soviet regime was to substitute for this bourgeois domination the hegemony of the proletariat, a measure indispensable for the creation of a socialist economy: it would be impossible to break bourgeois resistance without recourse to dictatorial methods during a "transitional" period, which might be prolonged. The new doctrine subordinated the individual to the state, whose power was to be limitless when taking measures designed to achieve "revolutionary goals."

The ideology of fascism was expressed—three years before Mussolini's *coup d'état*—by Oswald Spengler, when in 1918 he published *The Decline of Europe,* which was soon to sell one hundred thousand copies. Democracy is nothing but an illusion, for universal suffrage offers "no real rights": the electorate is at the mercy of the party steering committees who dictate their will through propaganda. Parliamentarianism, which was "a continuation of the bourgeois revolution of 1789," had lost its attraction, either because it had served as an instrument of economic power, or because it was overshadowed by the operation of economic and social forces outside of its jurisdiction. According to Spengler, this breakdown of democracy paved the way for the "irresistible" march toward the cult of the "strong man." The masses were prepared to trust in leaders who were capable of curbing vested interests, of making people aware of the need for sacrifices, leaders who would be able to form a ruling class in order to assure the continuation of their work.

There was a social crisis: in all the belligerent nations the war had brought about a sweeping transfer of wealth. Monetary inflation distinctly altered the relative standard of living. The peasant masses, which had on the whole suffered the greatest losses in manpower, profited from the urgent need for food. In large parts of Central Europe they also benefited from land reform, which the governments of new or "reconstructed" countries hoped would counteract the spread of communist ideas, and would at the same time destroy the power of the great landed proprietors, whose interests and sympathies lay with vanished political regimes. But the working classes found themselves in a far more difficult predicament when the hostilities came to an end. In most of the belligerent countries, the rise in wages, particularly among "skilled" laborers, had been slower than that of the cost of living. The situation improved somewhat during the last weeks of 1918, but real wages dropped again when demobilization threw millions of men onto the labor market. By the end of spring and during the summer of 1918, social protest began to appear in Britain, France, and Italy.

These strike movements were in fact not revolutionary in nature: in January the Socialist parties in all three countries had refused to join the Communist International and, during a conference at Berne in February, condemned the forceful seizure of power and the dictatorship of the proletariat. And yet the anxiety aroused by labor agitation forced the governments, in drawing up peace treaties, not to prolong this period of incertitude, which was slowing down the rebuilding of the economy.

Finally, there was the rising tide of nationalism. During the war both camps had used the "principle of nationalities" continually as a propaganda weapon. The Allies, who had hesitated while Russia was still czarist, gave their support during March of 1917 to the "national committees" formed by Czech, Polish, Serb, and Croat émigrés. In 1916 the Central Powers tried to encourage the Irish nationalists against Great Britain and the nationalism of the Baltic and Finnish peoples against Russia, and even tried to turn the Polish nationalist movement to their own advantage. How could these appeals to sentiment fail to continue to provoke severe agitation, even after the armistice? Should not the principle of nationalities, according to the Wilsonian program, dominate the settlement on territorial questions in the peace treaties?

The European peoples involved in this problem were fully aware of the impossibility of applying this principle in all the border areas where the linguistic map showed mixtures of races. Where therefore was one to find the clearly recognizable line of demarcation—the subject of Point 9 of Wilson's message—between Italians, Slovenes, and Croats? How was one to determine a territorial division in Bohemia between the Czechs and the Germans who were, furthermore, bound by economic ties? What frontier was one to fix in Transylvania, where Germans and Magyars had formed communities within a Rumanian majority, some of which went back to the thirteenth century? And how was one to determine the nationality of the inhabitants of Macedonia, where linguistic groupings—Bulgarians, Serbs, and Greeks—did not always coincide with the religious groupings of the three rival Orthodox churches?

The "nationalities" were prepared for battle immediately after the armistice. The new states, in the euphoria of the victory which had been won virtually for their sake, were inspired with a fighting spirit and set about preparing arguments to support their territorial claims. They did not stop at invoking the principle of nationhood but added both "historic rights" and economic interests. The mixtures of populations, they said, were often nothing short of a colonization by the former masters of a territory; it would be an act of straightforward justice to remedy such situations, even when they were centuries old. And should not these populations, liberated from foreign domination, receive the mineral deposits or railroads upon which their economic life depended, even if the rights of nationalities should suffer as a result? Strategic arguments were rarely overtly invoked; and yet these arguments often inspired all the others.

But even as the political and social concepts that had prevailed in the nineteenth and early twentieth centuries crumbled, a new concept of international relations was emerging in the minds of statesmen and in the temper of the masses—a concept that stemmed from a movement fostered in certain liberal and democratic circles.

Prior to 1914 the notions of a "United States of Europe" or of a "league of nations" were not much beyond the "academic" stage and had had no influence on international political relations. Although the war had frustrated these hopes, it did not discourage the pacifist organizations: after all, in order to bear this trial, humanity needed to believe that a better world would emerge from the crisis. The initiative came from the neutral countries. The League to Enforce Peace was founded in January 1915 in the United States under the leadership of former President Taft. This society outlined a plan for a league of nations that would be charged with arbitrating international conflicts and with imposing respect for its rulings through economic, financial, or even military sanctions. In April 1915, at The Hague, Dutch and Swiss pacifists created the Central Organization for a Lasting Peace. The idea was then taken up by intellectual groups in the belligerent countries: in London, the League of Nations Society and in Paris a magazine called *La Paix par le Droit* drew up similar plans. Even in Germany a group of lawyers and political writers, the *Bund neues Vaterland,* also developed similar plans. In May of 1916, President Wilson pledged the support of the greatest neutral power for these ideals. He evoked a response in Great Britain, where the Secretary of State for Foreign Affairs agreed to the idea in principle. He even found an echo in Berlin, where Chancellor Bethmann-Hollweg was at that moment preparing a "peace offensive." But the idea became a reality only after the United States had entered the war, when the President undertook the role of arbitrator of the future peace: the message of January 8, 1918, brought to the foreground, among the main points of this peace, the idea of the creation of a "general society of nations," capable of giving all the would-be member states "mutual guarantees of political independence and territorial integrity."

It was only natural that in 1919 these ideas found strong support in public opinion. The exhausted populations wanted a new order that would assure stability and security in international relations—just as they had after all the great international crises of the nineteenth century: in 1815, in 1849, and in 1871. They hoped that this new order would prevent a return to the agonies suffered by a large portion of the world during the space of more than four years. The Wilsonian ideal corresponded to their most profound aspirations.

Also, it is important to mention the new direction of these concepts. Whereas before 1914 the formation of a "United States of Europe" had been the central thesis of this movement, we now see the European project being absorbed into a universal design. This was the necessary consequence of a world war in which the intervention of the United States had been decisive. But it was also the proof that Europe sensed the need of this American presence to ensure the future organization of peace. Was this a prelude to the "decline of Europe"?

The Fate of European Imperialism

What was to happen to the colonies or zones of influence in the "new countries" during this decline? The predominant position held by Europe up until 1914 was now being challenged.

The European countries, obliged to devote all their strength and resources to the struggle, were forced to suspend their efforts in the area of economic expansion. Engaged in mutual destruction, they had lost the prestige that their successful methods had gained them in the past. Finally, they had seen the foundations of imperialism undermined by criticisms and by slogans which were adopted by the intellectuals in the colonies or in the zones of influence. The position in world economy that the belligerent states had held up until this time had been largely lost through the mobilization of industries for war needs and through the lack of maritime transport. Even Great Britain, who at the beginning of the war strove to maintain her normal economic activity to the best of her ability, had soon been obliged to abandon this effort: her exports, which in 1913 reached £630,000,000 sterling, dropped to £532,000,000 in 1918; taking into account the rise in prices, this decline in export volume amounted to approximately 40 per cent. In France goods exported in 1918, calculated by weight, represented only one third of those exported before the war. European commerce had therefore lost a share in foreign markets which was quickly picked up by the United States and Japan. This was of course to be a temporary loss! But when were these markets to be recovered?

In regions under the political domination or the predominant influence of the Europeans, the spectacle of the war in Europe encouraged the hope of escaping this ascendancy. In certain instances the initiative taken by the belligerent states even unconsciously favored this hope.

In order to counteract the chronic shortage of manpower, Great Britain and France recruited natives from their overseas colonies: India furnished 943,000 men, 683,000 of whom were soldiers; the French colonies and protectorates furnished 928,000 men, of whom 690,000 were soldiers. The mobilized natives came into contact both with their fellow soldiers and with militant trade-unionists in the munitions factories; when they went home, therefore, they brought back new ideas; they had become "thinkers," stated a French politician who was an authority on colonial matters.

On the other hand, in order to frustrate Turkish policy, to avoid the risk of a "holy war," and also to protect the Suez Canal from a Turkish offensive, British diplomacy encouraged the Arab nationalist movement and promised the Emir of Hejaz that he would be placed at the head of a great independent Arab state. This move opened the way to success in the Palestine campaign—but by the end of 1918 it had placed Great Britain in a difficult situation in Palestine, Iraq, and even in Syria, where the promises given the Arabs contradicted secret Franco-British agreements. The British cabinet had roused a people who temporarily had rendered it a service, but who became a burden and even a threat before the war was over.

Finally, in 1917 Great Britain and France, who since 1842 had imposed a status of political inferiority upon the Chinese government through the system of "unequal treaties," desired and obtained China's entry into the war. They had obtained several immediate advantages (the recruiting of Chinese labor to work in French industry or public works; the confiscation of German ships that had taken refuge in Chinese ports since 1914); but above all they particularly wanted to convince the Chinese government that it could expect their diplomatic support at the peace conference, and thus lead it into resisting Japanese pressure. The fact that China was to participate at the peace conference on equal footing, at least theoretically, with the great powers, meant that she could certainly profit from the situation to demand the annulment of the "unequal treaties."

But these aspirations for emancipation were particularly encouraged by the diffusion of the Wilsonian ideas and by communist doctrine which, as opposed as they were on certain matters, in this case found common ground in the condemnation of "colonialism." In his public statements the President of the United States declared that the power of all governments should rest on the consent of the people. He applied this principle of free self-determination of people to colonialism. He did recognize the necessity of economic expansion and the importance of foreign markets; thus, he granted that an industrial nation might force a "new country" to open its commerce to the more highly developed nation through coercion or even temporary military occupation.

But he also recognized the right of a people to demand its freedom the moment it was prepared for self-government. Domination should only be transitional. Wilson also declared, in his message of January 8, 1918, that in the settlement of colonial matters "the interests of the populations concerned must have equal weight with the equitable claims of the government whose title is to be determined." During a speech given on July 4, 1918, he added that all territorial questions should be settled "upon the basis of the free acceptance of that settlement by the people immediately concerned." He therefore desired to avoid extending colonial domination over new territories; to hand over these territories to a nation that would receive a mandate to administer them; and to entrust the League of Nations with control over mandatory power. This "mandate" system would ensure the development of a territory for the sake of its inhabitants and would protect them from abuse such as forced labor or confiscation of lands. The President of the United States wanted, it is true, to apply his ideas cautiously, for he did not wish to clash with the interests of France and Great Britain. But the intellectuals among the native populations of European colonies were interested only in the doctrine of self-determination and were not concerned with Wilson's mental reservations.

European world interests were even more directly menaced by Communist propaganda. In September of 1917—even before the Bolshevik coup—Lenin published *Imperialism, Highest Stage of Capitalism,* in which he offered a general interpretation of the history of European expansion. The concentration of industry has given finance capitalism the dominant role in economic life; the accumulation of capital has reached such proportions that investments outside Europe have become indispensable: the export of capital, even more than the search for foreign markets, has thus been the motive behind imperialism, be it colonial conquest or a "semicolonial" domination resulting from the policy of spheres of influence. Consequently we have, on the one hand, the birth of new rivalries between the great powers, since the attempted common exploitation of new countries amounted to a "truce." According to Lenin, the First World War had been a war "for the division and distribution of the world, the distribution and re-distribution of colonies, of zones of influence, of finance capital." On the other hand we have the development of a "universal system of colonial oppression," which had placed "more than half of the world population" under the yoke of the great industrial powers. However, the penetration of these imperial powers modified the ancient social structures in these new countries; it put an end to "the thousand year isolation of agriculture": the oppressed people thus became aware of their national identity. At the same time capitalism met with an ever increasing resistance although, ironically, it was capitalism itself that opened the prospect of emancipation to these peoples.

The practical conclusion toward which Lenin's thesis was leading was expressed in March 1919 in the final resolution of the first congress of the Communist International: struggle against imperialism whether colonial or "semicolonial"; encourage "movement of emancipation"; destroy this imperialism, which is indispensable to the stability of capitalism—that must be the program.

This program thus attacked all forms of European economic expansion, going considerably further than Wilson's critique, which applied only to "colonialism," and which, said the Communist Congress, amounted to a mere "changing of labels."

What were the respective parts these two influences, American and Russian, played in the emancipation movements that in 1919 destroyed the achievements of European expansion. It would be hardly worth while to attempt to answer this question, for the historical information is still too fragmentary to draw valid conclusions. Besides, this critique of imperialism would have to confine itself to intellectual circles. The deepest influences motivating the masses were doubtless an automatic xenophobic reflex, the sufferings created by the economic situation, and finally religion.

It is important to outline the nature of each of these anti-European movements in the colonies and in the zones of influence.

India was the "jewel" of the British empire. The British presence in this enormous mass of humanity—approximately 320,000,000 inhabitants in 1919—was minimal: 60,000 soldiers, 25,000 civil servants, and 50,000 colonists, technicians, or businessmen. And yet, since the great uprising of 1857, British domination had not been directly threatened, thanks to internal dissent—religious, linguistic, and social—among the natives. Even though the intellectual and commercial bourgeoisie had sought an autonomous status similar to that of a dominion after 1885, and especially since 1905, the "National Congress" had not succeeded in overcoming the resistance of the British government. But the World War had given the nationalist movement new strength, and in June of 1916 the Muslims, to mark their hostility to Great Britain's Arab policy and their support for Muslim unity, agreed to collaborate with the Hindus. The British cabinet thought it necessary to offer a compromise. The memorandum issued in July of 1918 by the Secretary of State, Lord Montagu, and by the Viceroy, Lord Chelmsford, on Indian constitutional reform, envisaged the creation of assemblies, recruited in part by an electoral system, which could participate in formulating legislation on certain matters. The National Congress considered these concessions insufficient. This offer was not in vain, however, for—as Lord Montagu mentions in his *Journal*—India was quiet throughout the spring of 1918 while awaiting these reforms—that is to say, during the critical hour of the war in Europe. But from early 1919 on, nationalist protest gained renewed strength. This protest was first directed, in March, toward exceptional police powers which the administration wished to retain although hostilities were over; and within a few days it took on the appearance of a mass movement: a general strike lasting twenty-four hours was prelude to a campaign of "civil disobedience." On August 10 at Amritsar disturbances ended in a massacre (379 rioters killed, hundreds injured)—owing to the nervousness of a British general. The Emir of Afghanistan, Amanullah, opened hostilities, with the hope of provoking a general uprising in India; he was beaten but obtained a peace treaty recognizing the independence of his country and finally putting an end to the quasi protectorate that Great Britain had exercised since 1879. Although the British government had repelled the attack, it was too apprehensive about the situation in India to embark upon a campaign against Afghanistan. The British Parliament learned a lesson from this crisis: it decided to vote in favor of the reforms promised by the Montagu-Chelmsford memorandum.

Why this sudden spurt of nationalist activity? Economic conditions certainly contributed to provoke the crisis; the peasants had good reason to complain. During the World War the price of manufactured goods rose, as did taxes. In 1918 they were afflicted with a poor harvest which condemned part of the country to starvation during the first months of 1919. Above all, the actions of an exceptional personality played a dominant role: Gandhi inspired the masses through the powerful attraction of his disdain for material goods, his spirit of sacrifice, his desire to establish harmony among people, and the strength of his religious feeling.

In Egypt, where Great Britain—after more than thirty years of illegal occupation—had established its protectorate in November of 1914, the "National party," under the leadership of Zaghlul Pasha, demanded independence directly after the armistice in the name of Wilsonian principles. The demand was immediately turned down by the British cabinet, which subsequently arrested Zaghlul. This action resulted in an uprising which rudely shook British domination for three weeks in March 1919, until Anglo-Indian mobile units arrived from Palestine. The nationalist leaders then adopted another approach—namely, "passive resistance"—which perpetuated a state of alert. The High Commissioner, General Allenby, recommended that the British government adopt a policy of appeasement, and freed Zaghlul. In September the government flatly turned down the demand for independence and announced its intention of establishing a regime that would accord an important legislative role to elected representatives of the Egyptian people. This marked the beginning of long and bitter controversies, which were to end with the abolition of the protectorate by the declaration of February 28, 1922. In this Egyptian movement, nationalist resistance was not limited to the group of Muslim intellectuals who prior to 1914, as in the case of India, had been the militant agitators: Zaghlul formed an alliance between the Copts and the Muslims and was able to rouse political interest in rural districts by exploiting the unrest provoked by the requisition of manpower, beasts of burden, and foodstuffs during 1918 for the needs of the expeditionary force in Palestine and Syria. There again, the economic and social situation favored nationalist propaganda; but it was an outstanding personality who provided the impetus.

The Union of South Africa was inhabited by 5,000,000 blacks; 1,500,000 Europeans, of whom 480,000 were British and 800,000 were Boers; 200,000 Hindus, the labor force of the Natal plantations; and 600,000 Chinese, imported for working the mines. Social life was dominated by the racial antipathies and the rival economic interests of these heterogeneous elements. Here was a situation favorable to the maintenance of British domination, for no nationalist movement could unite these disparate groups. The whites—British and Boer—feared being eventually overrun by the blacks, whose numbers were rising more rapidly since the British occupation had brought with it peace and medical care. But the two elements of this white population were divided by the memories of the South African war, by language, and even by life styles. To be sure, the "South African party," to which the majority of the British belonged, also counted among its members "reconciled Boers"; but the "National Boer party," whose supporters were the small rural landowners, was anti-British. In January of 1919 this nationalist party decided to claim independence for the Transvaal and for Orange in the name of President Wilson's principles; yet at the same time it did not attempt to step beyond the bounds of being a legal opposition.

France met with far less serious resistance in her colonies and protectorates. There was no active opposition, either in Algeria or in Indochina. In Morocco, between 1914 and 1918, the far-sightedness of Lyautey succeeded in maintaining French authority in areas that had been "pacified" despite the retreat of the major part of the occupation forces. The resident general nevertheless conceded that the Wilsonian principles and the events in Egypt gave rise to a flow of ideas, of comments upon world events and on the condition of the Islamic peoples, and councils among the native elite. He also recommended to the French government that they should accord the necessary satisfactions to this elite without delay. A protest movement developed in Tunisia, whose leader, Abdel Aziz Taalbi, had studied in Cairo and had been in contact, prior to 1914, with nationalist leaders in India. The "Destour" party, without going as far as claiming independence, invoked the Fourteen Points to ask that the ministry formed by the Bey be responsible to an elected legislative assembly. But this resistance did not involve the use of force.

The Italian domination in Libya, on the other hand, was almost completely eliminated. In October of 1914 the Senoussite sect, strict Muslims and fervent Arab nationalists, forced the Italian troops to abandon all the interior of Tripoli and Cyrenaica. Through an agreement signed in April of 1917 with the Grand Senoussi, Mohammed Idriss, the Italian government had promised not to attempt any expansion of her zone of occupation, which was in fact reduced to five or six fortified bases along the coastline. In November of 1918 the native leaders, probably urged on by Turkish officers, invoked the right of free self-determination of peoples and announced the existence of a "Republic of Tripolitania." The Italian government felt it could not ask the nation to make the effort required for a colonial expedition, considering its present state of economic exhaustion. It preferred to negotiate a compromise. In April of 1919 the Kallet-ez-Zeituna agreement established a system of "association" which would grant Italian citizenship to the natives, who could vote for a legislative assembly, and turned over the administration to Arab civil servants. Italian sovereignty was likely to be reduced to appearances.

The Spanish presence in northern Morocco was equally precarious. Since 1915 a native resistance movement had to all intents and purposes confined the military occupation to the coastal areas. In 1919 the leader of this movement, Abd-el-Krim, asked the Spanish government to abandon the military administration and appoint a civilian governor. He was not unaware that certain high-ranking Spanish army officers had considered relinquishing this Moroccan region, where the rebellion had never been put down. General Primo de Rivera had supported this thesis in a lecture he gave at the Royal Cadiz Academy in 1917.

Finally, Holland encountered serious difficulties in its Indies. The Dutch government had hoped to prevent these problems by convening a "People's Council" toward the end of 1918, whose powers were only consultative, but which accorded a place to the representatives of the "native elite." This elite had not been satisfied with this modest concession. In 1919 two opposition movements were formed; both of them were nationalist, but one was liberal, the other communist. The association of *Sarekat Islam,* which had two and a half million members, expressed the opinion of the merchants and the liberal professions; it did not demand independence and was content with autonomy. Even while taking a stand against Bolshevism, it campaigned against "tyrannical capitalism"—that is, against the large European companies that, thanks to a privileged regime, hindered the development of native enterprises. It wanted to organize a labor movement, with the goal of establishing social legislation, and also to develop a subordinate personnel for the nationalist movement. Communist propaganda, which had been promoted by Dutchmen, hardly penetrated the Moslem populations and was directed mainly toward soldiers and sailors. The new development was the emergence, at the head of the movement, of a Javanese called Semaoen, who in the following year was to affiliate the "Dutch Indies Communist party" with the Third International. The Dutch press gave full coverage to the riots and plots that threatened the security of the colonists; but it indicated that the nation was determined to hold out.

It was not only these movements for autonomy or independence in the colonies which curbed European predominance. The "new countries," in whose economies European interests played a major role and thus opened the way to political influence, also tried to emancipate themselves.

During the crises that the Chinese empire had undergone in 1894–1895, 1900–1901, and 1911–1912, foreign observers were struck by the passivity of the populace: save for a limited number of groups—intellectuals, members of Sun Yat-sen's Republican movement, and members of secret societies—there was no sign of patriotic feeling. It would be true to say, however, that in 1915, on the occasion of a threat of conflict between China and Japan, the urban populations, at least in the large cities and in the ports, had appeared to wake up to the needs of the country; but this reaction was very temporary.

During May of 1919, a nationalist Chinese movement, at first directed against Japan, emerged on the occasion of the peace settlement. It also opposed "unequal treaties"—that is, the privileges obtained by foreign powers in China between 1842 and 1914.

The intellectual renaissance and the desire to further their economic interests were the determining forces behind this nationalist movement.

The civil war, which once again had been ravaging China since the end of 1916, in no way interfered with the activity of the intellectual movement: philosophical studies, which neglected neither current European thought nor the "pragmatism" of the American John Dewey; historical research, in which an effort was made to evaluate documents; discussions in literary societies which tried to outline social tendencies in the novel. The spectacle of fruitless political agitation and the disorder of the country appeared to cause the intellectuals to widen their horizons. These intellectual debates focused on the conflict between partisans of Chinese civilization and partisans of Western civilization; the latter were divided into admirers of Europe or of the United States and supporters of Soviet communism.

Loyalty to the Chinese traditions found its most authoritative expression in two men who had both studied European civilization before condemning it: one was a philosopher, Chang Toun-sun; the other a political thinker, Leang Ki-chao. On returning to China after having lived for several years in Europe, Leang published a series of articles on "The Intellectual Bankruptcy of Europe." What was the reason, he asked, for the increasing social conflict to be found in the large cities of England or France in 1919? European society "lived in a depressing atmosphere," because it had lost sight of moral standards and because it had placed its confidence in scientific progress, the source of "every evil." Chinese civilization was "more complete and more perfect." It would be doubtless desirable to adopt certain techniques borrowed from Europe; but one must preserve the intellectual and moral concepts that mark the superiority of Chinese thought.

Western civilization, on the other hand, proclaimed Ho-che, a young professor at the University of Peking, has been called upon "to rule over the entire world," because it "frees man from the influences of environment, from the tyranny of habit, from the blindness of superstition." To preach the superiority of Chinese civilization is to favor the "inertia and vanity" of the Chinese people. Ho-che, who had studied at American universities, did not hesitate therefore to challenge the very foundations of Confucianism. He not only advocated the adoption of European political concepts, liberalism and democracy, but he accepted the idea of the emancipation of women and children within family life. He maintained that a whole new civilization had to be "created." This reconstruction would encourage China to resist Japanese pressure and to reject the "unequal treaties" imposed upon her by the European countries. His goal was therefore nationalistic.

But other professors at the University of Peking thought, on the contrary, that the kind of civilization that the great nineteenth-century European countries had fostered in the Far East had brought about a "degradation" of China, since this penetration had come hand in hand with imperialism. Disenchanted with the Chinese republic, which had wanted to adopt Western methods of political organization and had only achieved further confusion, these intellectuals looked upon the Russian Revolution with sympathy. The advent of a communist regime, wrote Li Ta-chao in May of 1919, demonstrates that "capitalist imperialism" is not invulnerable. On May 25, 1919, the Soviet government declared itself prepared to renounce the "unequal treaties." Would not communism afford the best means "to frustrate the aggressive policies of the capitalist countries"? According to these advocates, adherence to the Leninist doctrine was less important than the manifestation of nationalist sentiment.

Social conditions favored this nationalist movement, but they were in fact a minor influence. Directly after the signing of the armistice, Chinese industrialists and merchants, who had profited from the decline of European economic influence between 1914 and 1918, were once again competing with merchandise imported from Europe and saw foreign factories set up on Chinese territory return to capacity production; they could not expect protective measures, since the "unequal treaties" had limited the Chinese tariff rate to 5 per cent *ad valorem* and had afforded foreigners extraterritorial privileges, very useful in business. The owners of these Chinese enterprises, who suffered these disadvantages from 1920 on—especially between 1925 and 1929—were naturally inclined to blame the unequal treaties for their misfortunes. The workers in modern industries—it would appear that there were approximately three million of them in 1919—had reason to complain about their employers, for between 1914 and 1919 the cost of living considerably exceeded the rise in wages; but their social protest movement was also concerned with national problems. Chinese capitalism had joined forces with foreign capitalism, helping the latter to exploit China. Was this not sufficient reason to condemn it?

A vigorous national awakening was thus the new feature of Chinese life, whose future seemed so uncertain. There is a clear relation between the movement of May 1919 and the xenophobic movements that were to expand so much between 1925 and 1926.

Nationalistic movements broke out with even more vigor in the Turkish and Arab regions of the Middle East.

The Turkish nationalist movement found its doctrine in the work of a writer, sociologist, and poet, Ziya Gokalp, who had been a member of the "Union and Progress Committee" from the Young Turk revolt of 1908 until the end of the First World War. According to Gokalp, the decadence of the Ottoman empire was due to an overemphasis on Islamic civilization—whose origins were Arab and Persian rather than Turkish—in guiding the destiny of the state. The confusion between political power and religious power in the person of the Sultan Caliph, and the application of the precepts of the Koran to everyday life, had hindered the adoption of European technology. The reform measures should therefore include the separation of church and state, then adoption of Western scientific and technical methods, and finally the establishment of a political system that would give power to the intellectual elite. Only the Turkish regions of the Ottoman empire should benefit from these reforms. The Turkish state would be based no longer on the community of religious faith, but on the idea of nationhood. When in July 1919 Mustapha Kemal, inspector of the army of Anatolia, took a stand against the Sultan's government, he criticized it for agreeing to the demands of the victorious armies. And when at the end of 1919 he caused the Assembly to convene at Ankara to ratify the "National Charter," and then in April of 1920 decided to found a Turkish republic in Anatolia, he retained the essence of Gokalp's ideas: the secularization and Westernization of Turkey. This effort at national reform can be in certain respects likened to Japan's accomplishments between 1870 and 1890.

The awakening of Arab nationalism had become a political force only between 1904 and 1914, without causing much of a stir. The World War gave it new blood, because it had been to Great Britain's advantage to play the Arab world against the Turks. In 1918 the proclamation issued by General Allenby in Jerusalem promised independence to the Arabs of the Ottoman empire. The British government had doubtless, through the agreements concluded with the Emir of Hejaz, Hussein, and with the Emir of Nejd, Ibn Saud, laid the groundwork that would, it was hoped, give it a predominant influence in these independent Arab states. But its position was still precarious, even though these diplomatic precautions were bolstered by a policy of subsidies. These precautions might have been effective insofar as the leaders of native movements were involved in personal rivalries, also as "orthodox Islam" feared the success of the Wahhabite sect, of which Ibn Saud was the symbol. The situation might have been reversed if the sovereigns of the new states had been wise enough to unite through an alliance, or perhaps through federation, and to conduct a joint program against the direct or indirect domination of the Europeans.

The same forces were at work in all of these movements of resistance to European expansion, which opposed political in-

THE PEACE SETTLEMENT [144]

fluence, or sometimes even economic influence, but nevertheless did not deny the attractions of Western culture. Economic and financial difficulties, which had been the result of the war, had given rise to resentment in the masses, which sometimes took the form of violent protest; but even more potent was a nationalist awakening or a wave of religious sentiment, which were sometimes linked together (as in Egypt and India), sometimes separate. In the Middle East the economic aspects were of only secondary importance: the will for independence motivated the activists—that is, the intellectuals—who were more often than not indifferent to religion; religious fervor, however, led the masses to follow the movement. In China economic interests partially explain the solid support for the nationalist movement in urban areas, but they had no influence at all over the intellectuals. In South Africa the difficulties confronting the British administration lay in the contrasting civilizations.

Although each of these nationalist movements had a particular character, they were successful only when inspired by the action of a great man. Sun Yat-sen, Mustapha Kemal, Gandhi, and Zaghlul were hardly newcomers; each man already had a large audience in his country. It was their moral authority, as much as their political astuteness, that brought them to the foreground in this effort to establish resistance to Europe in 1919.

The Peace Conference

If it had not been for the promise that President Wilson exacted from his associates—namely, that the peace treaties be based on the Fourteen Points outlined in his message to Congress on January 8, 1918—the peace would probably have been a stringent one. But these Wilsonian formulas were so vague and poorly adapted to certain realities that they laid themselves open to contradictory interpretations. The losers therefore did not give up the hope of being able to strike bargains by turning the conflicting interests of the winners to their advantage.

The Participants

Among the five major powers associated with the victory, one, Japan, had taken no part in the European war; she had expansionist designs only on eastern Asia; however, her ambitions in this area were vast.

Nationalism had from far back deep roots in the collective psychology of the Japanese ruling classes; between 1894 and 1914 it had started as an expansionist effort which corresponded to the necessities of the economy. Nationalism had at no time found a counterbalance in this country, where socialist ideas had hardly spread at all, and where the internationalist doctrines of the pacifist movement had met with no apparent response. Had these conditions changed by 1919?

The nature of the collective psychology had hardly changed. Socialist propaganda began to appear in the press, in which the government tolerated criticisms directed toward the "excesses of capitalism" and the intervention of the military in politics; but socialist newspapers were careful not to stress internationalist tendencies, perhaps because they were aware that these ideas would hardly be compatible with the cult of the Emperor or with the faith that the majority of the working classes still had in this tradition. Communist ideas were doubtless circulated despite government ban. One hundred thousand copies of *Das Kapital* in the abridged Kautsky version were circulated, so the story goes, under wraps; but as soon as the first partisans tried to form a party, they were arrested. There was, therefore, no organized resistance to the current wave of nationalism.

Demographic conditions strengthened support for imperialism. In 1914 there were fifty million inhabitants in the Japanese archipelago. There were nearly sixty-five million by 1919. This rapid increase posed the obvious question of overpopulation: the insufficient supply of food; the impossibility of allotting even the smallest piece of land to a surfeit of "candidates." What were the possible remedies? Voluntary birth control? The government forbade all dissemination of birth control propaganda of which, incidentally, the people disapproved. An increase in the amount of land devoted to agriculture? To obtain a 20 per cent raise, by means of irrigation projects, would have required twenty years and a huge financial outlay—a slow and costly solution. As for immigration, the Japanese peasant was never very willing to leave home; and, apart from that, the countries bordering on the Pacific where land was still available closed their doors to Orientals. The only remedy, therefore, was industrial development, which would provide ample work for the peasant and permit the purchase of food from abroad in return for the export of manufactured goods. Nevertheless, Japanese industry still had to find markets and supplies of raw materials abroad. This indispensable economic expansion could develop under the easiest and surest conditions, provided it was supported by territorial expansion.

And yet Japan only played a limited role in the general settlements of the peace, for, except on rare occasions, her delegation did not participate in the discussions between the chiefs of state over the European matters.

The three major European powers who bore the brunt of the war operations, though unequally, were in a very different situation with regard to imminent diplomatic prospects.

At the outset Italy, through the defeat and dismemberment of the Austro-Hungarian empire, achieved her most important objective: she found herself relieved from the pressures which the great empire had formerly been able to exert upon her frontiers, and whose alliance she had accepted or suffered for thirty-three years. She met no further obstacles in recovering the disputed lands and hoped that the possession of Trieste, the maritime outlet for Central Europe, would permit her to play a role in the economies of the countries that "succeeded" the Dual Monarchy. In order to complement this success, she would obviously have to assure herself of a dominant position in the Adriatic Sea, where she tried, during the course of the armistice negotiations, to limit the expansionist designs of the new state of Yugoslavia. Finally in the eastern Mediterranean she was able once again to work on the projects that she had planned and had begun to realize between 1911 and 1914. All of these objectives—or nearly all of them—were agreed upon in April of 1915 in the Treaty of London and enlarged upon two years later in the St. Jean de Maurienne Agreement. Italy's main objective, therefore, was to obtain the fulfillment of these promises. Why did France and Great Britain not uphold their commitments in regions where they had no direct interest? The support given by Russian diplomacy to Serbian claims in 1915 had evaporated since the fall of czarism and the Bolshevik government's struggle with the Orthodox Church. The obstacle to the realization of the Italian program lay in the Wilson formula: Point 8 stated that the Italian question should be resolved by taking into account the clearly recognizable "lines of nationality." It therefore ruled out the Italian claims to the regions with German-speaking peoples (in the southern Tyrol) and Slavic-speaking peoples; but it was literally inapplicable in Istria and Dalmatia, where small nuclei of Italian-speaking people were scattered throughout. It was a perfect opportunity for controversy.

Great Britain had no territorial claims to present in Europe; she looked only for acquisitions in Africa and in the Near East. And yet the continental questions were of concern to her in the sense that she wished to eliminate the risk of a hegemony which would endanger the security of the British Isles, and where she wanted to retain export markets for her manufactured goods. She had always refused to allow the partition of Germany, which would have delivered the Continent into the hands of the French, and desired that the conditions of the peace should not prevent Germany from becoming once again England's principal European client. Furthermore, she did not wish to risk seeing this large country place "her resources, her brains, her powers of organization" at the disposal of Soviet Russia, and acquire advantages in the Russian market that British interests would be unable to recapture when the time came. The most serious danger in the situation, said Lloyd George in May of 1919, was the risk of seeing Russia "enter the German orbit."

France impressed upon the Allies the burden imposed upon her in the rebuilding of her devastated areas (368,000 houses destroyed and 559,000 damaged; 116,000 hectares where the amount of labor required to bring it back to working condition was more than the value of the land); of factories that had been destroyed, and of machinery and stocks of raw material that had been pillaged, in regions that in 1913 possessed 41 per cent of her steam-driven machinery; of mine installations that had been destroyed in the north and in the Pas de Calais; and of works of art that had been destroyed in railroad accidents. She was unable to count on the support of the United States in this matter, for the latter did not accept the demands outlined by the Minister of Commerce in December of 1918. And yet these economic and financial preoccupations took second place to the desire of safeguarding the security of her territory. The memory of the three invasions suffered during the course of one hundred years, the conviction that a German "retaliation" was probable and could only be delayed—these were the essential motives behind French policy. Public opinion was fully conscious that the victory would have been impossible without the help of the Allies or "associates," and that of these, only one could be counted on for support in 1914: would the circumstances be as favorable in the future? It was therefore necessary that France should first and foremost seek guarantees, through the peace settlement, against the possibility of a retaliation: "physical" guarantees, to increase the distance between her borders and the "point of departure" of an invasion; diplomatic guarantees, to avoid having to carry alone the burden of a future war. At the time of the armistice, however, she no longer had the authority she had had before in the coalition, because for four and a half years she had made a greater military effort than her allies. How could she have possibly saved her strength, since the war had been fought on her soil?

Was the United States, whose role had been decisive in the outcome of the war, going to arbitrate the dispute between her European "associates"?

The moment she entered the war, the United States proclaimed her disinterest: she sought neither territorial expansion nor political advantage. Her essential role in the war had been to stop German militarism and to assure France and Great Britain, whose political regimes respected liberal and democratic principles, and whose economic and financial interests coincided with hers, a victory that was all the more desirable since it no longer was liable to turn to the advantage of Russia. This goal had been achieved; therefore, it was unnecessary to go any farther: the "destruction" of Germany had been strictly ruled out by official American declarations.

And yet personally Woodrow Wilson had larger plans in mind. He wanted to found the League of Nations so that the peace treaties should not be mere precarious diplomatic arrangements but should pave the way to a new concept of relations between countries. He wanted the debates of the peace conference to be conducted along these lines, and he wanted the right to arbitrate. This role implied a direct participation in the safeguarding of future peace. The United States was therefore to renounce her traditions and to assume direct responsibilities for the protection of the independence and territorial integrity of member states of the League. The President, during a speech at the time of senatorial elections, outlined this plan on the day the armistice was signed. If the electorate did not confirm the majority held by the Democratic party, he said, it would "certainly be interpreted on the other side of the water as a repudiation of my leadership."

Out of thirty-seven seats to be filled, the Republicans won six: henceforth they more or less balanced out the Democrats and could therefore hope to defeat the President's policies. On November 27, 1918, former President Theodore Roosevelt declared that President Wilson now had "absolutely no authority to speak for the American people" and should therefore give up taking initiatives in the general peace settlement. Of course, the President would not resign himself to playing a passive role: he questioned the significance of the election results, since he felt that, as usual, their outcome reflected more concern over domestic issues than foreign policy. He continued to say, perhaps to believe, that the great majority of the American people were in favor of the League of Nations. Therefore, one might say he only trusted public opinion.

However, American public opinion exercised a more direct influence over the orientation of foreign policy than it could in France or even Great Britain; for the Senate, which played an important role in the ratification of treaties and in the nomination of top diplomatic posts, keeps an ear to the temper of the electorate, which states its feelings in letters or telegrams and through lobbies. What, therefore, was the nation's stand on foreign affairs?

While the electorate paid close attention to all economic, social, and financial questions that constituted the fabric of American domestic policies, it on the whole had very little knowledge of international problems. It had a few basic, traditional ideas with regard to these problems, the central theme of which was isolationism—or, to be more precise, the desire to avoid direct participation on the part of the United States in the intricate controversies between other great powers, and the desire to refuse all commitments that might risk leading the United States into playing an active role in foreign affairs and its immediate preoccupations. Intervention in the European war in 1917 had been necessary in order to defend the prestige and protect the economic interests of the United States. But this was only to have been a temporary measure. As soon as these goals had been achieved, it would be wise to return to the traditions that had been those of American foreign policy since the time of Washington and Jefferson, and that remained linked in the minds of most Americans to the further prosperity of the United States.

These traditions corresponded to essential characteristics of the collective mentality. The security of national territory was assured by the geographical position of the country. Why, therefore, should Americans take part in finding solutions to foreign problems that were no danger to them; and why should they be interested in these perpetual European quarrels? Furthermore, if she were to undertake commitments abroad, the United States would have to establish a large permanent army and, as a result, a system of obligatory military service. This would be contrary to Anglo-Saxon ideals and would also cause resentment among a good number of "foreign-born" Americans.

The basis of isolationism, therefore, lay in the conviction that the protection of national interests did not demand the pursuit of an active foreign policy. This stand was backed by the Republican party: as soon as President Wilson announced that he was in favor of active participation in foreign affairs by the United States, and had made the Democratic party adopt this program as part of its platform, the Republicans considered it "good politics" to exploit the latent isolationism of the electorate, and therefore took a stand against Wilson's platform.

But did this policy, which would have been both feasible and fruitful during the nineteenth century, correspond to the current world situation? The United States had become a great world power; she had increased her capacity of industrial production to such an extent that she now needed to find markets for her goods.

She now had a merchant navy whose presence was in evidence all over the world. She had acquired a leading position in the international capital market. How could she reconcile these economic and financial preoccupations with a policy of isolation? This contradiction came to the attention of the eastern bankers and exporters and also of academic circles. In order to check the isolationist movement, the President counted on support from these circles and also on his personal prestige. But what were these hopes worth?

Undoubtedly the outlooks and personalities of the four statesmen who personally laid the groundwork of the negotiations accentuated the different national interests of each country. These were the heads of the American, British, French, and Italian governments who, during the course of one hundred and fifty meetings, examined and decided on the reports and suggestions of experts, behind closed doors and in *tête à tête* conversations, without any permanent collaborators other than a secretary and an interpreter. This method of working allowed for the quickest possible solution to be reached on the vast number of problems on the agenda. It meant that personal contact was of major importance. The Italian representative, Orlando, played a rather minor role during the "Councils of the Four," for he rarely intervened during the debates when Italy's interests were not directly in question; thus it was the personalities of the "Big Three" that counted.

Clemenceau and Lloyd George were both famous parliamentarians, both polemicists, incisive and mordant, but their manners and temperaments were scarcely alike. Clemenceau was the pessimist who was contemptuous of humanity as a whole, a realist who sneered at the "noble candor" of the President of the United States, an opponent whose ungovernable strength of character and boundless energy accommodated neither the forms of traditional diplomacy nor the nuances of parliamentary opinion. Lloyd George was the opportunist, more remarkable for the finesse and flexibility of his mind and his agility in discussion than for the strength of his opinions; his main concern was to keep in touch with British public opinion and with the tenor of his parliamentary majority—a rather shaky coalition. He adapted himself readily to the trends of public opinion, and thus was inconsistent, but with all the ease and all the authority of a great business lawyer.

Woodrow Wilson was still marked by his past. For twenty-five years a professor of political science, he believed in the power of ideas and in his mission; this conviction gave him an air of moral superiority compared to his partners, whom he thought were too inclined to sacrifice the more important question of world peace for national interests. He was confirmed in this conviction by the extraordinarily warm reception he received from the people of Paris upon his arrival in January of 1919 to chair the conference. True, this intellectual, this idealist, was also a politician, the leader of a party, a man who did not lose sight of votes. And yet he was unable to concede to the traditions or to the prejudices of the American parliamentary majority. He knew very little about Europe —which he had visited twice as a tourist ten or twelve years previously—and he was far from understanding the difficulties, sometimes inextricable, posed by the linguistic, ethnographic, or economic realities in the application of a peace program based upon the principle of nationalities, upon the right of free self-determination of peoples, and upon free economic exchange. When he found himself confronted by the delegates of small countries or national groups, each with its own set of statistics and maps, and when he declared that he had learned from experience the difficulty of obtaining a truly democratic plebiscite, he clearly understood the gap that existed between his intentions and the means of action at his disposal.

The Nature of the Solutions

Let us examine only the most prominent features of these solutions, both in and out of Europe, since in a work of this nature it would be pointless to try to study them in detail.

In Europe, where the breakup of the three great empires had just liberated a new force, that of the "nationalities," the fate of the great Hapsburg monarchy had been decided by the will of the people two months before the opening of the peace conference.

The territories that had belonged to Austria-Hungary were now divided into seven countries, two of which, Czechoslovakia and Poland, were "new." The authors of the peace treaties had the difficult task of adjusting frontiers between the successor states, not only those separating victorious and conquered nationalities —German, Austrian and Magyar—but also those separating Poles from Czechs, Italians from Yugoslavs; these latter boundaries were obviously more difficult to trace, since the disputes could not be settled by the criterion that tended to give preference to the victors: the peace conference found no basis for a compromise either at Teschen or at Fiume. In the Balkan peninsula, where the collapse of Bulgaria and the Ottoman empire had given Rumania, Greece, and Yugoslavia the opportunity of making large territorial acquisitions, the Big Four had only to ratify a *fait accompli*. Finally, in the Baltic region the countries that had been detached from Russia by the Treaty of Brest-Litovsk and had in 1918 been subjected to German occupation began after the armistice to lead a politically independent existence. The four small countries that were in the process of being created—Finland, Estonia, Latvia, and Lithuania—were still threatened by Soviet Russia, whose access to the sea they blocked. Furthermore, they had great difficulty in getting rid of the German troops who sought to remain in these Baltic countries for several months. Here again, the Big Four confined themselves to taking note of an undertaking that was conducted along Wilsonian lines but that was not acted upon directly by the great powers. And yet Wilson announced his intention to force the German troops to evacuate these territories— but by what means? He stated that the United States could not send troops there—and yet six months later this was exactly what had to be done.

Here, therefore, was a vast area of Europe where the intervention of the "great powers" was minimal. Although the question of Germany commanded their full attention, the Four were far from being unaware of the importance of Eastern Europe, where a reconstituted Poland was meant to form a screen against Soviet Russia, while at the same time threatening Germany with a war on two fronts if she were to decide to attempt a retaliation.

The German question, the Polish question, the Russian question—
these were the main problems.

Great Britain and the United States were violently against the
French plan for settling the German question. Public opinion in
France, except in Socialist circles, had, first of all, been skeptical about the German revolution of November 1918, which it
tended to interpret as "camouflage" on the part of the imperial
regime. And yet in December, during the Spartacist movement,
the French people had thought for a time that Germany was dis-
integrating; and despite the dangers implied in the spread of communism, they were pleased with the prospect of this eventuality.
However, in the beginning of January 1919, when the Paris conference began, the German government once again took the
situation in hand and proved itself capable of maintaining German
unity.

Marshal Foch's plan was based on the prospect of a German
retaliation after an interval of twenty to thirty years. The memorandum submitted by the marshal on January 20, 1919, asked,
therefore, that the territories along the left bank of the Rhine
be detached from Germany, and that under the aegis of the League
of Nations they should form one or more "independent" states,
to be placed under Allied military occupation, whose duration
would not be specified.

This solution, which would ensure the security of France
but which was obviously contrary to Wilsonian principles, was
rejected by the United States and by England because it would
"throw Germany into despair" and risk pushing her into the arms
of Soviet Russia. The compromise suggested by Lloyd George
substituted this territorial guarantee with a military and diplomatic guarantee: Germany, whose army, reduced to 100,000
men, would be deprived of aircraft, tanks, and heavy artillery and
would be forbidden to station troops or maintain fortifications
in her territories along the left bank of the Rhine or in a fifty-
kilometer zone along the right bank of the river; she would be
subjected to a military occupation of the Rhineland and of the
Bavarian Palatinate during a period of time which in theory

should not exceed fifteen years; France would receive from Britain and the United States the promise of armed support in case of German aggression or in case of German violation of the statute of demilitarization established in the Rhine area. The weakness of this plan lay in the impracticality of imposing a permanent restriction on German sovereignty. There was also the chance that the United States Senate might refuse to ratify a commitment to an alliance that, even more than the Covenant of the League of Nations, was contrary to all the traditions of American politics.

The application of the Wilsonian principles—the rights of national minorities and the free self-determination of peoples—was once again in direct conflict with French interests over the question of Austria. If the population of this new republic, which was entirely German-speaking, were to invoke these principles in demanding union with Germany, the Reich would be able to acquire a territory that, with its six and a half million inhabitants, its mineral resources, and its banking enterprises, would compensate for the loss of Alsace-Lorraine, Poznan, and northern Schleswig. German strength would therefore be intact, despite the loss of the war. The Austrian Chancellor requested the adoption of this solution on January 9, 1919, for he did not believe his country could survive with a head that was too large for its body—namely, a capital city inhabited by almost a third of its population. On February 16 the elections for the Austrian Constituent Assembly returned a Socialist majority, which voted without reservation in favor of "union." The members of the American delegation attending the peace conference seemed prepared to agree to this request; the majority of Lloyd George's collaborators were of the same opinion. Needless to say, the French government was violently opposed to this "union." On March 27, Clemenceau made the following points in a speech at a meeting of the Big Four: France wanted to eliminate this threat, which as far as she was concerned, meant the realignment of Austria with Germany; that in her opposition to this, she was hardly flouting the right of self-determination. This motion was supported by Orlando, who dreaded the thought of German territory extending as far as the Brenner Pass. In a similar case neither Lloyd George

nor Woodrow Wilson himself would consider immediate application of the principles inscribed in the Fourteen Points to a situation that would endanger the balance of power on the Continent.
Therefore, France and Italy had little difficulty in getting their
motion adopted: Article 88 of the Treaty of Versailles, confirmed
by Article 80 of the Treaty of Saint-Germain, forbade the republic of Austria to surrender its independence. And yet Wilson
intended to provide for the future; he caused the right of "unification" to be recognized, provided that it had the consent of the
League of Nations.

Compared to these two essential points, the Saar question was
only of minor importance. And yet this question gave rise to the
most passionate argument among the Big Four. The Americans
and the British were willing to grant that France had a right to
compensation for the destruction of the mining installations in
the Pas de Calais and in the north—in the form of a temporary
requisition of coal from the Saar Valley. But why did the French
government want to claim the annexation of half of the Saar
territory? The historic argument—a return to the frontier of 1814
—was of dubious value and openly contradicted the Fourteen
Points which, accepted as "the basis for the peace" by the "associates" of the United States, expressly stipulated the re-establishment of the French frontiers of 1871. The argument founded on
free self-determination or on the rights of nationalities was unacceptable for, among the 335,000 inhabitants of the territory,
only some 10,000—those from Saarlouis—appeared to have
French sympathies. Why, asked Lloyd George on March 28,
1919, repeat Germany's mistake with respect to Alsace-Lorraine?
And how can one forget, added Wilson, that the victors, upon signing the armistice, made definite commitments to Germany? To which
Clemenceau retorted that it would be foolish to "treat the Germans
with justice," for they will never forgive us. This bitter controversy
can doubtless be explained by Clemenceau's concern for domestic
politics. Many supporters of the 1814 frontier in the French parliament agreed with the President of the Republic. And yet the compromise solution, which would deprive Germany of the entire region
of the Saar—which would be placed for a period of fifteen years

under international administration—and which would grant France the ownership of the mines, was not seriously questioned by French public opinion, which was far less concerned about "historic rights" than were the parliamentarians.

There was a distinct contrast between the bitterness of these discussions relative to territorial clauses and the more accommodating atmosphere of the debates over economic and financial clauses. And yet the most important stipulation, concerning reparation for war damages, gave rise to an open disagreement between the victorious powers.

The principle had been put forward in the note of the Allies and associates dated November 5, 1918, imposing these reparations on Germany. But how was the debt to be calculated when the total value of the damages had not yet been evaluated? And what were to be the arrangements over the schedule and the terms of payment? France and Belgium, who had been subjected to invasion, wanted Germany to foot the bill for reconstruction. Great Britain, who had suffered no material losses other than the destruction of part of her merchant fleet, wanted Germany to pay reparation for the damages suffered by her people, thus earmarking for herself a larger portion of Germany's payments. Thus, the total amount of the German reparations rose even further. When the French delegation put forward the figure of 220,000,-000 gold marks, the American delegation protested: it would not be conceivably possible for Germany to make payments of such a size, even if they were to be distributed through yearly payments over a period of half a century. Although the German debt had actually been increased through the actions of the British delegation, the latter threw its support behind American objections, whereupon the French made a declaration of principle: "Germany will pay." This disagreement among the experts led the Big Four to entrust the calculation of the debt, after further investigation, to an inter-Allied commission—a delay tactic that in effect implied a reduction of this debt, for it is impossible to believe that two years of reflection would have eliminated the obstacles.

The authors of the Versailles Treaty further increased these difficulties, in their belief that it would be useful to establish a causal relation between the imposition of reparations and the origins of the conflict. Article 231 stipulated that Germany had to pay for war damages "inflicted on the allied governments and their peoples, as a result of the war which had been imposed upon them by the aggression of Germany and her allies." In short, this article duly noted Germany's guilt in the manner of a civil law indictment; but German public opinion interpreted it to mean a moral responsibility. Therefore, by engaging in a historical controversy over the causes of the war, they also endangered the negotiations for the reparations. This was an opportunity from which the German government would be able to profit.

This settlement of the German territorial or financial questions gave rise to an obvious reproach: it is bound to provoke German protest but does not deprive the Reich of the means to retaliate. To force Germany to sign a statement that she would interpret as being an admission of her guilt for having started the war; to oblige her in theory to work for fifty years to pay off her debt; to impose a military occupation upon her for fifteen years, which would be a constant irritation to the German people; to insist that the Reich accept the right of nationalities when it would work against German interests, but to refuse it the advantages to be gained in the case of German Austrians and Sudeten Germans— these are the penalties traditionally imposed by the laws of war, but they foster a desire for revenge. The Versailles Treaty left intact German unity and the industrial wealth of the Reich. Although it disarmed Germany, it left her with a career army which could easily become an army of officers. It stipulated that the army occupation that was to guarantee the reparation payments was to last fifteen years, while the payments themselves should continue for from forty to forty-five additional years. It would be difficult to dispute the value of these criticisms, and yet there is no way of knowing what should have been done instead. During debates in the French parliament, criticism dwelled upon maintaining German unity—the heart of the matter for a large number of Frenchmen. They were of the opinion that the partition of Germany would have been the only effective guarantee. Clemenceau had no trouble in demonstrating that the blame lay with the others, for neither the United States nor Great Britain would consider dismembering Germany. How could the French government bring them to change their minds? The victory had been won through a coalition; and a coalition had decided upon the principles for the peace settlements. France was in no position to argue the point.

Although during the discussions there was little mention of Soviet Russia, the subject was constantly on the minds of the Big Four.

Since the summer of 1918 the Allied powers and associates had in fact conducted a policy of intervention in the Russian civil war, in eastern Siberia and in northern Russia, on the Murmansk coast. On November 6, 1918, the Soviet Congress had declared that Russia was prepared to start peace talks if the Allied powers abandoned their intervention. In December the latter replied by sending an expeditionary force under French command to land at Odessa, where it was to assist General Denikhin's White army. However, during the opening discussions of the conference, Lloyd George directly confronted the Russian problem. He thought that the policy of intervention in the civil war would lead nowhere because it was impossible to count on the Whites ("it would be like building on sand") or on being able to deploy enough Allied forces on Russian territory to obtain a decisive result (an attempt to do so would risk mutiny among the troops, who were impatiently waiting to be demobilized). It would therefore be foolish to try to put down Bolshevism by force. Wilson shared this point of view. Negotiation was therefore imperative. This suggestion was adopted with reservation by the French government.

Why was there still no decision? During the negotiations that were opened in Moscow at the end of February 1919 by William Bullitt, a member of the American delegation to the peace conference, the Allies and associates envisaged the withdrawal of their troops from Russian territory on two conditions: that the fighting in the civil war come to a halt, on the basis of the *status quo*—that is, that the White army would keep the territories it occupied; and that there be a resumption of commercial relations between Russia and the other nations. But the Soviet government demanded that the retreat of the Allied troops precede the demobilization of the Red army, evidently because they counted on the collapse of the White government as soon as it was reduced to its own forces. Neither Wilson nor Lloyd George had any intention of adopting such a course. The discussions therefore came to an end. It is hard to believe that had they been pursued, they would have resulted in a lasting settlement, considering that the settlement would have been based on a division of Russian territory.

However, this setback did not cause the Allies and their associates to increase or even to pursue the policy of intervention. The French expeditionary force retired from Odessa on April 3, 1919, under conditions that confirmed Lloyd George's prognosis. The British renounced their intention of protecting their oil interests and evacuated Baku on May 10. In September the Murmansk coastline was in turn evacuated. However, the Big Four continued to lend support to Admiral Kolchak's government in Siberia in the form of war materials and subsidies, although no troops were committed. Marshal Foch's plan, which suggested the establishment of a "defensive barrier" to "contain" Bolshevism by giving support to Poland and Rumania was not accepted by the United States and Great Britain. In short, toward the end of June, President Wilson conceded that the Allies and their associates had not succeeded in formulating a policy on the Russian question.

What actions could they have proposed? A massive intervention —with several hundred thousand men—would have caused the collapse of the Soviet government (Lenin was to say as much years later). But where would they have found the troops? Neither the United States, the French nor the British governments were prepared to undertake further military operations after having just come out of the Great War. It would doubtless have been possible to call upon Poland for a contribution. The Polish government would hardly have any reason for favoring the reconstruction of a powerful Russia. And yet even if this massive intervention had been feasible, would there have been any tangible results? The reports from British agents consistently mentioned that in regions held by White armies, the peasant population of Russia feared that a victory for Denikhin would mean the restoration of the great landed proprietors. The Allied representatives attached to Admiral Kolchak, who had with great difficulty persuaded him, in the event of victory, to agree to establish a parliamentary regime, had no faith in the execution of such a promise. Furthermore, since the proposed armed intervention would benefit the White generals, the Allies ran the risk of seeing it turned against their own interests.

The fact that the restoration to power of the military and reactionary elements of old Russia could lead to a *rapprochement* between Russia and Germany was doubtless the reason for the unwillingness of the Big Four to take any action.

In the absence of a solution to the Russian question, the Polish settlement could only be partial, for the tracing of the new nation's borders had been left unresolved. The determination of her western borders had been easier since it consisted of annexing German territories. And yet when the commission of experts suggested to the Big Four that they should give Poland all the territories where two thirds of the total population were Polish-speaking—that is, the major part of Poznan, of eastern Prussia, and of Upper Silesia —two of three points were turned down. It was decided that the city of Danzig, whose population was German, should not be annexed by Poland and should receive an international status; it also entrusted settlement of Upper Silesia's status to a plebiscite, although the American experts said that the plebiscite would probably not be free of coercion, considering the dependence of the Polish population on the great German landowners and industrialists. In the two cases it was Lloyd George who caused the Polish claims to be denied. Did he take this action simply because the British government did not wish to bolster a country that would provide a center for French hegemony? Economic motives were more likely behind this move: the port of Danzig, the outlet for the Carpathian oil and mining regions, should remain completely open to the British merchant navy; the coal and iron ore resources of Upper Silesia were necessary to the economic vitality of Germany.

The authors of the treaties did not attempt to dispute the fact that the peace settlement was fragile, in that it left open the important questions posed by the "absence" of Russia and by the Balkanization of the Danube region. However, contemporary observers did not appear to be concerned with these omissions.

With regard to the questions outside of Europe, no serious difficulties arose when the former German colonies, under cover of a system of mandates, were divided among Great Britain and her dominions, France, Belgium, and Japan. This distribution merely consolidated the results of military operations in central and southern Africa, in which Italian troops played no role at all. The Italian delegation to the conference confined itself to asking for compensations in favor of her colonies on the Red Sea and also in Libya. Once again Italy did not press her claims too hard; she essentially had little active interest in these colonial affairs and thought it preferable to concentrate her efforts on the Adriatic question, which was more important for Italian prestige. Incidentally, she did not succeed in realizing her goals. The bitterness that the colonial settlement was to provoke among the Italian people after the triumph of the fascist movement had not yet manifested itself in 1919.

Only the question of Asia gave rise to sharp debates.

In the Far East, where Japan managed with little difficulty to arrange that she be given a mandate over the German archipelagoes in the Pacific, north of the Equator, and the right to maintain a provisional military occupation of the maritime province of Russian Asia, the distribution of the "rights and interests" that Germany possessed in the Chinese province of Shantung was the occasion for bitter controversy.

The Japanese government took possession of these "rights and interests" after 1914; she accepted the settlement whereby they were given back to China, but on condition that she receive all the advantages that had been promised her in the Sino-Japanese accords of May 1915, and that would assure her considerable influence over the Chinese economy. The Chinese delegation replied that the 1915 treaties were invalid, since they had been imposed under conditions of an ultimatum, therefore by violence; in order to obtain the restitution of Shantung, without asking for anything

in return, she cited the principle of free self-determination of
peoples. France and Great Britain were aligned with Japan through
secret treaties which they had signed at the beginning of 1917.
But the United States was free from any commitment.

President Wilson attempted to act as mediator. To Japan he
said that the future peace in the Far East depended upon Sino-
Japanese relations, and recommended she not risk "setting fire"
to a country of four hundred million inhabitants; he reminded
China that the honoring of a treaty, even if it were signed after
an ultimatum, was an "imperative rule." The compromise he envisaged would be a revision of the 1915 treaties—that is, a restriction on the advantages promised to Japan. The Japanese delegation
refused to comply. On April 30, 1919, the Big Four abandoned
the discussions: they decided that German "rights and interests"
in Shantung would be handed over to the Japanese, thereby
admitting that the major powers should not be involved in the
restoration of this territory to China or in the conditions of such a
transaction. This step in effect meant adopting the Japanese thesis.
Thereupon, the Chinese delegation refused to sign the Treaty
of Versailles.

Why did the President of the United States yield? He exposed
himself to Clemenceau's irony ("Wilson speaks like Jesus Christ,
but he operates like Lloyd George") and, more important, to the
displeasure of American public opinion which was notoriously
hostile to Japan. But he feared seeing Japan taking reprisals
during the debates over the League of Nations Covenant. The
Japanese government would have wanted this Covenant to recognize the principle of equality among races and to forbid all "dis-
criminatory" practices contrary to this principle. This amendment,
which would have obliged the United States, Canada, and Australia to accept Japanese immigration, was rejected. Japan made
it known that if she obtained satisfaction over Shantung, she would
not insist on the question of inequality of races; but that if she
did not obtain it, she would refuse to become a member of the
League of Nations. It was in order to "save the Covenant," which
he saw as the greater part of his work, that Woodrow Wilson, despite the urgent advice of his personal collaborators, renounced his

intention of supporting the Chinese cause. Was the Japanese threat a bluff? According to Secretary of State Lansing, in 1919 the American Senate was convinced that it was, and criticized the President for having yielded too quickly. Thirty years later, however, documents found in the Japanese archives were to prove that Wilson was correct, and not Lansing.

In the Middle East, Great Britain wanted to settle the fate of former Turkish territories. The 1916 Franco-British treaties had foreseen a distribution of Arab countries between France and Great Britain, with the exception of the Syrian interior, which was to be made into an independent state and turned over to Hussein, Emir of Hejaz. The St. Jean de Maurienne Treaty of April 1917 had promised Italy not only southern Anatolia—the Adalia region—upon which Rome had already had designs in 1914, but also the region of Smyrna, whose population was Greek. Lloyd George asked for and was granted revision of two of these points. In December of 1918 the territory of Mossul, with its oil wells, passed from France to England; in May of 1919 the region of Smyrna, despite vigorous protest from the Italian delegation, was "provisionally" granted to Greece, one of Great Britain's clients.

The question of primary importance was obviously the fate of Constantinople and the Ottoman Straits. British diplomats first suggested that this doorway to the Mediterranean should be given an international status, under the aegis of the League of Nations, the administration of which could be handed over to the United States. But President Wilson, without giving a final refusal, stated that under no circumstances would he consider the idea of sending American troops to Constantinople, for the United States had never been at war with the Ottoman empire. One would therefore have to obtain the peaceful consent of the Sultan's government. This possibility was rejected when the Turkish delegation arrived at the peace conference on June 17. The Turks appeared to reject this motion, even though it concerned the question of the Mossul region and Silesia, whose fate had already been decided by the victors. Therefore, in order to finish with the matter, would it not be convenient to consider dividing all the Turkish territories among the great powers by allocating mandates? Lloyd George considered this plan but rejected it when a delegation of Indian Muslims protested a division that would weaken the authority of the caliphate. The Big Four parted without having outlined the basis of a solution. On June 25, 1919, Clemenceau noted that "as for the manner in which we are to dispose of the territories of the Turkish empire, I have no idea where we are any more."

Only six months later—after the withdrawal of the United States—Great Britain, France, and Italy once again resumed the study of the Ottoman peace. On August 10, 1920, the Treaty of Sèvres transferred four fifths of the Sultan's territory, which had formerly been part of the ancient Ottoman empire, and left him only Central Anatolia besides Constantinople. In the settlement Great Britain received the better part of the bargain, with the protectorate of Egypt and the mandates of Palestine and Mesopotamia. She extended her protection of the Suez Canal to the north, and through Baghdad she held the land route to India, while at the same time she received important oil resources. She forced the decision to demilitarize the Dardanelles and the Bosporus, where an inter-Allied commission assured freedom of passage at all times. British policy would never have agreed to this solution when czarist policy was capable of seeking access to the Mediterranean, but it conformed to British interests when Russia was weakened. Finally, the Aegean Sea had become a "Greek lake," where Great Britain counted on having a decisive influence. These advantages had been acquired at the particular expense of Italy and also of France. However, Italian policy in the Adriatic and French policy in the Rhineland had too much need of British support to oppose Lloyd George's initiatives in the Middle East. But the result of this settlement was certainly precarious: the authors of the treaty hardly dared hope that the Turkish nationalist movement would resign itself to accepting their decisions.

It is almost impossible to discern any new ideas in these negotiations: the Wilsonian formulas were respected only when they corresponded to the interests of the victors. The only notable feature was the abstention of the United States, which had no desire to assume responsibilities for the Middle East or the Far East. When in May of 1919 the British cabinet wanted to erect a barrier against a possible Russian attempt at expansion, by suggesting the mandating of Armenian territories, President Wilson was cautious in his reply, because he was fully aware that the Senate would not accept this responsibility. The American tradition of prudence and isolation was stronger than interest in economic expansion.

The Lacunae

The peace conference had been the moment of triumph for the former "national minorities" of Europe, for the populations who had lost their identity under Russian, German, and Austro-Hungarian domination. True, the application of "the right of free self-determination" had met with difficulties in the border cases, where the mixtures of populations had been almost inextricable; and the principle had been distorted when it was found in conflict with economic or strategic interests to which the doctrine of "historic rights" had often served as an opening. And yet the political map established in 1919 was, from the vantage point of the nationalities, far more satisfactory than it had been in 1914. Before the World War the total number of people who protested against belonging to a country where they had the feeling of living among strangers amounted to some sixty million, one fifth of the total population of the world; after the application of the peace treaties it was reduced to approximately thirty million.

Did this mean that the stability of boundaries was more secure? In fact the protesting groups held a far more important position in the realm of international politics than they had before, for the "new minorities" were most often composed of those very people who five years previously had belonged to that segment of the population whose role had been a dominant one in the administration, and who retained a sense of superiority despite the upset.

Again, this situation not only set victors and losers, beneficiaries and victims of peace treaties against each other; it often brought the new countries into conflict, stirring up nationalistic feelings over the delineation of their mutual frontiers. And in many cases the authors of the treaties, through lack of valid information or sufficient time, left the settlement of these disputes to the future.

What were the sensitive areas in this outburst of malice and covetous desires?

In northeastern Europe the heart of the controversy lay in the determination of the frontiers of reconstituted Poland.

The German-Polish frontier determined by the Treaty of Versailles ran through an area containing a mixture of Poles and Germans and gave the Polish state approximately one and a half million Germans. The German protest centered around the separation created between the Reich and East Prussia: what right did the treaty have to grant Poland this "corridor"? The Polish government replied that the corridor was in fact a territory extending eighty-five kilometers from east to west, with a population that speaks the Kachoub dialect, whose distant kinship with the Polish language is indisputable. Germany retorted that when the Kachoubes belonged to the Prussian state prior to 1914, they gave their votes—except in the case of three constituencies—to "German" candidates rather than to protesting Poles; that this population was unaware of being Polish! Here was an occasion where there were differing opinions over the rights of nationalities. The Germans appealed to the "Latin" doctrine, while the Poles leaned on the "Germanic" theory, which understood linguistic kinship to be the essential characteristic of nationality. The argument of principle, as on many other occasions, was used to further political and economic interests.

At first sight the question of Upper Silesia was much more important. In this great industrial region of the German empire, two thirds of the inhabitants in 1914 spoke Polish; this indisputable numerical superiority had given the Polish government, during the course of the peace conference, the right to press for the Wilsonian principles. The Germans brought forward an argument similar to the one it had invoked over the question of the "corridor": the Poles of Upper Silesia, separated from the Polish state since the fifteenth century, had not "protested" any more than had the Kachoubes. Furthermore, the Prussian government, which had ruled over this territory since 1740, had raised the standard of living and made the area into an important center of the metallurgical industry; and the Germans, who formed the majority of the urban population and who held all the capital, were indispensable to the very existence of this center. Finally, how would Germany be able to pay the reparation damages if she were deprived of part of her production facilities? These were the arguments that were exchanged on this question, not only between Germans and Poles but in public debate everywhere, particularly in England, in anticipation of the plebiscite finally ordered by the authors of the Treaty of Versailles. But what was the value of the Polish worker and peasant vote—most of them were illiterate—since they had been subjected to the pressure of German officials and landed gentry? And what line of demarcation would it be possible to trace without hindering the daily activity of the labor force and without destroying systems of transportation that were the backbone of economic activity?

The allocation of the region of Vilno gave rise to a bitter debate between Poland and the new state of Lithuania. Before 1386 the city had been the capital of the grand duchy of Lithuania; after the creation of the Polish-Lithuanian union it had become "Polanized"; at the time of the first partition of Poland in 1772 it was turned over to Russia and remained Russian until 1918. According to the latest Russian statistics of the time—they dated from 1897—the population of the town itself (200,000 inhabitants) was 40 per cent Jewish, 31 per cent Polish, 24 per cent Russian, and only 2 per cent Lithuanian; but in the province of Vilno the proportions were quite different: 61 per cent were Russian, 17 per cent were Lithuanian, 12 per cent were Jewish, and 8 per cent were Polish. How was the principle of nationalities to be applied? Compared with the Lithuanians, the Poles had a relative majority within the city but were in the minority in the country. Both were less numerous than the Russians. The Treaty of Versailles had been unable to determine a frontier, for the state of Lithuania was not yet recognized by the major powers. The Supreme Allied Council was entrusted with the mission of bringing about a settlement: on December 8, 1919, it gave Vilno to Lithuania but declared that this decision was provisional, thus leaving the way open for Polish protests and replies.

After having considered, then abandoned, a negotiation with Soviet Russia over the Russian-Polish territories, the peace conference did not attempt to allot these lands. The differences were particularly serious in White Russia. Doubtless the large majority of the population was Russian-speaking and Orthodox; but in the southern region the Ruthenians were more numerous than the Russians, and throughout the area that had belonged to Poland before 1772, the Poles still held powerful positions among the urban bourgeoisie and the landed gentry. The Polish government, therefore, invoked "historic rights"; to avoid the application of the principle of nationalities, it insisted that neither language nor religion could be valid criteria, for the White Russians had no patriotic feelings toward Russia proper. The government's principal argument rested on the role that the Polish state could be called upon to play in the new Europe: should not this region form a barrier against communist expansion? In December of 1919 the conference of ambassadors—without making any contact with the Soviet government, with whom diplomatic relations had not been established—traced, according to the suggestions of the British Minister for Foreign Affairs, Lord Curzon, a provisional frontier, to be approximately bordered by Grodno, Bialystok, Brest-Litovsk, and Przemysl. The "Curzon line," which divided White Russia, was evidently ignored by the Soviet government; it was considered unsatisfactory by the Polish government, which wanted to revert to the frontier of 1772.

In Central Europe, where the peace treaties had placed 7,000,000 Magyars under the domination of Czechoslovakia and another 1,300,000 under the domination of Rumania, Hungarian protests were the principal threat to the new territorial status. However, she was not the only country to complain, because the determination of frontiers between new states gave rise to arguments that the peace conference left unsettled. The allotment of the territory of Teschen in Silesia—2,000 square kilometers with 426,000 inhabitants—gave rise to a diplomatic conflict between Poland and Czechoslovakia. On this occasion the Polish government could invoke the principle of nationalities, whose application it had disputed in White Russia: the territory was 55 per cent Polish, 25 per cent Czech, and 18 per cent German. The Prague government claimed "historic rights," for Teschen had belonged to Bohemia for three hundred years before being annexed by the Hapsburg monarchy. However, behind these arguments there also lay the determining factor of economic interests: an important railroad and the Ostrava coal mines, which produced 6,000,000 tons annually, were the chief motives behind Poland's demands for the territory. In November of 1918, Czech and Polish troops occupied the territory and established a provisional line of demarcation while awaiting the arbitration of the great powers, who, incidentally, restricted themselves to consolidating the existing situation.

In the valley of the Drave, along the Austria-Yugoslav border, the fate of the region of Klagenfurt (21,000 square kilometers, with 230,000 inhabitants) had to be decided by a plebiscite, which did not take place until October of 1920 and turned out in favor of Austria. And it was also a plebiscite that decided the fate of the small territory of Sophron, claimed by both Austria and Hungary. Finally, the Banat of Temesvar, in the southern regions of Hungary, was claimed by both Rumania and Yugoslavia.

The question of the Adriatic, bitterly fought over during the meetings of the Big Four, remained open. The Italian government, needless to say, claimed the territories it had been promised in 1915 by the London Pact, and was satisfied. Though he was not tied by previous promises when the United States entered the war, President Wilson finally allowed that Italy should receive—apart from Trieste and the parts of Istria and of Dalmatia with their Italian-speaking populations—the valley of Upper Adige, inhabited by approximately two million German-speaking people, thus extending her frontier as far as the Brenner hills. Thus the principle of nationalities yielded to strategic interests. But these advantages seemed insufficient to Italian diplomacy, which, in addition to the promises obtained in 1915, claimed the port of Fiume, despite protests from Yugoslavia.

On the strength of their respective principles, the Italian delegation and the Yugoslav delegation could invoke the right of nationalities, since two thirds of the city's population was Italian-speaking, and the suburb of Susak was almost entirely inhabited by Slavs. Here once again was an example where it was impossible to trace the "clear, reasonable line" among different national groups on which President Wilson, as he said in his message to the Congress of the United States, thought he could count. Also, historic and economic arguments had been superimposed on the Wilsonian principles. Did not Italy have the right to this eastern coast of the Adriatic which in so many respects still bore the imprint of Venetian civilization? And could Yugoslavia surrender a port behind which all the land belonged to her?

In order to defeat the Italian claims, the President of the United States rigorously asserted his personal authority, without paying attention either to the protests of the Italian delegation to the peace conference, or to events in the Italian parliament, or even to Orlando's government, which fell on June 29 for having been unable to defend Italian interests in the Adriatic. In August of 1919 he succeeded in causing the adoption of a compromise: Fiume would remain a "free city." But on September 12 a corps of Italian volunteers under the leadership of Gabriele d'Annunzio took possession of the city; and the Roman government, overwhelmed by the patriotic surge provoked by the success of this coup, refused to acknowledge the compromise. Wilson, however, stuck to his solution; he declared his conviction that public feeling on the matter was artificial; furthermore, he thought that Italy was in the midst of economic and social difficulties that she would be unable to resolve without American aid. While the Treaty of Trianon settled the fate of the Hungarian territories, it reserved decision on the question of Fiume, which for four more years was to be the occasion of diplomatic conflict between Yugoslavia and Italy.

In the Balkan peninsula, where prior to 1919 religious passions and national hatred had been particularly vehement, the wars between Bulgaria and Serbia in 1915, between Bulgaria and Rumania during the autumn of 1916, and then in 1917 between Bulgaria and Greece had left in their wake sufferings and bitterness which were certainly not dispelled by the Treaty of Neuilly. How was one to determine "national allegiance" among these Macedonian populations without taking into account linguistic groups, where Bulgars, Greeks, and Serbs formed complex "centers," and where the Orthodox churches fought among themselves over the faithful? The frontiers established by the treaty placed the territories where the majority of the population through language or religion belonged to the Bulgarian national group under the domination of the "Serbian, Croat, and Slovene" state. And how was one to determine the rights of Greece over the region of Cavalla, where the commerce of the port, it is true, was owned by Greeks, but where the immediate environs were in part inhabited by Turks?

The question of Bessarabia—namely, the region situated between the Pruth and the Dniester, on the shores of the Black Sea—was one of the last examples, and one of the more typical, of the difficulties faced by the application of the principle of nationalities. The population of this region was a mixture of Russians and Rumanians, Jews and Germans. The Rumanians were undoubtedly in the majority, for they formed perhaps two thirds of the population. Was this a "valid" majority? Bessarabia, once part of the Ottoman empire, had been annexed by Russia in 1812, which in turn ceded the three southern districts to the principality of Moldavia and subsequently took them back in 1878. During the period between 1856 and 1878 Moldavian colonization had been active in these three districts, where certain elements of the Russian population were "Rumanianized." It was impossible, therefore, according to the Russian thesis, to consider as Rumanians these Russians who now spoke Rumanian. The Rumanians replied that if this were the case, then one would have also to discount the influence of the Russian colonization which had expanded during the first part of the nineteenth century. In April of 1918—one month after Soviet Russia had been forced to sign the Treaty of Brest-Litovsk—a "Supreme Bessarabian Council," most of whose members were Moldavian, had decided to reject Russian domination and voted for union with Rumania. This was a genuine case, said the Bucharest government, where the right of free self-determination of peoples is undeniable: how could the great powers refuse to recognize this manifestation of Rumanian nationalism? But the Soviet government protested, for the members of the Supreme Council had not been elected and therefore could not presume to represent public opinion; it called for a plebiscite, which the Rumanian government refused to consider.

Therefore, there were a number of disputes in Europe for which valid solutions were impossible without rejecting the Wilsonian principles—which the authors of the peace treaty quoted as their authority. Settlements had to be sought through compromise. But was it possible to count on an atmosphere of reconciliation when, here and there, the various nationalisms were still aggressive toward one another? There could hardly have been a better opportunity for the great conquered powers to seek a means of maintaining and exploiting these troubled areas to their advantage!

Was there a means of counteracting these threats? The principle stated in President Wilson's Fourteenth Point had envisaged the creation of a "general association of nations [for the purpose] of affording mutual guarantees of political independence and territorial integrity." Application of this principle could lead to the protection of the territorial status established by the peace treaties, thus preserving it permanently for the benefit of the victors. To what extent did the authors of the Covenant of the League of Nations wish for this result, and did they work to ensure it?

The guarantee of political independence and territorial integrity that Article 10 gave to all the member countries of the League was per se a guarantee of frontiers. Was this wise? wondered the Foreign Office in December of 1918. Throughout almost the entire European continent, for many years to come, the peace settlement was to give rise to protest and to encourage long-lasting quarrels between the "nationalities." It was, therefore, quite possible that the protection of territorial integrity would be a heavy burden, for there were very few regions where sentiments of nationhood were expressed "with indisputable authority." Furthermore, economic transformations and the resulting migratory movements would alter the population of several regions and thus pose new political problems. If these frontiers could not be considered as definitive, the task of guaranteeing them would have to be made more attractive. The British champion of the League of Nations, Lord Robert Cecil, went even further, in saying he considered it opportune simply to eliminate the promise of protection against outside aggression. Woodrow Wilson was absolutely against this, for it would have meant the destruction of the "keystone" of the Covenant. However, the final compromise took into account the British objections, for while maintaining the guarantee, it weakened its effectiveness. "In case of any such aggression," read the amended text, ". . . the Council shall advise upon the means by which this obligation shall be fulfilled." This meant in effect that Article 10 was restricted to a statement of principle, thus opening the way to all kinds of qualifying interpretations and casting a shadow over the notion of the stability of frontiers.

The British delegation wished further to obscure this principle by providing for a possible revision of the territorial status. Article 19 of the Covenant aimed at empowering the League of Nations Council to "recommend" the settlement of frontiers or even the transference of territories. If the states in question refused to adhere to these recommendations, to what danger would they be exposing themselves? According to the British plan, they would lose the right to call on the protection of the League of Nations, which meant in effect that aggression against them would become legal, and that the clause of territorial guarantee would cease to operate. But this threat struck the French government as far too excessive, for France feared it would weaken Poland or Czechoslovakia, the necessary nucleus for a system of "rear alliances." In its final form Article 19 was restricted to provide for a resort to "friendly pressure" which would allow the guarantee to stand. The revision of frontiers was, therefore, nothing but a pious hope: for, after all, is there such a thing as a friendly invasion?

This, therefore, according to Wilsonian concepts, was how the principle of guarantee was to be maintained. It remained to establish the ways and means of exercising this guarantee. What kind of sanctions would the member states impose upon a country that had violated the Covenant? The American plan, which was a combination of Wilson's fears and the more subtle ideas of his experts, foresaw economic or financial sanctions and "military" sanctions but avoided suggesting what these might consist of. The British delegation was skeptical. "We have doubts as to whether or not the member states would agree to undertake these commitments, and we express even further doubt as to whether they would fufill their obligations if the situation were to arise." These reservations were directly influenced by the doctrine of British pacifism, which had not once during the previous hundred years approved of the use of force. The British plan, therefore, suggested "moral" or, at the very worst, economic sanctions, to the exclusion of military or naval sanctions. On the other hand, the French plan, approved by the Italians, placed the accent on military sanctions but went far and beyond the American suggestion: it proposed entrusting their execution to an international force, provided with a permanent military staff and manned by contingents that all the member states would be obliged to supply.

The French plan was quickly rejected during the debate that took place in April of 1919. How could a sovereign power, said the Anglo-Americans, consider subjecting itself to the decisions of an international military staff? And would not the smaller countries be anxious about the existence of an international force that would in effect be at the disposal of the great powers? Article 16 of the Covenant established a compromise between the British and the American proposals: economic or financial sanctions would be obligatory for all member states and should be applied automatically against any state resorting to war, in violation of the commitments inscribed in the Covenant. But the military or naval sanctions would still be optional, meaning that in each particular case they would be the subject of a recommendation, passed unanimously by the Council of the League. The member states would be free in their decision. If they refused to participate in the sanctions by not sending a contingent, their only obligation would be to accord free passage over their territory to the international force charged with fulfilling the resolutions of the Council.

Therefore, the guarantee offered by this Covenant was still dubious. A victim of aggression could not be certain that the members of the Council would be unanimous in declaring that the law had been violated; it could not be sure of armed rescue, even when the Council recommended military sanctions; it failed to specify the space of time that might elapse between the alarm and the rescue. This was one of the fundamental lacunae in this system of organizing the peace.

Dissension Among the Victors

Conquered Germany had preserved her unity; she was still a great country and was assured of recovering the basis of her power after a delay of perhaps twenty or thirty years. She would therefore be able to dream of revenge. In December of 1918 this prospect found its expression in an article in the *Deutsche Allgemeine Zeitung*: "Nothing will have changed the fundamental point of Bismarck's continental policies as long as unified Germany stands." This was confirmed the moment the Treaty of Versailles was signed.

When the conditions of the peace treaty were made known in May, the Independent Socialists agreed with the Social Democrats, the Catholic Center, and the Conservatives that this "peace of violence" was contrary to the principles formulated by President Wilson in the Fourteen Points and introduced in the note of November 5, 1918, as the basis for the peace negotiations. And yet while the Independent Socialists considered that Germany should sign because she was sure that the application of the treaty would not be lasting, the Conservatives preached refusal with equal confidence, as they were sure of not having to carry out the policy they were earnestly recommending. Government circles, aware that German resistance would be futile, wanted only to attempt to obtain an extenuation of the conditions of peace. The "counterprop-ositions" presented at the peace conference proceeded along this line.

When they were almost entirely rejected, and German public opinion understood that the victors were standing firm, the partisans of the "refusal policy" diminished in number: on June 23 the treaties were accepted by the Weimar Assembly with 237 votes in favor, 138 against, and 48 abstentions: Social Democrats, Center Catholics, and Socialist Independents respectively. How could Germany possibly risk invasion and perhaps even partition?

Nevertheless after the signing of the treaty, the discussions con-tinued in the German press, especially over the great debate before the National Assembly on October 23, 1919. Three trends were particularly noticeable.

To the right were the "national Germans" (they were to pick up 3,700,000 votes during the general election in June 1920) who conducted a violent campaign against France, accusing her of wanting to demean Germany; they declared that the treaty was "impossible to fulfill." Henceforth certain among them considered playing the Russian card; either because collaboration with Russia, even Soviet Russia, was necessary to hold Poland "in check" and to regain outlets in economic markets which German industry very much needed, or because these German-Russian relations could cause anxiety to either France or Great Britain. And yet, the manifesto of the Executive Committee of the Communist Inter-national had just confirmed that the Treaty of Versailles imposed excessive burdens on Germany, the brunt of which would fall on the German worker!

The "Populist" party, through which the interests of great in-dustrial concerns—especially Stinnes—were served by the political talent of Gustav Stresemann, was equally hostile toward the terms of the treaty. But it was in fact more flexible, because it wanted to keep open the possibility of negotiation along economic lines with the European powers that in 1913 absorbed 31 per cent of the total German exports. During the elections of 1920 this party was to gain approximately the same number of votes as the "nationals."

The parliamentary majority—that is, the Social Democratic party (5,600,000 supporters) and the Catholic Center party—adopted a policy in favor of the treaty and rejected any idea of seeking support in the East; it wished to act by "reason and persuasion," to show the victors that they should bear in mind Germany's "vital necessities," and thus bring them to abandon part of their rights, at least in the area of economics. "Foreign policy in the decades to come," declared the Minister of Foreign Affairs, Hermann Müller, a Socialist, "should above all be a policy of economics."

Although they might have been divided over the policy that should be pursued during the near future, all the German parties at least agreed that the Treaty of Versailles should be revised as soon as possible. It was easy to predict that this revision would first aim at adjusting the borders, or even the status, of the new countries—Austria, Czechoslovakia, Poland—which were within immediate reach.

The governments of the three major victorious European powers —France, Great Britain, and Italy—which up until the signing of the peace treaty continued their inflexible stand against Germany, even when they had differences of opinion, no longer hesitated to voice their disagreements once the document was endorsed.

Through the Treaty of Versailles, France gained important territorial advantages. The recovery of Alsace-Lorraine satisfied national feeling and erased the memory of 1871, while at the same time it brought her the iron ore from Lorraine and the potassium from Alsace. Colonial territories were to be enlarged, though, on the whole, public opinion had not expressed any desire for this increase. The Congo territories, ceded in 1911, were regained; a mandate was granted over the Cameroons and parts of Togo and Syria. On account of the Russian Revolution and the German defeat, France had become the only great military power and held incontestable sway over the Continent: the balance of strength in Europe had thus been profoundly altered. This appeared to confirm the optimistic views of the Premier and his closest collaborator, André Tardieu. But would these results last? The work accomplished by the peace conference was exposed to a double threat: the possibility of German retaliation and the economic and political imbalance, whose principle cause was the "absence" of Russia.

The French negotiators of the peace treaty continued to fear German retaliation. It was also expressed by Jacques Bainville in May of 1919 in *L'Action française*: "Sixty million Germans will not resign themselves to paying a regular tribute of several billions to forty million Frenchmen for twenty or thirty years. Sixty million Germans will not accept as final the shrinking of their eastern frontier or the partition of the two Prussias. Sixty million Germans will laugh at the small state of Czechoslovakia." The same anxiety appeared during the French parliamentary debates that in September of 1919 preceded the ratification of the treaty. It was obvious to the majority of people who spoke during these debates that the German people, despite their defeat, would still harbor their sense of superiority acquired during the nineteenth century; that they would soon recover their "desire for power"; and that the essential traits of their collective psychology—a respect for hierarchy, a sense of discipline—would in no time allow them to overcome their current lapse of morale. It was clear to everyone that Germany, whose means of production were almost intact— since she had not been subjected to invasion, except for a small area of East Prussia—would once again make an effort to expand her economy when her stock of raw materials had been replenished. Critics from the extreme right maintained that in order to avoid this danger, it would have been better to destroy German unity. Clemenceau replied that he could not break this unity, or even isolate the left bank of the Rhine, without provoking a rupture of the alliances that would have meant the "failure of the victory."

Which guarantees could France count on, therefore, in the event that Germany tried to avoid the application of the treaty and perhaps attempted a war of revenge?

The treaty did not determine the total sum of the reparations or the amount each victorious country would receive when Germany paid off the debt imposed upon her. In the Chamber of Deputies, the spokesmen of the Socialist party and of the Center right both regretted the inadequacy of clauses in the treaty and stressed the danger threatening the French debt. "How are we to be paid? It should be written down in black and white: we know absolutely nothing about the matter at all," declared Louis Dubois. And Vincent Auriol repeated, "Guarantees of payment? Where are they? I have read the treaty; I see nothing but uncertainties. . . . I am glad the war is over. But I am afraid that the battle of reparations is about to start."

The direct guarantees that the clauses of the treaty offered against the risk of German retaliation were still undecided. Of course disarmament was imposed upon Germany for an unspecified period of time, but as a prelude to general disarmament. It was therefore quite likely that after a brief period the conquered nation would attempt to force France to reduce her military forces. Furthermore, the demilitarization of the Rhineland should have been permanent; but the Allied occupation was to end after fifteen years—precisely when, according to Marshal Foch's remark, the Reich would be in a position to prepare for retaliation; and the small German army, recruited on a voluntary long-term basis, would become a "professional" army, with men ready to become underofficers or squad leaders in a large army of the future.

Would the indirect guarantees that were inscribed in the Covenant of the League of Nations and in the security pact accepted by Wilson and Lloyd George be of any value? While economic sanctions as provided in Article 16 were in force, military sanctions were only for the future. In case of aggression, it was true, the Council of the League of Nations had the "duty" to recommend to member states the use of force; but it was not forced to fulfill this moral obligation. If the recommendation were made, the governments then had to accept it unanimously. Only then would troops be ready at hand. "Would not the League of Nations army always arrive too late?" This was the fear expressed by the French jurist Larnaude. As for the security pact, the chairman of the Chamber of Deputies, Louis Barthou, wondered if it was of any value at all: would it be ratified by the United States Senate?

Furthermore, the moderate deputies felt that the "absence" of Russia was dangerous to the security of France. Was this only because the Russian Revolution threatened political and social stability throughout Europe? It was also and especially because France had lost the "counterbalance" that the Franco-Russian alliance had assured her for twenty-five years. The recognition of Poland and the formation of a large Rumania were only palliatives: there was no reason to suppose that "these countries could in the future replace the power of Russia." And was there not something to fear in a Russo-German alliance? Russia might perhaps look toward Germany for the support necessary for her recovery; these two countries which were the losers in the war might even be tempted to "unite in the hope of a common revenge."

André Tardieu and Louis Loucheur objected to these fears with boundless optimism. The former was sure that the solution adopted for ensuring the security of France was the "best possible." The other pointed out that the recovery of the reparations was entirely possible, for Germany's means of effecting payments would be quickly regained. But Clemenceau was not so easily convinced. He was aware of the treaty's imperfections. Could it have been otherwise in a coalition peace? The clauses signed at Versailles were, he said, nothing but "a collection of possibilities," and their final success would depend upon what France would be able to make of them.

On October 2, 1919, after a prolonged debate lasting five weeks, the Chamber of Deputies voted an overwhelming majority in favor of ratification (327 votes against 53, with 74 abstentions). And yet this majority had "neither enthusiasm nor illusions."

Although Italy was among the victorious powers and had acquired considerable advantages through the destruction of the Austro-Hungarian empire, she felt she was being treated as a poor relation. For example, she was unable to obtain all the advantages she had the right to expect according to the terms of the treaty of April 1915 and by the accord concluded in 1917 at St. Jean de Maurienne. In the Adriatic she received only part of the Dalmatian coast; the other part had been given to the new state of Yugoslavia, which became a rival after the armistice. Over the question of Fiume she had surrendered to the will of President Wilson. Furthermore, she did not receive her share of "mandates" of former German territories. In the eastern Mediterranean she kept the Dodecanese which she had occupied since 1912; but the policies of Lloyd George had frustrated her in the role she had counted on playing in the southern zone of Anatolia. The attitude of her partners seemed to her all the more unfair, since she considered that she had played a very important role in the defeat of the Central Powers. After all, it could be argued that the Piave victory had forced Austria-Hungary to negotiate for an armistice, which, as a result, had been the immediate cause for the German surrender. This was the opinion Mussolini expressed on November 2, 1918, in the *Popolo d'Italia*. His personal actions in 1915 had been important in the movement favoring entry into the war: "The Italian victory supersedes that of all the other armies." One must add that in France and Great Britain public opinion was far from prepared to attribute this pre-eminence to the Vittorio-Veneto armistice, which was further reason for Italy's feeling slighted.

The bitterness was expressed in most of the press, even the day after the signing of the Treaty of Versailles: the Allies had not fully appreciated the part played by the Italian army in their common victory; they had not granted Italy her "rights." There was no question of delaying the ratification; and when the government, without waiting for the results of the legislative election scheduled for November 15, decided on October 17, 1919, that this ratification would be passed by decree, political circles manifested no serious indignation over a solution that was nevertheless highly questionable. They were doubtless delighted to be able to avoid the responsibility of accepting or refusing it. In December 1919 the government insisted before the new chamber that it was essential for Italy to remain "united" to France and Great Britain, and in short recommended acceptance. The plea resulted in a majority vote, but only a very modest one. Parliamentary opinion, however, did not hide its disappointment; and yet it did not dare reflect this disappointment in its vote.

Why was there so much hesitation in the expression of such deep-rooted bitterness? This caution can be partially explained by the low level of morale and by social troubles: the war, which had been denounced by the majority of Socialists and by a large number of Catholics, had left behind "a wealth of passions and hatreds" in political circles. During the summer of 1919 strikes broke out not only in industry but also among farmers. But above all, these government decisions were influenced by the economic and financial situation. On July 12 the Minister for Foreign Affairs, Tittoni, announced that the Italian railroads had enough coal for a few weeks only, and that even the food supply could not be assured without resorting to imports. He added that if Italy was to be able to pay for her purchases, it was imperative that she obtain a foreign loan of six or seven billion lire. How was she to manage this at a time when the financial agreements she had made with Great Britain and the United States during the war had just expired? These conditions, said the Minister, "prescribe" the course of foreign policy. In conclusion, he said that the treaty had to be ratified; "otherwise, the national machinery would come to a halt within a few weeks." During the month of August the Minister of Finance outlined Italian needs for raw materials, foodstuffs, and Anglo-American credit before the Supreme Economic Council in London. What economic and financial aid could Italy expect if she refused, or even if she delayed the ratification?

Public and parliamentary opinion in Great Britain reacted fairly favorably to the treaty after it was signed. Only the Labor and the "orthodox" liberal press, hostile to the coalition cabinet, thought that the burdens imposed upon Germany had been too harsh. The Conservative or Liberal Unionist papers were inclined to recognize that the treaty was "as satisfactory as could be expected," because it signaled the destruction of Prussian militarism and founded the League of Nations. On July 21 the ratification was passed after brief parliamentary debates which did not give rise to any particularly heated comment in the press. But four or five months later, public opinion began to swing in the opposite direction. The principal cause of this change in attitude was undoubtedly the publication, at the end of November 1919, of John Maynard Keynes's *The Economic Consequences of the Peace*.

Keynes maintained that the destruction of the European economy had been started by the war, and that it risked being completed by the application of the Treaty of Versailles, which would weaken the economy even further. Prior to 1914 the European economic system had centered around Germany, who was still foremost client and supplier of Russia, Austria-Hungary, Italy, Belgium, and Switzerland, and who held an important position in the foreign trade of Bulgaria and Rumania, and who had second place, after India, in British foreign economic relations. This economic progress was based on the exploitation of German underground resources—coal and iron ore—and on overseas trade. The peace treaty deprived Germany of all her merchant fleet, all her colonies, and all the rights and privileges she possessed outside of Europe in her zones of economic influence; it confiscated her oil wells in the Sahara, and the iron ore from Lorraine, which she had annexed in 1871; it might even cause her to lose Upper Silesia. It also wanted to impose upon her the payment of reparations, which she could honor only by increasing her exports of manufactured goods. The fact that the economic rehabilitation of Germany was necessary to the economic reconstruction of Europe was not understood by the authors of the treaty. This, concluded Keynes, was the catalog of errors committed by Lloyd George and even more so by Clemenceau.

This thesis had a thundering success (the book was translated into eleven languages and sold 140,000 copies) and, despite its exaggerations, met with no serious criticism. It was twenty-five years before it was closely examined by a young French historian. The Keynesian critique contributed considerably to discrediting the clauses of the treaties among intellectual, economic, and business circles. It became even more important when in 1921 the British economy went through a severe crisis.

But it was not only that general anxieties and trends differed in Paris, Rome, and London, but their immediate interests clashed as well.

The Tunisian question, which had disappeared from the political horizon for almost twenty years, threatened to provoke new difficulties between France and Italy. The French government, concerned over the expansion of the Italian colony—which, owing to the privileged status it enjoyed from the 1896 conventions, was tending to form a "state within a state"—denounced these conventions in October of 1918. It was an impeccable decision from a juridical point of view, for the terms of the Italian occupation were drawing to a close. However, it was debatable from a political point of view. After having fought a European war together, was this the opportune moment to protest vigorously against Italian interests? The decision warranted careful thinking, for the application of the conventions would be "renewed" on a short-term basis. Every three months the Tunisian Italians might well fear the loss of their privileges. The French government estimated that the precarious situation would doubtless lead them to ask for French naturalization, and thus result in their leaving the Italian "community." It is hardly surprising that public opinion and official circles in Italy protested against this pressure.

There was friction between the policies of France and Great Britain in the Middle East. Great Britain, who had used the presence of her expeditionary force in Syria and her navy in the Aegean to dictate the terms of the armistice to the Ottoman empire, had held the dominant position from the end of 1918 on. She particularly wanted to protect the Suez Canal by governing Palestine through a mandate; to ensure the economic superiority in Mesopotamia which she already possessed prior to 1914, and to consolidate her strategic positions in the Persian Gulf, essential for the security of India. France concentrated all her efforts in the direction of Syria, where for many years, through her schools and missions, she had maintained an intellectual influence in non-Muslim circles and had in 1913 obtained a zone of economic influence when the great European powers were arranging the terms for distributing the railroads in the Ottoman empire. These Franco-British agreements concluded during the war were revised in December of 1918: Great Britain arranged that the Mossul oil wells, which had been given to France by the 1916 agreement, be placed in the British zone of influence; in exchange for this concession, France would be allowed to exercise, through a mandate, a "political" and administrative control not only along the coastline of Syria but also in the regions of Aleppo, Moms, and Damascus—that is, the areas which had been promised to the Arab state, and which, since October of 1918 and with the consent of the commander in chief of the British expeditionary force, had been placed under the control of Emir Feisal, son of Hussein. However, when the French government wanted to extend its military occupation into the interior of Syria, it met with resistance not only from the United States but also from Britain, who was caught between the contradictory promises she had made to the Arabs and the French. Lloyd George refused to withdraw the British troops, whose presence was protecting Feisal's authority; and in May of 1919, Clemenceau declared that if the mutual agreements were not honored, he would refuse to associate his policies with those of the British cabinet "in this part of the world." After five months of discussions the British government decided to announce the withdrawal of its expeditionary force, but on the condition that French troops did not penetrate the three cities of the Syrian interior where Feisal's troops were stationed.

These Syrian disputes brought French public opinion to take a critical view of British initiatives throughout the Middle East. When Britain signed an agreement in Teheran on August 9, 1919, which promised a dominant influence to British political and economic interests in Persia, practically the whole French press, from *L'Humanité* to *L'Echo de Paris,* announced that this treaty was equivalent to a protectorate.

These differences among former allies were nevertheless only minor aspects of the international situation. The "retreat" of the United States was decisive.

On July 10, 1919, the President of the United States submitted the Versailles Treaty to the American Senate; and on August 29, at a conference between Woodrow Wilson and the Senate Foreign Affairs Committee, the discussion centered around Article 10 of the Covenant of the League of Nations, which the President declared was the "backbone" of the treaty, and which the opposition considered contrary to the Constitution. With a view to underlining the defects of the treaty, and to pointing out that the President made essential decisions without paying attention to objections from his collaborators, the Senate committee decided to open an extensive hearing, calling sixty witnesses. In order to force the Senate's hand, Wilson made a direct appeal to the electorate; but on September 25 he was stricken with a paralytic attack and was unable to conduct his campaign. There were no warm feelings between the President, who although in excellent spirits, was unable to work, and the Senate committee. On November 20, 1919, the ratification of the Treaty of Versailles was thrown out of the Senate, as it lacked the two-thirds majority required by the Constitution.

And yet the defeat did not appear conclusive. The chairman of the committee, Senator Lodge, announced he would agree to the ratification provided the text were accompanied by fourteen reservations, the most important of which would indicate the desire on the part of the United States to assume "no obligation whatsoever" with reference to Article 10 of the Covenant, and to refuse the League of Nations the right to intervene in questions concerning either the Monroe Doctrine or the customs and immigration laws of the United States. But the President declared that these reservations were unacceptable. Wilson's resistance was sufficient to defeat Lodge's proposition.

Then the Senate, with a simple majority—in this case sufficient —passed a resolution that, "ignoring" the Treaty of Versailles, demanded the conclusion of a peace treaty between the United States and Germany—a vain undertaking at this particular moment, for the President vetoed it. The electorate decided the outcome of the debate. During the presidential campaign of November 1920, the opponents of the treaty and the League of Nations amassed nineteen million votes as opposed to little more than nine million. After the legislative elections the Republicans had a solid majority in the Senate—fifty-nine seats against thirty-nine. The repudiation of Wilson's policies was indisputable.

"Isolationism" was the central issue of this great debate. After having abandoned the accustomed line of conduct for almost three years, American political circles spontaneously returned to the traditions that had been those of the United States since her founding. They certainly did not regret having taken a decisive part in the World

War; but they were astonished at the frequency with which their European "associates" resisted their opinions during the peace conference. They therefore did not want to be directly responsible for the execution of the treaties and even less for the maintenance of international order. The essence of Lodge's criticism of Article 10 of the Covenant of the League of Nations was that it would give the right to any nation, large or small, to call for American troops to help put down local squabbles. Most of the people shared this feeling, because they did not understand the quarrels of the Old World and perhaps also because American soldiers had been disillusioned in their European experiences.

These profound currents of public opinion were strongly reinforced by party spirit, and by the personal views of the political leaders.

The leaders of the Republican party took an opposite stand to the Wilsonian thesis, either because they did not want to let a Democratic President leave his personal imprint on a world peace settlement and thus confirm his prestige, or because they expected that their appeal to traditional isolationism would find sympathy with public opinion. The result of the forthcoming American presidential election was of more concern to them than the future of world peace. One comes across so many similar cases in the study of international relations.

The President's attitude played into the hands of his adversaries. In November 1919, on the occasion of the senatorial elections, Wilson intervened in the campaign by closely linking foreign policy to the controversy between the parties. The Republicans won six seats, thus rendering virtually impossible the formation of the two-thirds majority required for the ratification of the treaty. And yet the President had pursued his objectives at the peace conference and had declared, in a speech dated March 4, 1919, that he was certain he had the support of the great majority of the American people. In short, Wilson played the classic game in the history of American politics: the call to public opinion against parliamentary opinion. But he had also annoyed his opponents. He did not have the physical strength to carry this hazardous course to the end, and found himself, in November of 1919, confronted with the Senate's pure and simple refusal to pass the ratification. Why did he not therefore accept a compromise? Ratification with "reservations" would probably have been carried by a two-thirds majority if the President had advised his Democratic friends to vote with Lodge's resolution. Is the fact that he did not resign himself to such a course proof of his pride, his intransigent egotism, or of his grave illness? The last interpretation is often the conclusion of American historians; and yet it is not very convincing, for Wilson did not pursue an "all or nothing" policy to the very end: on March 4, 1920, before the Senate's last vote, he declared that the treaty had to be either abandoned or accepted without modifications that could change its meaning. He was thus not refusing to allow certain reservations, but those of Senator Lodge annulled Article 10 of the Covenant, which was undoubtedly the masterpiece of the Wilsonian system. Is it surprising that the President did not agree to this capitulation?

Conclusion to Book II

A brief glance at the settlement of world peace in 1919 brings two facts to light:

Western Europe had managed, despite its impoverished economic situation and its moral crisis, to maintain nearly everywhere (except in Libya) the positions it had occupied prior to 1914 in other continents under colonial or semicolonial form. By the end of 1919 it appeared—at least for the time being—to have sorted out the claims of nations that a few months before had been a threat; it had even established "political control" over the Arab countries through mandates in Palestine, Syria, and Iraq—the heart of Islam—where previously it had had only economic or financial influence. How had this change come about? Success had been facilitated by the state of affairs among the natives: in Egypt, as in India, the mass movements, which during the spring of 1919 had been the great surprise, had turned out to be a flash in the pan, doubtless because they had been poorly organized and insufficiently staffed. This success was due also to the attitude of President Wilson who, after having encouraged the claims—perhaps without having taken full account of the implications of the principles they represented—had agreed with Lloyd George not to allow the Egyptian delegation and the envoys of the Boer nationalist party access to the peace conference; the delegation of Indian Muslims was admitted—but on the insistence of the British government and only to offer an opinion on the Turkish treaty. In short, the President did not wish to aggravate the problems of the British empire.

But the more valid explanation lies in the military effort. Although the British government was eager to demobilize its army rapidly, it had sent considerable forces into Egypt and India, despite the hesitations of a section of public opinion and an attempted mutiny in a regiment due to take up overseas duty. The French government did not hesitate to send a military expedition into Syria. In order to prevent future troubles, the Governor General of Indochina, in a speech dated May 8, 1919, warned that France would use maximum forces to put down "elements of disorder." The two European powers showed that they had no intentions of withdrawing. And yet the United States, while trying not to frustrate the imperialistic ambitions of France and Great Britain, abandoned the Treaty of Versailles, the security pact promised to France, and refused to participate in the League of Nations. This withdrawal, so significant for the fate of the treaties and for the general peace, profoundly shook an already delicate structure. Did the authors of the Treaty of Versailles foresee what would ensue and try to avert the consequences; or did they, on the contrary, prefer to turn a blind eye?

After the senatorial elections of 1919, which gave the Republicans forty-nine seats as opposed to forty-seven for the Democrats, Wilson was aware of the difficulty he would have in finding a two-thirds majority; and yet he counted on the Senate's being forced to bow before public opinion. But his entourage did not share his optimism. On March 20, 1919, when Wilson and Lloyd George had just offered Clemenceau the security pact, Colonel House doubted that the Senate would accept this convention; but he felt that since Clemenceau was satisfied, the United States could pursue its real objective. The French ambassador to Washington had on three occasions between February and March of 1919, warned his government of the possibility that the entire treaty would not be ratified. These warnings were not brought to the attention of the French Chamber of Deputies, before which

André Tardieu had only hinted at a possible rejection of the security pact. Did he therefore consider the ambassador's warnings to be valueless? Or did he judge it opportune to keep the parliament in the dark?

EUROPE AND THE WORLD
BETWEEN 1920 AND 1929

Introduction to Book III

For a period of ten years, both within and outside Europe, the consequences of the war continued to dominate international relations.

Application of the peace treaties was the core of diplomatic activity and the movements of public opinion in Europe; but although the prospects of economic reconstruction solicited less direct attention, they were none the less immensely important. The efforts on the part of Germany and Hungary to obtain partial revisions of the treaties or to escape the burdens of reparations should not draw attention away from the difficulties that sprang basically from the "absence" of Russia and the Balkanization of Danubian Europe. It is quite easy to establish a link between the machinations of political interests and economic preoccupations.

Beyond Europe it was the fate of European possessions that commanded attention: competition between the interests of the United States or of Japan and those of Europe; the rise of nationalistic aspirations, along the lines already established in 1919. The Chinese republic, the Arab countries, and Latin America were, in this respect, scenes of major transformation.

And yet between 1928 and 1929 the most pressing difficulties were resolved. Was peace to be lasting? Contemporary observers were doubtful, though they did not predict an imminent crisis. What were the causes for this uneasiness? This is the last question that this essay will attempt to answer.

8

The New Influences

In this convalescent world, as it were, where so many pressing questions demanded decisions from governments, diplomatic activity took on new forms: personal contacts between statesmen increased either through sessions of the Council of the Assembly of the League of Nations or during international conferences; these deliberations met greater repercussions in public opinion and in the press than they had in the past. Did the economic situation and the tendencies of the collective psychology exercise an influence over this diplomatic activity? And what direction was taken by national politics?

The Economic Recovery

Between 1920 and 1923 the economic situation, which had been so critical in Europe since 1919, was still precarious; and the instability of the whole picture was also the most striking characteristic in other parts of the world.

In Europe, where the crisis of underproduction was gradually disappearing, the transformation of the political map profoundly changed the distribution of raw materials and sources of energy between countries. The customs barriers that rose along the new frontiers impeded commerce and narrowed the markets; industries had to try to adapt themselves to these new conditions. Monetary inflation continued to maintain the rise in prices; it is true that it gave production a temporary "boost" and in France and Germany eased the financial burdens of industrialists, who were in fact partially relieved of their debts; but it discouraged capital investment and, as a result, delayed industrial redevelopment. The importation of raw material from non-European countries was still difficult, on account of a lack of means to pay for them: Europeans, who before 1914 had financed imports by the revenues earned from capital they had invested in these countries, were now unable to buy from abroad. Furthermore, the countries that sold raw materials used to purchase industrial products in Europe; but when they ceased to be suppliers, they also ceased to be clients. Finally, the industries that had been created in South America or in Asia between 1914 and 1918 resisted renewing ties with Europe. World commerce, whose progress had been rapid and constant at the end of the nineteenth and the beginning of the twentieth centuries, was now subject to sharp fluctuations. Europe's part in international commerce was now no more than 41 per cent, compared with 61 per cent in 1913. British exporters, more aware than all the others of the general condition of the European and non-European markets, received a nasty shock. After an anxious period of waiting they experienced a moment of euphoria between October 1919 and August 1920, which was followed by an economic crisis that continued for almost two years.

And yet European industrial production maintained its technical superiority, which assured it a decisive advantage in the field of "heavy" industries over all the non-European countries—except for the United States. The hope of a recovery lay in these industries.

But although this European recovery was late in materializing, one should not forget the difficulties that were also besetting the great competitors of Europe during this period of readjustment—namely, the United States and Japan.

After having experienced a great boom during the course of the World War, because the activity of the Europeans and even of the

United States in the Far East and in southeastern Asia had in large part been paralyzed, Japan went through an economic and financial crisis which reached its peak between March of 1920 and June of 1921 and continued, although diminishing, almost until 1925. The full extent of this major crisis included a steep decline in the export of manufactured goods and a similar decline in industrial prices, which dropped from 317 points (1914:100) to 201 within eighteen months; a drop in gold reserves and foreign currency to pay for imports, and measures for tightening credit in order to break this movement; the bank panic of March 1920, which was the result of this credit squeeze; a drop in production which put a quarter of the workers in big industry out of work; a decline in the consumption of rice, for the unemployed could no longer eat their fill; a consistent decline in agricultural prices (the price of rice dropped 50 per cent between January and December of 1920); conflict between landed proprietors and farmers unable to pay their rent (in one year there were eighteen hundred serious cases of armed or incendiary attacks). These problems proved the decisive importance of export markets to the Japanese economy.

In 1919 the United States had succeeded in surmounting without serious difficulty the questions posed by the passage from a war economy to a peacetime economy. But a serious crisis occurred in October of 1920, whose causes were as much European as American. Europe was buying far less foodstuffs, since her agricultural production was once again approaching normal, and less cotton, on account of the exchange crisis. The United States government adopted a policy of deflation which diminished purchasing power, and the Federal Reserve Board, by raising the bank rate, forced banks to refrain from offering unlimited credit to industry. The drop in wholesale prices—the index fell from 229 in 1920 to 150 in 1921—was accompanied by a wave of unemployment (4,750,000) and bankruptcies (100,000 in 1921). But although the government did not think it should intervene, the crisis was practically over by the autumn of 1921, and the upswing of economic activity was quick. By the beginning of 1922 the return to prosperity was assured.

Thus by 1923 the crisis of readjustment, both within and without Europe, was overcome. And yet Europe was still far from having recovered the position she had held in the world economy prior to 1914. Of the total exports between continents just before the war, commerce between non-European countries constituted only 25 per cent of the world market; it now represented 40 percent. The capacity of industrial production dropped 18 per cent in Europe between 1913 and 1923, whereas it rose 41 per cent in the United States.

After 1924 economic recovery extended over the major portion of the world.

In 1925 agricultural production throughout Europe returned to the level it had attained between 1910 and 1913. Coal production reached the average pre-war figure to the nearest thousand ton; but while in 1913 it formed 50 per cent of the world's output, it now only formed 47 per cent. If steel production (35,750,000 tons) had dropped by three million tons from the 1913 figures, the number of spindles in the cotton mills was distinctly larger. Business was facilitated by monetary policies: stability was more or less restored in monetary exchange, and the credit operations of central banks were established in nearly all the states on a gold basis; ties between national economies therefore became closer, and the interdependence of the various countries allowed each to specialize in industries to which it was best adapted. In short, the situation evolved in a satisfactory manner and continued to improve during the coming four years.

In Japan the recovery, which came later, was also slower. Between 1922 and 1925 the industrial production index rose only from 68 to 82 (1928:100); but during the next two years it rose approximately 20 per cent. This recovery, it is true, ran into trouble in 1927 because of the failure of a huge metal concern—the Suzuki Company—which threatened to take the Bank of Formosa with it; but government intervention, which subsidized the bank and various other enterprises, sufficed to put a stop to this brief crisis. The upward trend began again between 1928 and 1929; within the space of one year the index rose 10 per cent. And yet this prosperity was both tentative and fragile.

In the United States, on the other hand, the industrial boom was astonishing. Between 1922 and 1929 the rise in steel production was 70 per cent, in chemical production 94 per cent, in oil extraction 156 per cent; it reached 255 per cent in the automobile industry, which in 1929 represented 12 per cent of the total value of industrial production. The two "stagnant" branches were the coal industry, where production even went down slightly on account of competition from electricity, and the textile industry, where production rose in volume by 17 per cent between 1923 and 1929 but diminished in value, as European competition forced a drop in prices.

It is true that agriculture was not as well off, particularly in cereal production: the purchasing power of the farmer, which in 1921 was 25 per cent less than the 1914 figure, improved only slowly. But since agriculture involved only 21 per cent of the population, this situation could hardly cast a shadow over the tremendous rise in prosperity. The national revenue rose within eight years from $56,500,000,000 to $87,000,000,000. The surplus of the commercial balance tripled within five years; the New York Stock Exchange index indicated that within three years the market value of stocks had at least doubled. Public opinion, in view of this success, was enthusiastic.

During this period of rising prosperity, when the economic structure was based almost entirely on foundations that had been laid during the previous half-century—the prevalence of private enterprise, state interference limited to financial policy and customs and excise—contemporary observers were struck by the inequality existing between the various national economies, and particularly the considerable difference between the level of "prosperity" in the United States on the one hand and the industrial countries of Europe on the other.

The great superiority of American industrial production was closely tied to the development of automation—particularly rapid in the automotive and chemical industries—and to the perfection of technological methods. For many reasons European countries were unable to keep up with this pace. While in the United States the national per capita income rose 25 per cent over a period of ten years, it was nearly at a standstill in Great Britain, Germany, and France; European industry, therefore, was unable to find the capital necessary for modernizing its equipment as readily as could American industry. Again, the increase in the number of frontiers and tariff barriers encouraged the continued use of old-fashioned, poorly equipped, or badly situated industrial plants with small returns. In 1929 the United States accounted for 44.8 per cent of the world's industrial production, Germany for 11.6 per cent, Great Britain for 9.3 per cent, France for almost 7 per cent, and Russia for 4.6 per cent.

The United States was also gaining an increasing superiority in the field of agriculture, particularly owing to the development of new machinery: in 1930, American farmers used 1,020,000 tractors, while European farmers, not counting Russia, had no more than 130,000. There again the condition of the capital market was the main reason for this discrepancy.

Finally, the United States played the major role in international movements of capital. In 1929 her foreign investments totaled approximately $15,000,000,000: $5,300,000,000 in Latin America, $5,000,000,000 in Europe, $3,000,000,000 in Canada and the rest in Japan, China, and the Dutch Indies.

And yet the answers to these questions concerning American superiority do not lie in technical and financial conditions alone: demographic conditions also had the same effect. The total population of Europe had dropped between 1914 and 1919 owing to losses during the war and the lower birth rate; it began to increase after 1920 at a faster pace than during the first years of the century. Prior to 1914 the rise had partly been offset by the great migratory movement toward the American continent; this movement met with an obstacle in the United States: the laws of 1921 and 1924. These laws had three aims: to prevent the "disruption" of national unity by an influx of Slavs and Latins, whose assimilation had become difficult; to protect the income level of the working class; and to place obstacles in the way of the "importation" of communist ideas. They established a quota system that resulted in immigration being reduced to 165,000 persons in 1925, 150,000 persons in 1927, while in 1913 there were almost 1,200,000 immigrants. The availability of manpower, therefore, rose rapidly in Europe, since the emigration of male adults had been curtailed. There were fewer jobs available than the labor market could accommodate. Between 1923 and 1927, depending on the year, unemployment among the working class in Great Britain varied between 10 and 17 per cent, in Germany between 7 and 14 per cent, between 10 and 12 per cent in Sweden, and in Denmark between 10 and 22 per cent. This excess of manpower encouraged a slowdown in automation.

This situation was particularly important for international affairs. The financial transactions between the United States and Europe affected political relations, whether it was a question of the payment of war debts between France, Great Britain, and the United States, the demand from European industries for American capital, or competition for stocks of raw materials and oil deposits between British and American trusts. The quest for raw materials and markets was one of the essential motives behind Japanese foreign policy. Even in Europe, Great Britain's continental policy was largely motivated by the desire to see Germany recover an important place in the economic community; the question of reparations, which was the ground for economic and financial contention between Germany and France during these ten years, was a factor that weighed heavily on political relations between these two countries. The interest, particularly on the part of German and British industry, in "reopening" the Russian market explains some of the political initiatives taken by the governments of Berlin and London with regard to the Soviet government. Finally public reaction in the European countries to both foreign policy and domestic policy varied considerably according to the economic and financial "context"—the monetary crises during the years 1920–1924 or the period of relative euphoria between 1925 and 1928.

Even prior to 1914 economic or financial factors influenced international relations; whether they acted as incentives or as instruments they played a role that historical interpretation should never lose sight of.

Changes in Collective Psychology

The influence of economic and financial conditions, however, is only one of the contributing factors that merit attention. The changes in collective psychology are no less important, whether it was a question of change in political ideas or of the temper of the nation. Furthermore, such tendencies became all the more apparent in that diplomatic action, in its new forms, addressed itself directly to public opinion.

The democratic and parliamentary institutions that had apparently survived the 1914–1918 war unchallenged were less resistant to the difficulties of the postwar period. In Germany the electoral system established by the Weimar Constitution led to the formation of coalition governments, which were condemned continually to arrange compromises among the parties they represented. In France political life was marked by a crisis over parliamentary membership, over the methods of parliamentary procedure, and especially over the authority of the executive. The desire for a reform of the state, for a rejuvenation of its institutions, began to make itself felt in 1920 and gained ground during the following years. Even in Great Britain the political "machine" creaked from time to time. In all three countries the parliaments were obliged temporarily to renounce their essential functions and, in order to provide against urgent necessities, to turn over legislative powers to the executive. "Rule by decree" was substituted here and there for "rule of law." This was a grave distortion of the principles that had been the basis of the rights of the people in liberal, democratic Europe before 1914. Public opinion finally showed such serious disenchantment for these principles of parliamentary democracy that in 1928 the Interparliamentary Union held meetings to discuss the problem.

The immediate cause of these difficulties was the contrast between "political society" and "economic society." The parliamentary system, upon which professional, economic, and financial groups can easily exert pressure, is often incapable of mediating conflicts of interest between producers and consumers or between groups of producers, or of making rapid decisions required by the economic or fiscal situation.

But basically the crisis was dominated by the existence in Europe of new regimes which rejected the concepts of democratic liberalism. After its victory in the civil war, Russian communism exerted its influence by means of the Third International, which guided the activities of the German, French, and Italian Communist parties but found a less favorable terrain in Great Britain, where membership lagged. After the success of Mussolini's march on Rome on October 24, 1922, and his accession to power, fascism attempted to promote a new solution to the "problem of state." It found a reflection in Spain in 1923 with the dictatorship of General Primo de Rivera, and subsequently in Poland in 1925, where General Pilsudski established an authoritarian political system.

The presence of these new regimes was a cause of instability in international political relations and posed a possible threat to peace. The antiparliamentary movements in France and in Germany looked either toward Moscow or toward Rome. The national Communist parties gave their allegiance to the international policies of Soviet Russia. The "bourgeois" groups sympathetic to fascism wanted French policy to serve Italian interests. The conflicts between ideologies helped to increase antagonisms between nations, while personal regimes needed to assert their desires for prestige and power in foreign affairs.

The irritations of nationalism and the rancor and hatred that application of the treaties could not help but create gave great importance to the "minorities" question in European countries where the population, sometimes numerous (30 per cent of the over-all population in Poland, 29 per cent in Czechoslovakia), considered as alien the government to which they were subject. Prior to 1914 the national minorities had sometimes been protected by the great powers—as in the case of the Ottoman empire, for example—but such action, rarely disinterested, had been intermittent. The authors of the treaties had wished to establish a more valid guarantee in the place of occasional protection. In order to minimize conflicts between the minority groups and the governments of countries inhabited by these populations, they had promised the members of these groups that they would be able to conserve their languages, their religions, and their educational or charitable institutions, and that, in order to defend their liberties, they might have recourse to all legal means—namely, freedom of the press, the right of assembly and association, and the right to vote. Fourteen "new" states had to pledge not to establish any discrimination with regard to the civil and political rights of their citizens who differed from the majority by race, language, or religion. This set of rules was placed under the supervision of the League of Nations, whose Council was to examine complaints that minority groups brought before it. Here was a work of peace established in response to a liberal sentiment which was often preached before 1914 and, while imposing restrictions on these states, at the same time protected them from irredentist movements.

But in practice this system far from satisfied the hopes of its sponsors. The cases that members of national minorities brought before the Council of the League of Nations were often inspired by a maneuver in which concern for the protection of individual or collective freedom was cited only to serve a political end. They resulted in the censure of certain countries by world-wide public opinion and protest, sometimes in separatist movements in the heart of the minority group. Thus, they induced a state of unrest, whereas they had been designed to ensure peace within the "new" states. The replies of the accused states were prompted by similar concerns. The governments would seek to obtain by diplomatic bargaining an attitude of "indulgent compliance" on the part of the Council of the League. They complained of being subjected to a rule of exception, since the system of protection of minorities applied only to certain states, and since in a number of others, minority groups suffered restrictions against which they had no recourse. Therefore, they demanded that the system be universally applied. But in 1922 the League of Nations Assembly refused to extend the application of the statute of minorities, not only because it would have encountered the opposition of certain great powers (was it conceivable that Great Britain would allow the League of

Nations to examine the Irish question?), but because it was afraid of "resuscitating" national minority movements in regions where these issues actually no longer existed.

Because of these debates, to which a substantial portion of the League's agenda was devoted, the nationalities question received a good deal of publicity. The result was too often "the intensive, hothouse cultivation of all the elements of disruption, disturbance, instability, and unrest." Thus, as noted by a statesmen closely connected with the work at Geneva, although the numerical importance of minorities in the Europe of 1919 was less than half what it had been in 1914, their political importance had greatly increased. In order to put an end to these difficulties, an "exchange of minorities" was contemplated. This was the solution applied to Turkey and Greece after 1923. But the material and moral difficulties imposed on these uprooted populations seemed to condemn this system to be abandoned.

Outside of Europe the movements based on feelings of nationalism were of a different nature. Of course, the question of "national minorities" was still in evidence. It was overshadowed, however, by problems world-wide in scope, in that they involved the fate of European interests in the other continents. It is true that these nationalistic tendencies were not always reflected in international politics. The protests of the Indian nationalists in 1921 and 1922, when Gandhi developed his campaign of "noncooperation," was still at the time a British problem. But two of these great movements, in China and in the Islamic countries, had a particular impact on international relations. Both of them began to emerge by 1919 but had been unable to exert any effective influence on the peace settlement. What new characteristic did they take on between 1920 and 1930?

The Moslem nationalist movements, which could call on some 250,000,000 men in Asia and Africa, gained momentum from 1920 on. The basic reason for this surge was most probably the indignation brought on by the peace settlement which, despite the Wilsonian promises, had extended European control over the

Arab countries of the Middle East. The leaders of these movements, in seeking to organize resistance against European hegemony, often adopted Western military and economic techniques
and on occasion even copied administrative or political institutions.
The "purists" who had demonstrated the most profound antipathy
toward Western civilization now moderated their intransigence,
aware that unless they accepted certain forms of this civilization,
they would be incapable of shaking off foreign domination.

The great force animating the masses behind these movements
was that of religion. This is what undoubtedly explained the daring
and persistence of the Turks, the Riff tribes, or the Senoussites.
The leaders and their lieutenants, however, were often removed
from religious concerns and were motivated rather by political
design. In Egypt, Zaghlul carefully refrained from taking a stand
on the question of the Ottoman caliphate. Nor did he want the
religious leaders to interfere in the organization of the nationalist
movement, in which he hoped that Christian Copts would join with
Muslims. In the Dutch Indies the Sarekat Islam association, which
was conducting a program of nationalist claims against Dutch
colonialism, accepted non-Muslim members. In Turkey, Mustapha
Kemal went so far as to proclaim the separation of church and
state. There was thus no question of a great surge of Moslem
solidarity between 1920 and 1926. These movements were or-
iented toward a "Western" notion—that of the national state—
and did not appear to consider the idea of coordinating their
efforts. Nor did they seek the support of the Communist International, since the Moslem masses remained unmoved by the
slogan of class warfare, while the leaders mistrusted the Soviet
program.

These initiatives were hardly encouraged by the sovereigns.
Wherever the Islamic dynasties continued to exist, they more often
than not wanted compromise solutions, since an adventurist policy
could lead to their downfall. The Sultan of Turkey was even
prepared to accept foreign protection if it would consolidate his
power. It was the new men, the dictators, who directed the nationalist movements. The dissension between the European nations was
their trump card, whether it was the conflict of interests between

Great Britain, France, and Italy, who were watching each other
and seeking, in their mutual troubles, to get the upper hand over
each other, and who, above all, did not want to pull a competitor's
chestnuts out of the fire; or the conflict of opinions, within each
of the three states, between those who advocated an imperial policy
and those who rejected the principle or refused to accept its responsibilities.

The Chinese nationalist movement which appeared in May of
1919 suffered a setback between 1920 and 1921 because of the
gravity of the internal crisis. The civil war, which had been "suspended" during the peace conference, resumed between the Peking
government—that is, the group of generals usually known as the
"An-Fou Club"—and the Canton government, stronghold of Sun
Yat-sen and the founders of the revolution of 1911. The two rival
governments were themselves at grips with dissensions or local
uprisings. Of the eighteen provinces that made up China proper
in 1922, four were under the actual control of Peking, two under
that of Canton, and the other twelve were virtually independent,
in the hands of generals whose *de facto* power was often contested
by rivals. The "war lords" adapted themselves willingly to this
chaotic situation, since it worked to their personal advantage.
However, two organizations began to take shape—the Kuomintang
party and the Communist party.

The Kuomintang was reorganized in 1923 by Sun Yat-sen, who
provided it with a doctrine in 1924 in his book *The Three Principles
of the People.* He said that China had become a "colonial market-
place" and that, oppressed by the imperialist powers, she was
"the slave of more than ten masters." There was no other way to
escape this fate than to borrow from the material civilization of the
Westerners, at the same time preserving the Chinese moral and
political philosophies. In this regard Sun Yat-sen's thinking did
not add a great deal to the traditional themes of "reformers" such
as Leang Ki-chao, for example. It did, however, differ insofar as
social and political factors were concerned. Sun considered that
China's economic situation differed too widely from that of Europe
to permit the adoption of Marxism. He therefore stopped at the

nationalization of essential industries but wholly respected private ownership of land, hoping only to correct by fiscal measures the most blatant inequalities. He said that the political organization would be democratic, that it would assure all citizens enjoyment of equal rights. It would not, however, take its example from the French or the British system, nor from the American, not only because the nature of Chinese society did not lend itself to the application of Western methods, but because these very methods were unsatisfactory. Thus China needed to bring forth its own solution, one that would give the leading role to the "intellectual elite" while according to the "masses" a mere right of control, which would only be exercised after a "period of education." *The Three Principles of the People* tended, therefore, to suggest a strong government, quite different from the one Sun had advocated in 1912. Was this evolution solely the result of the experiences and disappointments of "the father of the Chinese Revolution"? No doubt it had been influenced also by the example of the European revolutions that, in Italy as well as in Russia, had put authoritarian regimes into power.

Meanwhile the communist experiment, rejected by Sun Yat-sen, found its apostles who began in 1919 to propagate their ideas among university students. In July 1921, Chan Tu-siu, whom the Congress of the Communist International had designated to organize the Chinese party, held the first meeting in Shanghai where he was assisted by Li Ta-chao and Mao Tse-tung. He was surrounded by only a handful of men. At that point the party began to recruit members from among the workers in the industrial region of Honan—especially from the metallurgical works at Han-Yeh-Ping. It did not approach the peasantry until 1924.

Faced with these material or emotional forces, which were a permanent cause of difficulty and unrest in international relations, the counterbalancing forces began to decline with the break between the Second International and the Communist International which had been proclaimed at the beginning of 1919. The schism between democratic socialism and the communist movement was achieved in France by December of 1920, and also in Germany and Italy. Weakened by this rupture, socialism was even less able to exercise vigorous action in the preservation of peace than it was before 1914.

Basically the most effective counterbalance to the forces of disruption during the ten years following the signing of the peace treaties was the weariness of the people. Exhausted by too long an effort, they looked forward to stability, to a safe night's sleep. There was absolutely no appetite for war.

National Policies

In the great nations that were in a position to make their influence felt, the conduct of foreign policy was obviously dominated by the concerns that existed at the time of the peace settlement. However, certain new tendencies appeared in the currents of public opinion and in the strategies of statesmen.

In Germany the democratic regime improvised by the Weimar Constitution did not have deep roots in public opinion. The *Reichswehr,* whose officer corps was identical to that of the imperial army, was "a foreign body" in the Republic. Between 1920 and 1926, however, it refrained from taking sides over the political regime, since it wanted to be the organ of the great national interests, to embody the Fatherland, to be above involvement in political parties. But it also wished to avoid compromising itself, against the day when it would be able to reaffirm its primacy. General von Seeckt considered that the time had not yet come for the structure of the state to be altered. This attitude of apparent reserve did not, however, prevent the army from exercising a real authority on certain occasions. It was a "counterbalance" to civilian power because the government was unable to withstand internal difficulties without its support.

The chief characteristic of parliamentary life was the position adopted by the Populist party, urged on by Gustav Stresemann. Whereas the Populists had agreed in November of 1922 to be part of the Cuno government—a coalition cabinet that had advocated a policy of resistance to France on the reparations question—their leader adopted a policy of "fulfillment" in August 1923. Germany would thus cease to contest the principle of reparations, would respect its disarmament commitments, and would promise to harbor no more dreams of revenge.

Economic interests were probably the chief motive behind this sudden change of heart. In order to replenish her stocks of raw materials and to modernize her industrial equipment, Germany would need to call on foreign capital. "We have an urgent need for several billion," noted Stresemann in his personal diary. If the Reich could not come to an understanding with the capital-holding countries, it would suffer an "economic cataclysm," since "we no longer have the means to finance our enterprises." How could this be achieved unless English and American capitalists were reassured? This conciliatory attitude would also in time permit Germany to gain political advantages. Once she had been admitted to the League of Nations, she would manage systematically to obtain a revision of the Treaty of Versailles. Evacuation of the Rhine territories; diplomatic intervention for the relief of Germans placed under foreign domination in Czechoslovakia and, particularly, in Poland; rectification of the Polish border with a view toward doing away with the corridor; finally, but in the more distant future, the union of the Austrian republic with the Reich—these were the plans Stresemann outlined in a confidential letter addressed to the ex-crown prince of Prussia on September 7, 1925.

The adoption of this new line of conduct, which was to guide German foreign policy for six years, was simply realistic. According to Stresemann's thinking, Germany had to choose the "West." True, he did not refuse to negotiate with the Soviet government in the winter of 1925–1926, or to pledge, in April 1926, the neutrality of Germany in case the Western powers waged a war of aggression against the U.S.S.R. But he immediately made use of this Russo-German treaty as a means of pressure to obtain a permanent seat on the Council of the League of Nations. In the words of a German diplomat, Soviet Russia is a "trump to be played against the West."

As the development of this "fulfillment" policy progressed, however, so did the resistance engendered by intransigent nationalism

grow stronger among the German people. When Stresemann outlined his program in 1924 and 1925, he was criticized only by the
"German National" party which at that time represented just about
one fifth of the electorate. In the general elections of May 1928,
in which there were many abstentions, the parties in favor of the
fulfillment policy still gained 17,000,000 votes out of an electorate
that counted about 26,000,000 registered voters. But in September
1930 these parties lost 2,700,000 votes, while the National Socialist
party, which openly preached a war of revenge, gained 5,600,000.

The evolution of public opinion deserves our attention even
more than do the diplomatic incidents. Did the nationalist opposition consider the policy of fulfillment a failure? It did not question
the results, but it did condemn the principle. Was it the manifestation of unrest or even of anguish provoked by social and economic
difficulties? At that time, it is true, Germany's economic recovery,
which had progressed quite favorably between 1925 and 1929,
due partially to the influx of American capital, showed a noticeable
slackening. It was not, however, until 1931 that the Reich was
seriously affected by the world-wide crisis. Most of the German
press did not hesitate between these interpretations. This shift of
political strength, according to the newspapers, could be explained
by the surge of patriotism and the desire to wash away the "national shame"; the economy played no active role in this development.

In Italy the economic, social, and moral crisis, whose symptoms
had been apparent since the summer of 1919, continued for almost
three years. On two occasions the internal troubles were quite
serious. The transient governments—those of Nitti, then Giolitti
and Sforza, finally that of Facta—were able to conduct only a
tentative foreign policy.

Conditions changed with the *coup d'état* of October 30, 1922,
and the advent of the Fascist regime. Foreign policy was thenceforward directed by a man who was subject neither to the influence
of party or even in the first years to that of business. Since the
armistice of 1919, Mussolini had consistently rejected the trend
toward internationalism and had stressed the primacy of the state,

whose sovereignty should be "absolute and inviolate." He had stated his desire to restore the grandeur of Italy, not only by remolding her institutions, but also by a "spiritual transformation," and to cause her interests and her rights to be recognized by partners too inclined to treat her "as another Portugal." Finally he had announced his desire to inaugurate "a glorious period in Italian history." With these first public declarations upon taking power, he began proclaiming his intentions. If the Entente did not become a "homogeneous and balanced bloc," where members would have equal rights and responsibilities, Italy would resume her freedom of action. However, even if she were not forced into this position, she would avoid involvement in the League of Nations system because it was neither possible nor desirable to maintain perpetual peace, and because the guarantee of the territorial *status quo* was no more than an "Anglo-French" instrument. The peace treaties were "not perpetual"; they should be revised the moment they no longer suited reality.

Two plans of action derived from these premises. First, the Italian government should dominate the Mediterranean and expel the "parasites." The Mediterranean "should be and will be *mare nostrum.*" The Adriatic question, of course, was in the forefront of this Mediterranean program. Second, the reconstitution of Austria-Hungary, even under the guise of a simple Danubian confederation, would be dangerous to Italian interests, since such a confederation (unless it was formed under the aegis of Italy) would resume its expansionist designs in the direction of the Adriatic. The result would be the same if Austria were absorbed by Germany, since the Danube states would in the end gravitate toward the orbit of the German system, creating a paralyzing threat that would weigh "on Italy's back." Furthermore, on May 20, 1925, Mussolini declared that he could "never tolerate the patent violation of treaties that the annexation of Austria by Germany would constitute."

Fascist Italy's preposterous foreign policy was only superficially active. It would have to remain circumspect until Italy had been "rejuvenated" at every level—politically, morally, economically, and financially. Mussolini himself conceded this necessity in a speech in February 1923. Rejuvenation, however, proceeded slowly. Politically the regime underwent such a serious crisis in 1925 and 1926 that the fall of Fascism seemed imminent. Economically, industrial production, which received from overseas four fifths of its raw materials and fuel, remained very dependent upon foreign sources. The weakness of its military and naval resources could not be overlooked. In 1923 the Italian navy was inferior not only—it goes without saying—to the British Mediterranean fleet but to the French navy as well; five cruisers whose construction was undertaken at the time would not be completed until 1932. Plans for reorganizing the army were not perfected until 1926 and were realized only slowly. Here were causes for prudence. Thus *il Duce*'s contempt for the League of Nations—that lifeless, unimportant, "academic organization"—did not lead him to take the logical step. "I prefer, in general, being on the inside to being on the outside," he declared.

This was tantamount to admitting that the hour had not yet come to realize the "difficult, patient, and cyclopean" task that he had announced on the eve of his accession to power.

The great Russian nation, whose population (133,000,000 in 1923; 146,000,000 in 1926) constituted two-fifths of the entire population of the Continent, had in 1919 undergone a crisis that threatened to sweep away the Soviet regime. The hope cherished by the Third International that it would see the communist idea spread to Germany and Hungary had been quickly dispelled. The Soviet government found itself threatened, especially in April and October, by the converging offensives of the White armies. By the end of autumn, however, the Red army had succeeded in breaking these offensives and in resuming the initiative. But the policy of intervention, abandoned by Britain and France, was taken up by the Polish government, which in the spring of 1920 offered assistance to the last White army remaining in the field, that of Wrangel in southern Russia. This policy encountered fresh disaster. The Russo-Polish war did indeed allow Poland to extend her territories in White Russia, but it did not save Wrangel's troops, who were left stranded when the Russo-Polish war was over in November 1920.

It was only after that date that, having overcome immediate

dangers, the Soviet government was able to turn its attention toward its general foreign policy. In the formulation of this policy, psychological conditions and economic motives were given equal attention.

The Soviet leaders did not believe that "peaceful coexistence" was possible between Russia and the great capitalist nations in 1919: it seemed likely and logical to them for the Western powers to attempt to suppress the country that was the birthplace of communism. The failure of Anglo-French intervention had dispelled that fear. Certain among them, notably Lenin and Stalin, came to believe therefore that coexistence would be possible, at least for a while, on the condition that the Moscow government could "disrupt the capitalist front" and avoid the threat of a coalition. To achieve this it would be necessary to reassure the bourgeoisie. The means to be employed would include subduing the activity of the Communist International, putting a stop to waving the "banner of revolution" in Europe, limiting their designs to the establishment of communism "in one country," concluding nonaggression pacts with immediate neighbors, and obtaining *de facto* recognition of the Soviet regime from the countries of Western Europe. Such tactics need not close the door to the future, for the communist state needed only to set an example, and the world would topple sooner or later.

Trotsky rejected these political concepts, not only because they suggested an overly prudent opportunism, but because they were dangerous. To abandon the encouragement to world revolution, he said, was to run a grave risk, since if "capitalist" Europe remained intact, it would of necessity want eventually to destroy the Soviet regime.

This conflict remained dormant until the autumn of 1924; it erupted after the death of Lenin.

Economic necessities reinforced this policy of temporary conciliation. The civil war and the resistance of private interests to the application of government measures had brought about the collapse of industrial production, the decline of agricultural production, and the paralysis of the railways. In 1921 Lenin was forced, in his own words, to beat a "strategic retreat"—that is, to renounce partially the application of communist principles, and to reinstate the stimulus of private profit in order to gain an increase in production. The "new economic policy" (N.E.P.), expressly announced as a temporary expedient, was to continue for almost five years. It meant resorting to foreign technicians or even to foreign capital to reorganize productivity—and, consequently, resuming economic and financial relations abroad.

The N.E.P. was abandoned in 1927 when Stalin, having eliminated Trotsky, adopted certain points of his adversary's program. But Soviet planning in its two aspects—development of heavy industry and socialization of agriculture—laid heavy emphasis on efforts to provide mechanical equipment. Russian factories were no longer in a position to furnish machinery and materials. Thus the promoters of the first "five-year plan" were obliged to look abroad for these items. Economic relations with the great capitalist states remained almost as necessary as they had been in preceding years.

It would be foolish to speculate whether economic or political motives determined this state of affairs. They were two facets of the same concern, which was basically defensive in that its essential goal was to ensure the survival and the safety of the Soviet state.

This policy, however, was defensive only insofar as Europe was concerned. The same men who thought it necessary to adopt a position of withdrawal in their relations with the Western powers, which Stalin called "the center of world financial exploitation," wished to take the initiative in Asia, the zone of colonial or semi-colonial domination of these powers. By favoring the development of revolutionary movements in India, Iran, and China, Soviet Russia would provoke a "crisis for capitalism" in the Western countries—especially in Great Britain—whose industries had great need of these foreign markets and of these reserves of raw material. At the same time she would attempt to extend her own influence in areas of the world inhabited by the great masses of humanity—without requiring their allegiance to communism. "Extend our hand to eight hundred million Asians," stir up their xenophobic sentiments by telling them that "European capitalism" is responsible for their misery—this was the program that Zino-

viev had proposed to the Congress of the Communist International
in 1919. Lenin himself adopted this idea at the very time he was
applying a policy of "retreat" in Europe. The victory of Bolshevism in the world, he said in 1923, will depend on the success
of this collaboration with the peoples of Asia. "We shall be compensated one hundred times over for what we have lost in the
countries of Europe."

In 1920 victorious France was a powerful military nation. She
was the only continental power to possess a large army. However,
neither this victory nor this strength sufficed to give the French
people the feeling that they had won a war. Foreign observers did
not fail to notice this.

What were the distinctive features of this collective psychology?
The conviction that the German danger would reappear in the
future, owing to superiority of population and of industry; the
feeling that the victory of 1918 would not have been possible without the support of Great Britain and the United States, and that
these favorable conditions might not exist on a future occasion;
finally, weariness: after a crushing effort which had cost the nation
20 per cent of its active population, the public wanted a speedy
curtailment of military obligations and considered "power politics"
to be burdensome. These anxieties and this fatigue did not, it is
true, affect all of the French bourgeoisie. Certain circles, especially
among the political groups of the right, gave evidence of an
imperturbable confidence and an unshaken firmness. However, this
attitude was confined to a small segment of the population.

Economic and financial difficulties confirmed this uneasy state
of mind. The principal problems encountered included the considerable budgetary deficit (expenditures in 1919 amounted to
forty-nine billion francs, while receipts scarcely exceeded eleven
billion), the urgent need to re-establish transportation in the devastated areas and to indemnify industry for war damages in order
to rebuild it, and the prospect of having to repay the debts contracted in England and the United States during the war. It was
unlikely that France could count on help from abroad, since the
American Treasury had decided at the time of the armistice to

halt the extension of credit to the former allies of the United States. Therefore, payment of the reparations provided by the peace treaty appeared unavoidable. In 1921 the chairman of the budget committee wrote that if Germany did not pay, "the problem will be insoluble."

It is difficult, however, to reconcile these psychological trends with these financial necessities. Payment of the reparations would be possible only if Germany achieved a surplus balance of payments. Thus, the industrial recovery of the Reich would be a prior and necessary condition to these payments. But the recovery of this industrial power would afford the conquered nation a "war potential." This was an inherent contradiction that French public opinion was slow to grasp.

Thus the "German question" occupied center stage among foreign policy considerations. Any other difficulties, in the Mediterranean or the Middle East, for example, were secondary. Although they sometimes caused concern in political circles, they did not create a serious stir in public opinion. What policy should be adopted toward a conquered power whose weakness would only be temporary?

Politicians, diplomats, and military men agreed that in the absence of the security pact that the United States and Britain had refused to ratify, the security of France should rest on a system of "rear alliances." By signing treaties with Germany's neighboring states—Czechoslovakia, Poland, perhaps even Belgium—France would be able to contain a German effort toward expansion which, directed at first against the weak points in the new European structure, would later threaten France herself. In general the public did not question the necessity for these alliances. Business circles favored them, since a French "military protectorate" in Prague or Warsaw opened the way to an economic and financial expansion in which the big Paris banks worked hand in hand with the great metallurgical enterprises. However, starting in 1921, France's German policy became an object of discussion. The two opposing tendencies that emerged were linked to the temperaments and personal ideas of two statesmen—namely, Raymond Poincaré and Aristide Briand. They were reflected equally in public opinion.

There were some who said that France, enjoying a military superiority that she should strive to maintain, was in a position to enforce the application of all the clauses of the Versailles Treaty and, if necessary, to resort to coercion. Besides, this firm stand would have the advantage of strengthening the system of "rear alliances," since it would give confidence to the nations to which France was committed. The French government had an obligation to apply this policy without considering the possible objections of its former allies. Why should France agree to abandon even partially the exercise of her rights? Why should she fail to exact the reimbursement of war damages? Why should she consent to the limited independence of her decisions? This state of mind, reflecting the opinions of the political right, was shared by a segment of the radical parliamentary group between 1920 and 1923. The statesman who embodied this policy—Raymond Poincaré—was a nationalist from Lorraine whose legal inclinations were most satisfied when he had a solid brief to plead.

The others thought it would be impossible to keep Germany in a state of impotence by the occupation of the Rhineland, disarmament, and the payment of reparations. This theory was outlined clearly by Aristide Briand in a speech at Saint-Nazaire in October 1921. France, he declared, had to reckon with British public opinion, which disapproved of a policy of restraint. She could not consider a line of conduct that would lead to the collapse of Anglo-French solidarity. She could no longer ignore world opinion that wanted to see Germany freed from financial control and resume her normal place in the "world market." In the long run, therefore, France would be unable to prevent the rebirth of a strong Germany, since complete application of the Treaty of Versailles would be possible only through "collective" action—an unlikely hypothesis at best. One must seek therefore to channel the momentum of this rebirth toward peace. "Germany," wrote Philippe Berthelot to Briand in January 1923, "will be stronger than France in the space of twenty to fifty years." In order to avoid a new conflict in which France would be "doomed," it would be essential for Germany to relinquish the idea of a war of revenge. This would be accomplished by bringing about a change in the

German mentality, by showing that collaboration between the two peoples could be possible and fruitful. Collaboration, however, implies concession. It is not surprising that, after having followed the nationalist line in the spring of 1921 and verbally contemplated "putting a hand to Germany's throat," Briand adopted this new policy: for twenty years he had been convinced that politics was the art of smoothing out differences. It was hardly surprising that the majority of the French people were converted to the Briand program in 1925, since such a line of conduct satisfied its desire for peace. But it was surprising that even Poincaré, despite a certain amount of reticence, should come around to the policy of conciliation in 1928.

Great Britain's domestic policy in 1919 was dominated by her traditional concerns. The public outlook was characterized by peaceful idealism, day-to-day problems, and the spirit of compromise. The general outlook on foreign policy included the fear of a continental hegemony in Europe and the desire for the safety of the maritime routes outside Europe, which were indispensable to the existence of the British empire and to the restoration of British economic influence. However, there was no question of Britain's returning to her policy of isolation, which she had abandoned in the first years of the twentieth century, toward the continent of Europe. Great Britain had clearly learned that she could no longer remain aloof without endangering her own security. She was conscious of being "European." What were the implications of these general tendencies?

It seems that public opinion in Parliament as well as among the general population was influenced by three facts. Since German maritime power had been destroyed, Great Britain possessed a naval superiority in European waters that left the British Isles immune to invasion. The fear of "invasion by sea," which had existed for some years prior to 1914, had disappeared. However, a continental balance of power was not guaranteed, since France, with the only large army, was seeking to establish a system of alliances that would give her a hegemony. The British public had no notion of the desire for security and the feeling of uneasiness experienced by the French people, not only because the British rarely made the effort to understand another's viewpoint, but because they were unwilling to consider the future. As long as there was little likelihood of a German war of retaliation in the near future, why should France maintain "excessive" military forces and try to group the new nations around her? At heart certain British groups suspected the French nation of harboring "Napoleonic ambitions." Finally, this French policy, though less ambitious than it seemed, went against British interests insofar as it delayed a stable European settlement, which was essential to the restoration of continental economic activities. On the one hand, the promises made by French diplomacy to the new nations allowed them, in effect, to oppose the amicable review of peace treaties provided for by Article 19 of the Covenant of the League of Nations. The majority of the British people did not believe that the continent of Europe could remain in a "static state," and felt that the best method of dealing with the grudges that still existed would be a frank discussion over the claims of the "unsatisfied" nations—a point of view also reflected in the attitude of the Foreign Office. On the other hand, the policy of encirclement directed against Germany was undesirable, since it was likely to perpetuate the chronic feeling of bitterness and rebellion in the bosom of this great people. It would be impossible to establish permanent security by isolating the Reich, any more than could economic prosperity be revived by ruining the German people or by continuing to disrupt the continental market.

Great Britain should therefore not agree to accept extensive responsibilities in continental affairs.

It was nonetheless recognized in political circles that it would be advisable to take partial account of France's anxieties, even if they did seem exaggerated. But how?

The first possible solution would be the conclusion of a "guarantee treaty" with France, which would be applied in the event of an unprovoked German attack, even if such a step on the part of Germany was intended not to violate the border but to violate the demilitarized status of the Rhineland. This promise, which Lloyd George made to Clemenceau during the peace conference, had been forgotten following the defection of the United States.

Lloyd George was to take it up again at the Cannes conference in early January 1922 and, at the same time, to make a counter-demand—that the French government take part in a plan for the "economic reconstruction" of Europe—an immediate corollary of which would be the reduction in the war reparations owed to France.

The second solution, which was to be adopted by Austen Chamberlain in 1925, perhaps on the advice of Lord Curzon, was to grant a guarantee to Germany and to France at the same time. Thus Great Britain would not be taking part in "an alliance directed against a third party" and would avoid association with a group of powers. Rather, she would be subscribing to an "impartial" commitment.

This guarantee, however, would be limited to the status of the Rhineland. The British cabinet did not intend to guarantee the territorial status established by the Treaty of Versailles in eastern and central Europe. In particular, Austen Chamberlain felt that the "Polish corridor" could not endure for very long. He thought that in several years Germany would be in a position, owing to her economic power, to bring Poland to a reconciliation that would be followed by a border revision. In any case, he wrote, "no British government would ever risk the life of a single British corporal" over this question. By refusing to accept any responsibilities toward these new nations—France's allies—Britain was in effect admitting that the French army should maintain sufficient means to intervene alone for purposes of maintaining the *status quo*.

In short, British policy was based on the conviction that Germany would be satisfied with diplomatic means to obtain a gradual revision of the Treaty of Versailles.

In Great Britain's relations with the other continents, two new factors command attention. Both outside and within Europe the basis of British power before 1914 had been her naval superiority. This predominance had been strengthened in Europe but was disappearing elsewhere. To avoid having to run an armaments race in which the United States, because of her industrial and financial resources, would undoubtedly come out ahead, Great Britain had been obliged to accept parity of naval strength in the destroyer and cruiser classes. This deprived her of one of her most solid assets in the conduct of her foreign policy. On the other hand, the reorganization of the empire obliged the British cabinet to take into account the feelings and desires expressed by the governments of her dominions. It could no longer make commitments in their name without previous consultation, at least when it was a question of possible participation in an armed conflict. The government now had considerable difficulty in reconciling its concerns with those of the dominions, since the latter tended to take a "regionalist" point of view. This situation was especially delicate in the area of collective security. The dominions regarded the Geneva system with some reserve owing to the abstention of the United States. Great Britain, as a member of the League of Nations and of the Commonwealth, had to reconcile two sets of obligations. If the British government agreed to increase its commitments within the League of Nations, did it not run the risk of seeing the dominions refuse to follow suit "and ask for their freedom"? Thus, the British cabinet was forced to seek compromises.

These naval and imperial considerations led British diplomacy to attach increasing importance to the friendship of the United States. The new situation added the urgent need for such a friendship to the feeling of mutual understanding that already existed before 1914. The necessity of depending on the support of the American fleet in the Pacific, the desire to avoid the risk of having the United States exert pressure on Canada and Australia, the desire to cultivate the powerful American financial interests whose hostility would be dangerous for the City of London—these were the reasons that explained the docility of Great Britain in her relations with the United States. The British cabinet, unwilling to take steps at Geneva that might cause concern in the dominions, was even more determined in its refusal to make a choice between the League and the United States.

Thus, British policy could not be "frankly European"; and this reservation was the basic cause of Anglo-French differences.

The isolationist tendency in American foreign policy was further strengthened by the election of a Republican administration in

1920. The application of the principle was only partial, however.

Washington declined any responsibility and any initiative in its relations with Europe. The interests of the nation, said Secretary of State Hughes, are different from those of Europe, and as a result American policy should continue to maintain an independent position. Could this independence, considered indispensable to the field of politics, be fully realized in the economic and financial fields as well? American industrialists, bankers, and farmers were not in a position to ignore the European market, nor were American contributors to the settlements of inter-Allied debts. Businessmen were well aware that the economic recovery of Europe would depend in large part on the amount of capital invested, most of which would come from the United States. If American producers were to sustain or to enlarge their exports, it would be due to this movement of capital. The government therefore favored developing these investments. Of course, it left to the banks the responsibility for their decisions, but it offered them opinions, advice, and warnings and imposed its control in the case of a foreign loan issued on the American market, especially if it feared that the money thus raised would be used for the purchase of armaments. The most striking feature of this line of conduct was the contrast between the political attitude and economic action. The one pretended to be impartial; it was not totally so, since American diplomacy continued to favor treaties of arbitration and disarmament and often sent unofficial "observers" to international conferences where official delegates would have conflicted with American policy; but it refused steadfastly to make any commitment. The other concerned itself not only with protecting world-wide American commercial and financial interests but also with ensuring the official participation of United States representatives in economic, social, or technical international organizations. The Republican administration sought neither to lessen this contrast nor to use political means to achieve economic ends in its foreign relations.

This "isolationism" did not of course apply to the Far East or to Latin America.

The present and future American economic interests in China, which offered over four hundred million "consumers," the desire to safeguard the strategic positions acquired by the United States in the Pacific archipelagoes, and the propaganda of the religious missions were the factors that induced Washington to check Japanese imperialism. In order to do so, the United States would have to agree to accept certain responsibilities and to conclude an agreement with the nations of Western Europe, particularly Great Britain. The State Department, however, wished to confine itself to the application of diplomatic pressure and did not consider making commitments that would imply the use of force.

The strategic concerns that had been an important factor in Latin American policy before 1914 in the isthmus of Panama and in all regions giving onto the Caribbean Sea were now realized. The United States government needed only to protect its gains by employing a somewhat attenuated form of "dollar diplomacy." The decisive influences in this part of the world were now economic. They led the United States to extend her activity toward South America, where she held only second place in the exploitation of natural resources and in capital investment. The withdrawal of Europe during the 1914–1918 war had opened the way to her exporters and her businessmen. Her aims in this area were thus to widen these initial successes, especially in areas containing supplies of raw material, and to consolidate at the same time her dominant position on the continent. Thus, European interests were gradually eased out.

Japan's international position was still influenced by economic and demographic factors that forced her to conduct a policy of expansion. Could this policy be pursued by peaceful means, or did it presuppose resorting to force? In 1920 Japanese leaders were divided on this subject; and this rift was to widen during the years to come.

"Peaceful" expansion would have to be confined to the customary processes of commercial activity. The directors of the big trusts— Baron Mitsuei, who controlled 284 enterprises with a total capital of 26,000,000,000 francs, and Baron Iwasaki, head of the Mitsubishi group which included 92 enterprises—proposed to seek an "economic *rapprochement*" with China, which absorbed 22 per cent of Japanese exports, by proclaiming their respect for Chinese sovereignty and territorial integrity, by creating agencies that would be responsible for the purchase of raw materials, by choosing resources in countries that would not become enemies of Japan in the event of a general war, by seeking new export markets—for example, in European colonies where the clientele, more concerned about price than quality, would be inclined to appreciate the products of Japanese industry. The Keizai Club, headquarters of the Japanese economy and meeting place of the heads of the industrial associations, was equally favorable toward this program. These business circles had an important influence on political life, since they subsidized the parties, owned the large-circulation newspapers, and were not afraid to purchase votes at election time.

Such moderation was dangerous, said the partisans of armed expansion. Japan must not run the risk of being deprived of raw materials or of being boycotted. The only means of avoiding these dangers would be to establish direct dominion or a political influence over territories of essential importance as sources of raw materials or foreign markets. This was the mission of the Japanese people, who had been called upon to direct and to "unify" the people of Asia. This imperialist theory had its principal promoters in the general staffs of the army and the navy. It also had numerous advocates within the upper echelons of the administration and spokesmen in certain university circles. The first objective in such an armed expansion would be Manchuria; the second, northern China. Beyond that, the extremists—especially Kita Ikki in his book published in 1919 and entitled *The Basis of the Reconstruction of Japan*—went so far as to suggest expansion at the expense of the great European powers which possessed "exaggeratedly extended territories" in the Pacific area—Australia and far-eastern Siberia, for example. Obviously such a policy would have to be backed up by a huge arms build-up and considerable financial investment. The "ultras" were considering a partial confiscation of capital to cover the costs of rearmament.

From 1920 to 1930 the theory of peaceful expansion prevailed except during a brief interlude. Imperialist agitation, however, was incessant and sometimes threatening, since the extremists had formed a fighting organization, the Rosinskai Society, which employed intimidation methods and sometimes went as far as assassination. But the business bourgeoisie controlled the Chamber of Representatives, where the *Seiyukai* party represented its interests and held a relative majority from 1921 on. The economic crisis induced this party to demand a decrease in armament expenditures in 1922 in order to lighten the fiscal burden. It also advocated a moderate foreign policy, since any brutal pressure exerted on China was likely to provoke reactions harmful to Japanese exporters. For five years, from 1924 to 1927, then from 1929 to 1930, the Ministry of Foreign Affairs was directed by Baron Shidehara, son-in-law of Baron Iwasaki, and consequently was closely linked to the interests of the trusts.

It was a quite unexpected turn of events in the contemporary world for Japan to manifest conciliatory and prudent tendencies in her foreign affairs.

Perhaps it is unnecessary to underline the fundamental feature in this panoply of national policies. The position adopted by the government and by the public in the United States from 1920 on was and would remain the underlying cause of this precarious peace.

The German Question

France was chiefly responsible, through the Treaty of Versailles, for imposing the limitations on Germany's sovereignty and the financial payments that weighed down the economy of the Reich. It was she who wished to maintain them to ensure her own safety and to permit the reconstruction of her devastated areas. However, her concern for security and the payment of reparations was only of minimal interest to Great Britain, who wanted to see Germany's production and commerce resume its former position in the world market. German political circles had anticipated at the end of 1919 that this difference of interests between the victors would make it possible to obtain a systematic revision of the clauses of the Versailles Treaty. As of 1920 British policy confirmed them in this hope.

French policy wavered between two tendencies. Either Germany should be obliged by armed coercion to execute the clauses of the treaty in their entirety despite the reservations, perhaps even the resistance of Britain; or else France should move toward a policy of conciliation which would involve the attenuation of the clauses after a short time. These policies were both adopted successively, before and after May 1924.

The Franco-German Conflicts (1920–1923)

From 1920 to 1923 the German government, formed from a coalition in the National Assembly and dominated by the Catholic Center party, attempted to circumvent the limitation of arms and the payment of reparations. The social and political crises that shook the Reich furnished it with arguments which French opinion generally held invalid but which the British public was more willing to accept.

During the revolutionary uprisings of 1920 the military clauses of the Treaty of Versailles were not respected. The German army, which was supposed to have been reduced to 100,000 men, retained 200,000 soldiers on active service and was supported by "paramilitary" formations—militias, civic guards—which numbered several thousand men. In March 1920 regular troops of the Reich penetrated into the demilitarized zone of the Rhine to suppress a communist insurrection in the Ruhr. The French government responded to this violation of the statute of demilitarization by a military sanction, the occupation of Frankfurt and Darmstadt, which it maintained, despite British objections, until the German troops were evacuated. In the spring of 1921—that is, after the suppression of the German internal difficulties—the French demanded the passing of German laws, on March 22 and 23, that would reduce the strength of the army to the figure fixed by the treaty, and the dissolution of the militias. This time they obtained the consent of Great Britain.

The question of reparations gave rise to Anglo-French discord that facilitated Germany's resistance. First, there was the question of determining the figure, since the Treaty of Versailles had not been specific. During the conferences at San Remo, Boulogne, and Brussels, the French government put forward a considerable sum —230,000,000,000 gold marks—as much to ensure itself the resources needed for reconstruction as to retard the recovery of German economic potential, which was also a war potential. The British government refused to overburden Germany. The working figure adopted by the Reparations Commission on May 5, 1921, was 132,000,000,000 gold marks, which were to be paid off in annual sums whose amount would vary according to the progress of German exports. Although the German government declared it was unable to pay more than 30,000,000,000, it nevertheless agreed to the terms in order to avoid the threatened occupation of the Ruhr. But six months later it demanded a moratorium, declaring that the fall of the mark left it incapable of honoring its commitments. After lengthy Anglo-French debates the French government replied by occupying the Ruhr in January 1923, a measure in which Britain refused to take part. Germany put up a "passive resistance" which she abandoned after eight months. However, when Germany gave in, the French government came around to agreeing that the reparations question be put before an international committee of experts which would conduct its business "free from any political influences." This solution had already been proposed before the occupation of the Ruhr and had been rejected by the French cabinet, because it would inevitably have lopped off a considerable portion of the German debt, and because it amounted to treating the reparations question "as a bank transaction." It was adopted just when the use of force seemed to be effective.

The policy of force was thus used successfully in 1920 and 1921 in respect to German disarmament, but it did not withstand a new, more difficult test two years later. Here are the circumstances of this setback that ought to be considered.

In early January of 1922, twelve months before the decision to undertake the Rhine operations, the French government had received an offer from Great Britain: if France would agree to place the reparations question under the scrutiny of an international conference, which would doubtless cut the amount of reparations due, she would receive the promise of British armed intervention in case of German aggression—in other words, a return to the security pact Lloyd George promised to Clemenceau which had become invalid because of the position of the United States. Aristide Briand, President of the French Council, was prepared to negotiate on this basis, but his decision was refuted by Alexandre Millerand, President of the Republic, and by the majority of the Council of

Ministers, which considered the English proposal unacceptable. Why was the guarantee promised to France alone and not to Poland and Czechoslovakia, keystones of the "French system" on the Continent? Furthermore, would an international solution to the reparations problem not result in France's losing her right to resort to coercion in the event of a future German "default"? After the resignation of Briand, the government under Raymond Poincaré announced a new policy. If Germany did not pay the reparations, she would be obliged to turn over the state mines of the Ruhr to her creditors.

What did the government expect to gain from taking this "collateral"? According to the later explanations of the President of the Council, they foresaw two possible results: either the Germans would be obliged to resume the payment of reparations, or by default they would have to place the mines at the disposal of their creditors. The government, convinced of its debtor's bad faith, preferred the first of these two possibilities. The German government was using the monetary crisis as an excuse for discontinuing the payments, even as it was itself aggravating the crisis, either by calculation or by deliberate neglect. Why did it not take stricter measures to check the fall of the mark? And why did Germany's industries refrain from repatriating the foreign exchange earned through their exports? As to the technical difficulties involved in such transfers, the politicians preferred to ignore them. According to this outlook—one that was shared by most Frenchmen— it would be logical to believe that the German government would "desire to pay" the moment the occupation of the Ruhr imposed an unbearable burden on Germany's economy. The other hypothesis involving a "productive collateral," which would itself provide a direct means of payment, would oblige the French authorities to make a considerable effort in order to organize the exploitation of the mines. It would thus be wiser not to resort to this solution until the other had been tried.

The execution of either operation involved serious risk of either armed resistance by Germany or of British resistance. According to some witnesses, Raymond Poincaré did understand the gravity of these obstacles, which were also recognized by Marshal Foch.

He yielded nonetheless to the pressure of the President of the Republic and of his colleagues in the cabinet.

Was this policy demanded by public opinion? It does not seem that the press had exerted a strong influence in this direction. *L'Action française* was almost alone in advocating the occupation of the Ruhr. But once the decision was made, the operation was approved by the right and center newspapers as well as by the principal radical newspapers. Criticism came from the communists who denounced the greed of the French metallurgical industry; the socialists, who considered the method ineffective; and the "left" radicals, who felt that it was inopportune. In brief, the large majority of people felt that France was within her rights to take such a measure, in spite of its being a risk.

Was the decision of the government influenced by pressure from the big industrial concerns? This hypothesis might seem plausible since French metallurgy was in competition with that of Germany, which depended on coal from the Ruhr for its existence. However, the members of the Iron and Steel Committee were in fact split. Some, including Le Creusot, wanted to take this opportunity to break the competition. The others, particularly the great Lorraine companies, had reservations, because they were afraid of being deprived of their coke supplies. These differences precluded any attempt at a concerted influence on the public powers.

Thus, the occupation of the Ruhr was determined neither by the pressure of business nor by public opinion. It was, rather, the outcome of a political deliberation that chose to ignore the advice of economists.

When the French government put this operation into effect and met "passive resistance" from the Germans—namely, a strike by the miners and the railway employees, precipitated and financed by the German government—the attitude of Great Britain was the focus of attention.

Since the previous summer the British cabinet had consistently repeated that the occupation of the Ruhr would be a disaster for the entire European economy, and would inflict particularly heavy losses on British exporters. Thus, the German government put its hopes on this Anglo-French dispute. In the end it was disappointed. The British government, even though it had urged the abandonment of the French plan until the last moment, adopted an attitude of neutrality in the face of the accomplished fact. Not until August did it declare that the occupation violated the Treaty of Versailles, and that it was taking upon itself the role of mediator. But when it met a French refusal, it confined itself to caustic comments without persisting further. Nonetheless, with the exception of certain conservative elements in southern England, public opinion was on the whole against the French policy, which can be easily explained by reasons of economic interest. The textile industry had suffered a loss of half its sales to Germany. The chemical industry had been deprived of the by-products of Ruhr coke. The coal and steel industries, which should have been pleased at no longer having to face German competition, became anxious when the French and Belgian authorities began to prepare for the exploitation of the mines. This coal, which was to be diverted from the German consumer, would surely be thrown onto world markets to the detriment of the English coal industry. German metallurgy, its back to the wall, would no doubt agree to enter into a Franco-German steel trust, whose existence would threaten the British industry. Financial groups holding shares in the big German enterprises feared losing their investments.

Here were a good number of reasons that might have induced Britain's vigorous opposition to the French undertaking. The cabinet, however, ignored these entreaties, no doubt taking into account the political risks involved for Britain's world position in an open policy rift with France.

This prudence on the part of Great Britain led to the "capitulation" of Germany. By adopting the method of passive resistance, the Reich government had hoped that Great Britain would force a compromise on France; it had prolonged this resistance in spite of considerable risk. The results were disastrous, as the "support of the Ruhr" had involved enormous expenditures—3,500,000,000 marks, without any return, which the Reich government had had to cover by a monetary inflation. At this point the mark plummeted.

(The rate of the dollar, which had been 10,425 marks at the beginning of January 1923, reached 6,000,000 marks on the eve of the occupation of the Ruhr, on August 13, and 142,000,000 on August 27.) This monetary catastrophe paralyzed business. German industry, threatened with a dearth of coal, risked foundering if the French occupation authorities forbade shipments entirely. Finally, the working population of the Ruhr, which had been in an enforced state of unemployment for months, no longer disguised its discontent, despite the indemnities it was receiving. The Reich found itself "on the verge of collapse." The government had taken these risks as long as there was a hope of British mediation. As soon as this hope collapsed, there was no longer any point in prolonging passive resistance. The new Minister of Foreign Affairs, Gustav Stresemann, conceded as much on August 23. On September 26, 1923, German capitulation was announced. The end of passive resistance opened the way to the policy of "productive collateral."

But the French victory was brief. The President of the French Council, instead of announcing his conditions to the German government immediately, avoided any negotiations at all. He confined himself to a negative attitude which surprised his diplomatic agents and astonished his political colleagues. This apparent passivity continued for two months, leaving British diplomacy the leisure to assume the advantage. On October 20, 1923, the British cabinet proposed an international study to determine Germany's ability to pay reparations. This suggestion had already been made in January 1922 at the Cannes conference—though in vain—and had been renewed in August 1923 with no more success. On October 28, just as Poincaré had won a major victory and was in a position to exploit his "productive collateral" (since the mines provided considerable receipts even after the expenses of occupation), he accepted the English suggestion which would most certainly result in a major decrease of the German debt. How can this behavior, so paradoxical at first glance, be explained?

There were many interpretations of the motives that led the French Premier to adopt a waiting attitude in the autumn of 1923. Among the immediate witnesses to the events—politicians, diplomats, members of the government—there were those who said that

Poincaré had realized that he would be unable to exact the reparation damages from the "Ruhr victory" from a Germany whose economy and finances were in complete confusion. If he agreed to a reduction of payments on his own authority, he would risk being exposed to parliamentary criticism. But he could as a last resort accept, provided that Britain took the initiative and the responsibility. Others said that the Premier believed it wiser to "let events run their course." He preferred to await the development of the political results of the German disorder. If the German government did not succeed in mastering the revolutionary movements under way in Bavaria and Saxony, it would be forced to accept within a few weeks any conditions that France wished to impose upon it. Perhaps it must also be considered that this policy anticipated the success of the separatist movement in the Rhineland. On October 23, Dorten proclaimed the formation of an autonomous Palatinate state. The small minority that upheld this undertaking believed it would be protected by the presence of the French and Belgian troops and by the indirect aid of the occupation authorities. It did not last for very long, however. While shunning intervention and refraining from giving precise instructions to his diplomatic or military agents, the French Premier would seem to have preferred deferring any negotiations with the Reich government in order to allow the separatists to try their luck. In short, he seems to have subordinated financial interest—that is, the immediate settlement of the reparations—to the political prospects, which seemed to him more important. There is insufficient information available to permit a valid choice between these two hypotheses.

It is easier to interpret the reasons that influenced the French government to accept the English solution. Poincaré realized that exploitation of the "productive collateral," implying the continuation of the Ruhr occupation, would increase the Anglo-French misunderstanding, since it would tend to be harmful to British economic interests. He knew that the earnings of the Ruhr operation were largely the result of the seizure and disposal of stocks found in the yards of the mines, and that further exploitation of this prize would become more difficult and more risky. More than anything else, he took into account France's monetary difficulties. The fall of the franc, which had begun in the first weeks of the Ruhr struggle (the dollar had gone from 14.98 francs in January 1923 to 16.23 in February and to 17.05 in July), had persisted and even worsened, despite the diplomatic success of September 26. Even though the French government was asking sacrifices from the French taxpayers in order to re-establish a balanced budget, the franc continued to fall until the Morgan Bank, on March 23, 1924, accorded a line of credit to the Bank of France. But in order to obtain this assistance, the French government had had to pledge itself not to issue any bonds without voting corresponding fiscal resources, even for the reconstruction of the liberated areas. The British press indicated that the New York and London financial markets—the only markets to which the appeal could have been made—would refuse to extend itself further as long as French policy persisted in its desire to "pacify Europe by force." In short, as M. Etienne Weill-Raynall remarked, Raymond Poincaré's government under-took the Ruhr affair without having "made sure it was financially sound." This would not have been a major risk if the French public had agreed to hold out in the face of world opinion and had consented to a further increase in taxes. But there was little hope of this happening. This was what led the Council President to yield to British pressure.

It marked the end of a policy that had sought to force Germany to fulfill all of the obligations imposed on her by the Treaty of Versailles. To evaluate its failure, it would suffice to note that the French government had declined the British proposal of guarantee in January of 1922 at the Cannes conference because it did not want to submit the reparations question to an international tribunal; whereas in November 1923 it rallied to this solution without obtain-ing the political recompense that it had been offered twenty months previously.

The Attempted Reconciliation (1924–1930)

After the general elections of May 1924, in which the majority of the French electorate was against both an increase in taxes and the use of coercive methods against Germany, a policy of conciliation was inaugurated which was thenceforward to govern Franco-German relations for several years. Stresemann announced his intention to fulfill the clauses of the Versailles Treaty. He hoped to obtain in return the systematic revision of these clauses and a seat in the Council of the League of Nations, which would enable Germany to exercise a more effective influence on diplomatic interplay and to intervene in questions relating to the status of national minorities. She would acquire the additional immediate advantage of foreign credits needed for the economic rehabilitation of the Reich. Briand, once again President of the Council, accepted these prospects, convinced that to resort to coercion would involve considerable risk.

The German contribution to this policy included the resumption of reparations payments and the explicit recognition of the frontier established between France, Belgium, and Germany in 1919. Germany's compensation, requested in September 1926 and promised three years later, was the premature evacuation of the Rhine territories, to be carried out five years ahead of the date fixed by the treaty. The failure of this policy, however, became evident by 1931. To understand this failure, it will be necessary to study the circumstances, the intentions, and the impact of each of the previous decisions.

The resumption of reparations payments by Germany was established along the lines laid down in the spring of 1924 by the international committee of experts under the chairmanship of an American, Dawes. The "Dawes Plan" fixed the increasing annual sums to be paid by Germany, but only for a period of five years (one billion gold marks during the first year, two and one half billion during the fifth). It decided that the fulfillment of these clauses would be guaranteed by the remittance of bonds secured by the German railroads and German industry. This settlement considerably diminished the burdens that the payment terms of May 5, 1921, had imposed on Germany; but by the system of guarantees it established a new limitation on German sovereignty.

The Reich government and the National Assembly ignored the objections of the extreme right, who were ardent advocates of resistance. The acceptance of the Dawes Plan seemed necessary, first of all to obtain the evacuation of the Ruhr, but also to attract from the United States and Great Britain the capital indispensable for the re-equipment of Germany's industry. What chance could Germany have to obtain this capital if she turned down the plan outlined by the financial experts of these countries?

In effect, the Dawes Plan was carried out under satisfactory conditions, and Germany discharged her obligations punctually for five years, during which the yearly payments were remitted without difficulty. However, the ease with which this was achieved was due to an exceptional circumstance—namely, the extraordinary influx of foreign capital, two thirds of it American, but also British and Dutch—into the German market. International financial circles considered that Germany, whose territory had emerged unscathed from the 1914–1918 war, was in a good position to make a great economic recovery. Their investments included extensions of credits to German banks, bond issues floated abroad by the public services of the Reich and by German cities, and the purchase of German industrial securities or of real estate. In five years the total reached 23,000,000,000 gold marks, according to the calculations of the *Reichsbank*—or perhaps 30,000,000,-000 if one is to believe the French evaluation. In the same period the over-all sum of German reparations payments hardly exceeded 7,500,000,000. Herein lay the explanation for the ease with which Germany paid the remittances. The German press, the President of the United States (in a speech on November 11, 1928), and the economists were in agreement on pointing out this direct relation between the international flow of capital and the fulfillment of the Dawes Plan. In September 1926, however, John Maynard Keynes pointed out the precariousness of this mechanism. The United States loans money to Germany. Germany transfers the equivalent amount to the Allies. How long could this system last? "The answer to this question is a problem for the American capitalist." In fact, when a serious economic and financial crisis broke out in the United States in the autumn of 1929, the American investments came to a halt. The mechanism of German reparations payments was instantly paralyzed.

The principal purpose of the treaty signed at Locarno on October 16, 1925, was the reciprocal confirmation of the clauses of the Versailles Treaty dealing with the Rhine region. Through this "Rhine Pact," Germany, France, and Belgium exchanged the promise never to engage in "any attack or invasion" or to resort to war between each other unless military action was decided upon by the League of Nations. This maintenance of the *status quo* between the three countries applied not only to their frontiers but also to the demilitarized status of the Rhineland. This was placed under the guarantee of Great Britain and Italy "individually and collectively." Nevertheless, promises and guarantees dealt solely with Germany's western borders and not her southern or eastern frontiers, since the Reich government refused any commitment toward Czechoslovakia or Poland. To palliate the results of this refusal, the French government signed assistance pacts with these two states on the same day. Such were the general features of the "Locarno system." What was its significance?

The German initiative in this matter had been taken with the counsel and advice of Lord d'Abernon, the British ambassador to Berlin. But it was Stresemann who had reshaped the British suggestion. Recognizing the frontiers of 1919 amounted to abandoning the claims on Alsace-Lorraine and the territory of Eupen-Malmédy. This sacrifice was significant only in a moral sense, since Germany was in no position to undertake a war of retaliation (this is the argument proposed by Stresemann in his letter to the crown prince of Prussia). It did, however, constitute a retreat that would expose the government to the criticism of the "German nationalists." The advantages gained through this retreat, however, were obvious. The Locarno Treaty guaranteed Germany against a return to "territorial sanctions" and against any encouragement that France might offer to a new separatist attempt. It left open the possibility of obtaining a revision of her southern or eastern borders by "peaceful" pressure. Stresemann wished also to avoid the conclusion of a security pact that Britain and France might negotiate between themselves, along the lines of the plan proposed at the Cannes conference. He wished to offer proof to the American public that Germany was not thinking in terms of retaliation, thereby reassuring American lenders. Finally, he anticipated that by easing Franco-German relations, he would obtain the evacuation of the Rhine territories ahead of schedule.

France gained an important advantage from the Rhine pact: the promise of armed assistance by Great Britain if Germany should attempt a war of retaliation. This advantage, although of little practical importance at the time, since Germany had not rearmed, seemed to have considerable significance for the future. On the other hand, France abandoned any idea of resorting to force in order to coerce Germany to respect the rights to which she was entitled by the Treaty of Versailles. True, she reserved the right of doing so if it were a case of defending Czechoslovakia or Poland against German aggression. But if this were the case, she would be acting without the cooperation of Britain and Italy and would run the risk of finding herself in a delicate situation. Why did Briand agree to this incomplete system? Why did he, said his opponents, adopt "an ostrichlike policy"? He had thought it necessary, he declared, to show France's good will in the hopes of encouraging a "moral disarmament" in Germany. He had wanted to induce the German government to abandon any attempt at agreement with Soviet Russia and to consider a collaboration with the Western powers. Finally he wished to open the door to a "systematization of the European economic order." If one may judge from the attitude of the press, French public opinion was in favor of this policy. The only hard-core opposition came from the monarchist extreme right which saw in the Locarno Pact the workings of "Anglo-American finance" designed to "chloroform the French people," and from the extreme left which thought it saw the first indications of an anti-Soviet coalition. Certain right-center newspapers voiced some uneasiness, fearing that once Germany was a member of the League of Nations, she would start "revisionist" maneuvers. But these were subtle reservations, almost timidly expressed.

The British cabinet (now a Conservative cabinet since November 1924, headed by Stanley Baldwin) was satisfied with the active role it had played in the negotiations. The responsibility it had assumed for the maintenance of the *status quo* conformed to Great Britain's over-all policies, since she was bound to be interested in the maintenance of peace on the Rhine. True, public opinion had until then appeared very reserved on this subject, for it was against British involvement in a system of alliances. But this new commitment, which had been undertaken "impartially" with Germany and France, did not meet the same opposition. However, in accordance with the views expressed by Lloyd George in January of 1922, the British guarantee was limited strictly to the Rhine region. These, then, had been the goals of British policy —a compromise solution between France and Germany, and a peaceful revision of the Polish-German border. Austen Chamberlain saw the Locarno system as a "personal triumph."

German diplomats were of the opinion that the premature evacuation of the Rhine territories was bound to be the consequence of these treaties. Stresemann had already attempted to raise this question during the Locarno negotiations in a note of July 20, 1925, according to which the Rhineland occupation would become superfluous as soon as France was granted the benefit of an international guarantee. He had been obliged to abandon his project upon the strict insistence of Chamberlain, who feared that this demand would bring about the failure of the entire enterprise. He took it up once more of course on the occasion of Germany's entry into the League of Nations. His interview with Thoiry and Aristide Briand in September 1926 gave him some hope, though it was quickly extinguished. In Paris, however, in August 1928 the principle was agreed to, this time with Raymond Poincaré. Why this failure and why this success?

Stresemann not only asked Thoiry for the premature evacuation of the Rhine territories but alluded to the withdrawal of the military mission in charge of supervising German disarmament, as well as to the restoration of the Saar territory to the Reich. He offered in return a financial advantage, the immediate issue of "Dawes Bonds" to a sum of 1,500,000,000 marks—that is, the anticipated remittance of one year's reparations, which would act as a remedy for the monetary crisis France was undergoing at the time. Did Briand agree to these proposals in principle? The German report on the interview states that this was so, but it is largely contradicted by the French communiqué. In effect, no negotiations were entered upon after this exchange of views. The German government did not specify its financial offer, perhaps because it had been unable to obtain the indispensable cooperation of the American banks. The Council of Ministers and the general public in France did not react favorably to the premature evacuation of the Rhine territories. Stresemann's financial counteroffer soon lost its attraction, since the franc was on the road to recovery. The Thoiry interview therefore accomplished very little. It is of interest, however, since it sketched out the possible basis for a general settlement of Franco-German difficulties.

After a two-year wait the German government—Stresemann was still Minister for Foreign Affairs but in a cabinet headed by Hermann Müller, a Socialist—invoked Germany's "moral right" to obtain the premature evacuation of the Rhine territories in a parliamentary declaration on July 3, 1928. It stated that this was a necessary decision for an "effective" policy of international understanding. While in Paris for the signing of the Briand-Kellogg Pact, Stresemann succeeded in gaining the consent not only of Briand but also of Poincaré, who was the new Premier. In exchange he offered a "definitive" settlement of the reparations question in the form of a long-term plan of payments that would extend beyond the five-year period of the Dawes Plan. The French government was unlikely to consider this counteroffer. The reason is probably to be found in the difficulties then current in relations between France and the United States. In April of 1926 the French government had promised to reimburse the major part of the debts contracted in 1917–1918 in sixty-two annual installments. But the parliament had refused ratification, not wishing to make a commitment without knowing beforehand the duration and rate of German payments after the expiration of the Dawes Plan. To avoid this difficulty, Poincaré wanted to obtain a lasting payments plan for the settlement of the reparations, whereas it was to the advantage of the Germans to make only a short-term commitment. The price the French government agreed to pay for Germany's consent was the premature evacuation of the Rhine territories. This is the probable interpretation insofar as we can judge from the historical information available today. If it is accurate, it shows that the French made a mistake in believing it was to their advantage to allow a provisional reparations settlement in 1924. However, this may not be the important question. Poincaré's reversal merely corresponded to the state of French public opinion—too tired of strife to wish for the return to a policy of constraint vis-à-vis Germany and too aware of the problem involved in "power politics."

The prospects opened up by the Paris talks in 1928 were realized the following year. On August 30 and 31, 1929, the Hague agreements provided, on the one hand, a new system of reparations payments in the Young Plan, which spread out the annual remittances over fifty-nine years but reduced the "actual value" of the German debt by 17 per cent. On the other hand, the Hague conference called for the evacuation of the Rhine territories prior to the date fixed by the Treaty of Versailles. The withdrawal of the occupation troops was to take place in June 1930, after the ratification of the Young Plan by the German parliament.

What results had been gained from this policy of conciliation which had been followed since 1924? Even if she could count on the fulfillment of the pledges contained in the Young Plan, France would herself have to answer for most of the expenditures involved in reconstructing the devastated areas—precisely three fifths, according to M. Weill-Raynall. Besides that, she had relinquished the guarantee of security afforded by the occupation of the Rhine territories five years before the predetermined date, without having achieved in return the result that Briand and Philippe Berthelot had hoped for—namely, a change in the German outlook.

In 1929 and 1930 it became clear that the German leaders considered that the concessions made by the French government were merely a preface to a larger revision of the Versailles Treaty. The

German government, in November 1929, made a claim for the restitution of the Saar. In September 1929 it pointed out that according to the terms of the treaty, the disarmament of Germany was supposed to be the prelude to a general limitation on armaments, and it declared that consequently the Reich would have the right to rearm if the pledges of the other powers with respect to the treaty were not honored. It expressed the hope (in a declaration by President Hindenburg on July 20, 1930) that the demilitarized status of the Rhineland would soon be revised.

These demands were coming from the groups that formed the parliamentary majority at that time—namely the Catholic Center, the followers of Stresemann, and the most moderate wing of the Social Democrats. However, the general elections of September 11, 1930, were marked by a considerable increase in support for the National Socialist party, which had gained only 809,000 votes in 1928 but now obtained 6,400,000 votes and 109 seats. Thus, the power of a party openly hostile to France began to reveal itself just when a large segment of French opinion felt that the evacuation of the Rhine territories was about to pave the way to a Franco-German "reconciliation."

After the death of Stresemann the government was still in the hands of men who had supported his policies. In 1930 German leaders—as would be the case in 1931—did not contemplate war with France. This would have been impossible in any case, given the respective conditions of their armed forces, as Germany's "clandestine rearmament" was still minimal. They did not discount the possibility of a war against Poland, but only on the condition of being able to "neutralize" France—an unlikely possibility unless Poland were to initiate the aggression. In order to construct and test out on Russian soil prototypes of items that the Versailles Treaty forbade Germany to possess, secret contact was still maintained between Soviet and German military technicians without negotiating an official agreement. Although presenting themselves as conciliators, these men were easily influenced by public opinion. After the elections of September 1930, Chancellor Brüning issued more rigorous instructions to the German delegation to the League of Nations.

The French Minister for Foreign Affairs felt he had been personally slighted, and, in a speech given in Geneva, denounced the "cries of hatred" rising in Germany. André Tardieu, Premier since October 1929, conceded in a speech on October 19, 1930, that France could no longer rely on efforts to achieve peace through organization, and that she would henceforth have to defend her borders by "her own means." Thus the climate of Franco-German relations refuted indisputably Aristide Briand's policy.

Russia and Europe
(1920–1929)

The conditions of "coexistence" between Russia and the other European states depended, of course, on the designs and the methods of the Communist nation; but they also depended on the solidarity that the other nations might manifest vis-à-vis Russia. The formation of a "capitalist bloc" was a possibility much feared by the Soviet government.

Thus conquered Germany found herself in a position to play an essential role in relations between Russia and Europe. Certain German military and political circles had anticipated since 1919 that Germany could seek support in Russia to circumvent pressure exerted by her conquerors. She could even let it seem that she was prepared to collaborate with Russia—without seriously considering such a step, which could create dangerous consequences for German social stability—in order to disconcert Britain and perhaps even France, thus bringing them to alleviate the clauses of the Versailles Treaty.

The study of relations between France, Great Britain, and Russia is therefore intimately connected with that of Russo-German relations. The term "study" is too ambitious. One can make little more than a sketch of this problem in view of the inaccessibility of both the Russian and the German archives.

The Failure of the "Quarantine Belt"

Since 1918 Soviet Russia had been in conflict with her European neighbors along all her borders. In 1920 she decided to give up her attempts to "Sovietize" the Baltic states and, in order to retain a "window" on Europe, signed peace treaties with these young countries. Everywhere else, however, she persisted in her demands: to recover Bessarabia, which had detached itself from Russian sovereignty in 1917 and had thereupon been joined to Rumania in April 1918 by vote of the Bessarabian Assembly; and to keep eastern Karelia, claimed by Finland, under a regime of "temporary" administration. She refused to accept the Curzon line as her border with Poland, as did the Poles. Only in the case of Poland did the conflict become an armed one. Under cover of the Russian civil war, the Polish government attempted to seize Ukrainian territories. As soon as it had emerged victorious from the civil war, the Soviet government threw back the Polish troops and, in turn, sent its armies into Poland. On August 14, 1920, the Russian offensive threatened Warsaw, which was relieved two days later by the Polish counteroffensive.

What was the attitude of the Western powers toward these conflicts? Did they practice the "quarantine belt" policy that Foch suggested, giving support to the countries bordering on Russia and seeking to establish a lasting solidarity among these nations?

In the Russo-Rumanian dispute the Supreme Council, which included representatives of the Western powers, decided in favor of Rumania in March of 1920. Needless to say, the Soviet government protested this solution and demanded a plebiscite which the Rumanian government refused.

The two governments had some difficulty in coming to an agreement on the Polish question, over which British reservations had hampered French policy in 1919. They decided, however, on July 2, 1920, to furnish war matériel to the Polish army and to offer the counsel of General Weygand to the general staff in Warsaw without considering sending troops for the time being. This assistance was accorded, however, under a condition demanded by the British cabinet. The Polish government was to relinquish its "imperialist and annexationist" policies and content itself with ruling over "lands that are indisputably Polish." This condition was of little consequence, since the Polish army succeeded in driving the Russians beyond the Curzon line. The Russo-Polish peace preliminaries on October 12, 1920, shortly confirmed by the Treaty of Riga (March 18, 1921), only recorded the lines of the war map. The border was fixed close to Minsk and Pinsk, 120 miles east of the Curzon line. Poland had thus acquired a good portion of White Russia, a precarious advantage which the Russian government was to contest as soon as it had the means to do so.

Thus the Western powers demonstrated on these two occasions that they were prepared to give material and diplomatic aid to Russia's neighboring states but would not go so far as to consider armed intervention.

Nor were they able to surmount the obstacles to harmony among these states. Poland and Lithuania were disputing the possession of the Vilno region. When General Zeligowski seized this city on his personal initiative on October 9, 1920—an action that had in fact been known to and approved by his government—the Western powers ended in recognizing the *fait accompli*. Lithuania, however, protested vehemently. This antagonism sufficed to ruin the prospect of a projected Polish-Baltic states bloc. Besides which, Poland was involved in a dispute with Czechoslovakia since the conference of ambassadors had decided to divide up the territory of Teschen. This decision, designed to give the Ostrava coal mines to the Czechs, overlooked the presence of an important Polish minority in the territory. These two disputes, in which, as in so many others, the adversaries invoked first the principle of nationalities, then that of historic rights, quickly gave rise to a bitterness entirely out of proportion to the real value of the stakes. The diplomacy of the Western powers sought in vain to propose compromises and to calm emotions. The "quarantine belt" plan was in ruins due to the explosive passions of nationalism.

France and Great Britain drew different lessons from this failure.

In London the Lloyd George cabinet, which had been faced with an economic crisis since the summer of 1920, wished to recover Russian markets for Britain's coal and industrial products. On March 16, 1926, it obtained an agreement whereby Russian ports were reopened to British ships and British subjects authorized to do business in Russian territory. The Soviet government agreed not to impede the flow of commerce between Russia and Great Britain.

On February 19, 1921, the Paris government signed a political agreement and military convention with Poland. The agreement stipulated only that the two governments would "concert their efforts" in case either one was the victim of an unprovoked attack. It did not designate the possible opponent. The military convention, whose clauses were secret, explicitly dealt with the eventuality of German aggression against Poland or France and also with the subject of a new Russo-Polish war. But France did not commit herself to providing her ally with troops. She promised only the shipment of matériel and technical personnel.

This was a further manifestation of the different courses taken by British and French policy in Eastern Europe.

Recognition of the Soviet State

During the autumn of 1921 the Soviet government, having warded off immediate threats, attempted to emerge from political and economic isolation. Within the framework of the "new economic policy" which he had announced in March 1921 in order to avoid the collapse of the Soviet economy, Lenin felt that commercial relations with the capitalist states must be resumed.

First the Russian government proposed collective negotiations. On October 28 it suggested that an international conference fix the conditions under which these relations might be re-established. From the beginning of this conference, it succeeded in playing off Germany against her conquerors. The Rapallo Agreement of April 16, 1922, marked the resumption of diplomatic and commercial relations between Russia and Germany. Although this diplomatic success placed the Russian delegation at Genoa in a more favorable situation vis-à-vis the other participating states, the negotiations with Britain and France ended in failure.

Two years later, Russian diplomacy took up this task once again, but with a different approach. It engaged in separate negotiations with each of the Western powers and succeeded in restoring commercial and diplomatic relations. Thus, at the end of 1924 the Soviet government was recognized by all of the great European powers.

How did it achieve these results? No doubt through the desire of the industrial states to recover the Russian export market, but also because of political rivalries between these nations. The motives behind this conduct require explanation.

The German decision was made on the initiative of the diplomats; the leading role was played by the head of the Eastern Affairs Section of the Ministry of Foreign Affairs. It would be true to say that business circles, hoping to find export markets for its industrial products and technicians, had wanted to resume commercial relations with Russia. True, the German general staff had already been in secret contact with the Russian general staff since September 1921 in order to arrange for the manufacture of war equipment prohibited by the Treaty of Versailles on Russian soil under the direction of German specialists. But the choice was determined above all by political motives—to show the conquerors that Germany was capable of resuming diplomatic initiative, and to threaten France and Great Britain with the prospect of Soviet Russia's receiving the benefit of the organizational qualities for which Germany was noted. The maneuver was effective in this respect, since the Rapallo Agreement provoked serious concern in Great Britain. Could not this agreement pave the way to a Russo-German collaboration?

The government in Berlin was divided. The Minister for Foreign Affairs—the great German industrialist Walther Rathenau—who undertook the responsibility of negotiating the agreement, apparently considered the idea of little value. He did not contemplate making a diplomatic drive toward the east. On the other hand, the chief of the general staff, General Von Seeckt, wanted a Russo-German alliance, for it seemed to him the only means of restoring Germany's position in international affairs. He tended to think that Great Britain, jealous of France's hegemony on the Continent, would see no objection in such an alignment. Hostility toward Poland would be the most solid ground for understanding between Germany and Russia. Basically the ultimate goal of this alliance could be a new Polish partition, a fact that the head of the German army did not hesitate to indicate in a report addressed to the Chancellor in September 1922. Brockdorff-Rantzau, who had headed the German delegation at the peace conference, had been ambassador to Moscow for six years. A consistent opponent of French policy, which had imposed a "national humiliation" on Germany, he felt, on the other hand, a profound dislike for the Soviet government, which he considered to be a "gang of criminals." While approving of the line adopted at Rapallo, he assigned strict limits to it. There must be no alliance, no political agreements of any sort, no secret arrangements between general staffs. Germany must not, he wrote to the Chancellor, consider a "military adventure." Nor should she make any contacts, even in secret, that if exposed would lead Great Britain to make an alliance with France. She had every interest in remaining discreet, because she would thus bring the British cabinet ultimately to accept German rearmament. This idea was an obvious contradiction to that of Von Seeckt. However, Brockdorff-Rantzau's policy was also that of Germany's President Ebert.

In Moscow hesitation was no less pronounced. The prospect of wider agreement with Germany seemed acceptable to the Commissar for Foreign Affairs, Chicherin. It was contested, however, in September 1922 by other members of the government who considered collaboration with a "bourgeois" government repugnant, and who had not ceased to provoke communist revolution in Germany despite the failure in 1920. At the time of the German internal crisis which was affecting in different fashions Saxony, Thuringia, Bavaria, and certain parts of the Rhineland in October 1923, Soviet leaders felt that the hour was at hand. A letter from Stalin, published in *Die Rote Fahne,* the German Communist newspaper, said, "The victory of the German proletariat will undoubtedly transfer the center of world revolution from Moscow to Berlin." The failure of the German revolutionary movements soon caused the Soviet government to revert to the Rapallo strategy. The practical results, however, were still quite limited. The collaboration was not wholehearted, since Germany wished to encourage its relations with Britain, while the Soviet leadership considered her the "bastion" of capitalism. Moreover, each government felt that the other was merely conducting a temporary maneuver. The Russian government planned to grant economic concessions to German enterprises on the condition of being able to supervise them closely. But German businessmen were reluctant to risk capital in a country where the security of investments was doubtful. In fact, the great metallurgical enterprise, *Rusgetorg,* which had begun operations on Russian soil late in 1922, had had its contract broken in January of 1924, perhaps because it was playing too large a role in Russia's economy. Two years later the transport agency organized by the directors of the Hamburg-American Line met with the same fate.

Prospects for the future therefore were bleak. Russia had nonetheless obtained an appreciable advantage, since the Rapallo Agreement had broken the economic blockade against her.

The attitude of the two great Western powers was no less hesitant, especially because their interests were not always parallel. At the beginning of 1922 the British government was anxious to achieve the reopening of the Russian market, which could bring relief to the critical economic and social situation by providing an outlet for British industrial production. To achieve this result, it was prepared to recognize the Soviet regime and to authorize the granting of credits, which the Russian economy greatly needed. But it wished to obtain compensation for the British industrial or mining enterprises that had been nationalized by the Communists and which had invested 2,750,000,000 gold francs in Russia before 1914. On the other hand, the settlement of debts contracted by the Russian state prior to 1917 was only of secondary importance to Britain. As the French government had no such pressing reasons to desire the resumption of commercial relations with Soviet Russia, it tended to be less accommodating. Recognition of the debts contracted by the czarist government (9,200,000,000 gold francs) was the principal condition of the negotiations. This was of considerable importance to the French holders of Russian bonds—some 1,600,000 persons, many of them of modest means.

At the Genoa conference in April 1922, as at the Hague conference that followed it in June and July, financial questions were the main topic of debate. The Russian delegation, whose position had been strengthened by the rapid conclusion of the Rapallo Agreement with Germany, sought to obtain the prompt extension of sizable credits from Britain and France. They agreed to recognize debts contracted before 1914, but on the condition that reimbursement might be spread out over a long period and would not require the payment of interest. They offered compensation, by granting concessions, to foreign capitalists whose property had been nationalized. These conditions were deemed insufficient, and the negotiations failed.

What were the reasons for this failure? According to the Russians, the chief obstacle was the question of nationalized industries, especially of petroleum concerns. The Soviet government offered to grant concessions to these companies; and Royal Dutch, which prior to 1914 owned large deposits in the Caucasus, was prepared to accept this solution. But Standard Oil—which, although it was unable to invoke the same rights as its Anglo-Dutch competitor, had acquired in 1920 a share in the Nobel trust, the group that controlled 40 per cent of production in the Baku region—wished to prevent the formation of a combine from which it would be excluded. This great American petroleum company therefore raised a question of principle. Accepting the Russian offer would amount to admitting that the nationalized enterprises could be exploited without the consent of their former proprietors, thereby abandoning the defense of property rights. Eventually, under pressure from the American government, the Western powers adopted this principle. After the failure of the conference, the Russians sought to make it appear that the interests of the holders of Russian bonds and of industrial exporters were being sacrificed to those of the American oil concerns. They preferred to remain silent on the no less delicate questions raised by the extension of

credits to Soviet Russia: was it possible to grant unhesitatingly
these financial means to Russia without the certainty that the prior
debts were actually to be repaid?

Two years later the Russian government was able to obtain this
resumption of commercial relations, the price of which it had been
unwilling to pay during the Genoa conference, without difficulty
through separate negotiations. The initiative came from Italy. In
the first speech Mussolini gave as head of the government, he
announced his intention to consider relations with Russia exclusively from a "practical point of view." The Fascist government
concluded a commercial treaty with Russia on February 8, 1924.
On February 1, 1924, with the advent of the Labor government, the
Ramsay MacDonald cabinet announced that it was prepared to
recognize the Soviet regime and to negotiate a commercial agreement, which was signed on August 8. In December, after the elections of May 1924 had assured the success of the "left bloc," the
French government decided to follow suit.

These decisions were determined by economic interests. In
Great Britain, where the economic depression seemed to be turning
into a chronic condition, and where unemployment rose to one
million, the Labor cabinet was increasingly eager to reopen the
Russian market to British exports before German business secured
a decisive advantage within the framework of the Rapallo Agreement. The Italian government wished to buy raw materials from
Russia, which would be offset by the sale of machinery and chemical
products. French exporters had no intention of being left out of
this market.

Whereas in 1922 Britain and France had linked commercial
negotiations to financial negotiations, they were now willing to defer
until later discussions of the problem of reimbursing holders of
Russian bonds and the owners of nationalized concerns. True,
the Soviet government did not receive any credits, since they were
dependent on the prior settlement of the schedule of reimbursement.
But it did obtain *de jure* recognition and acquire commercial
facilities that it had badly needed, without having had to give anything in return but an assurance of good will.

Should this success be attributed to the Rapallo policy and the German strategy? There is no doubt that the open breach between the capitalist countries seriously weakened the position of France and Britain vis-à-vis the U.S.S.R. But the principal factor was most probably the stabilization of the internal situation in the U.S.S.R. When the Western powers had agreed to the convening of the Genoa conference, the Soviet government, after the famine of 1921 and the crisis in economic policy, was in great need of help from Europe—Lloyd George had said as much to the House of Commons in March 1921. After the summer of 1922 the prospect of a good harvest gave Russian diplomacy a freedom of action that enabled it to turn down the conditions attached to the resumption of commercial relations with Britain and France. As the Russian economic crisis eased and the Soviet market opened up under the impulse of the New Economic Policy, the U.S.S.R. gradually found itself in a better position to ask for favorable conditions. The leftist governments that had simultaneously come to power in London and Paris in 1924 bore the consequences of a situation that Mussolini had been the first to recognize.

The New Difficulties

These successes were, however, shortly to be negated. Between the end of 1924 and the end of 1927, the Soviet government, weakened by a serious internal crisis—the conflict after Lenin's death between Trotsky and Stalin over economic and political policies—was confronted with serious difficulties in its European policy.

The first cause of these difficulties was the return to power of the Conservatives in Great Britain after the elections of October 29, 1924. This party had taken a position against the August 8 agreement and refused to accept the possibility of an extension of credits to the Communist nation. The Baldwin cabinet, after having tabled ratification of the agreement, declined to open new negotiations. In October 1925 it ordered the arrest of seven important members of the British Communist party in order to seize and publish documents establishing the existence of close relations between this party and the Communist International. At the same time diplomatic negotiations under way in February 1926 between the Russian and the French governments on the debt settlement question showed that they were far from being in agreement. These developments seemed to cancel out the recent hopeful prospects.

More important still was the conclusion of the Locarno Agreements in October of 1925. The German government seemed to be abandoning its Rapallo policy and to be willing to join a "common front" with the Western powers. The Russian press declared that this move constituted a "war machine" intended to be used against the U.S.S.R. The Soviet government was further convinced by the attitudes of France and Great Britain. After the failure of the Franco-Russian financial discussions in February 1926, the French government signed a treaty of alliance with Rumania ignoring the Russian claim on Bessarabia. Because of the encouragement and financial support offered British miners by the Communist International in the great coal strike, the British cabinet, after three months of hesitation, decided on breaking diplomatic relations with the Soviet Union. Soviet leadership suspected the Foreign Office of working toward a *rapprochement,* perhaps even a coalition between Poland and the Baltic states: in short, of returning to the policy of the "quarantine belt."

As a countermeasure the Russian government engaged in new discussions with Germany to reanimate and broaden the Rapallo policy. The immediate object of these discussions was to obtain Germany's neutrality in the event of war between the Western powers and the Soviet Union. The German government was on the point of entering the League of Nations within the framework of the "Locarno System." It would thus assume the obligations provided for by the Covenant of the League, including Article 16, which would oblige it to grant passage across German territory to French or British troops in case the Council of the League ordered sanctions against the U.S.S.R. This could pave the way to an anti-Soviet coalition. Therefore, the goal of Russian policy was to obtain from the German government a restrictive interpretation of its obligations toward the League of Nations.

The new Russo-German treaty, signed in Berlin on April 24, 1926, gave partial satisfaction in this respect. Germany pledged to remain neutral if the Soviet Union were the victim of aggression by a third power. She also promised not to join a coalition whose purpose was to subject Russia to economic or financial boycott. Thus when he came to take his seat in the League of Nations in September 1926, Stresemann stipulated that Germany would not be associated with sanctions imposed against the U.S.S.R. unless the latter were named an aggressor by the Council of the League. However, he added that the Council could not take such an action without the consent of the German government. This amounted to saying that if Germany did not join in the League's decision, she would not join in the application of sanctions and, consequently, would refuse the right of passage. The Treaty of Berlin, said Litvinov, had blunted the "anti-Soviet edge" of the Locarno Agreements.

In short, the German government refused a choice between East and West. Although basically retaining a Western orientation, Stresemann understood "the value of Russia as a trump to play against the West." To his way of thinking, his Russian policy was a means of pressure in his relations with France and Great Britain.

The reservations that marked the Russo-German political collaboration did not apply to the contacts between military technicians or to economic relations. Regarding the former, the Social Democrats produced detailed information before the Reichstag in December 1926 and March 1927, confirming the existence of a German-Soviet collaboration in the field of arms manufacture. The government was exceedingly evasive in its denial of these revelations. As to the latter, the Soviet Union conducted 29 per cent of its foreign commerce with Germany in 1927 and 1928. True, the volume of these exchanges was not yet appreciable, but it rose rapidly in 1929 and 1930 owing to the credits accorded German industrialists by the banks, which in turn received guarantees from the government.

The most surprising feature of the Russian government's conduct in its relations with Europe was the persistent anxiety Moscow expressed over the prospect of a coalition of the "capitalist countries." These fears were constantly voiced within the Executive Committee of the party at the beginning of 1927. Great Britain was suspected of directing an "anti-Soviet campaign," of wishing to "strangle" the U.S.S.R. by a blockade, even of preparing for a war. The same theme was developed by Stalin before the fifteenth Party Congress. It is hard to make out upon what grounds these fears were based. But there is no doubt that they led the Russian leaders to conduct a moderate foreign policy. In November 1927, Trotsky wanted the Russian government to come to the aid of the peoples of Europe "in the struggle against their oppressors." Stalin responded by saying that the first duty of the party was to avoid the risk of conflict with the countries of Western Europe. Stalinist doctrine, which aimed only at the "building of socialism in one country," was based on this cautious approach.

Several days later Trotsky was expelled from the party and deported to Turkestan. His defeat paved the way for the application of Stalin's policy, which circumstances had made necessary.

The Danube and the Balkans

The Danube region and the Balkan peninsula together formed an area that, carved into numerous political subdivisions, was on the one hand in contact with Russia—who, despite the minor role she was currently playing in Europe, was fundamentally a powerful nation—and on the other within reach of Germany, who was undergoing a rapid economic recovery between 1924 and 1929. The new Turkish state retained only a part of Thrace in the Balkans, and the little Albanian nation had only 800,00 inhabitants. Bulgaria with 5,400,000 inhabitants was hardly more populous than Greece, which had 5,000,000 in 1922. In the Danube region, whereas Hungary was reduced to 7,500,000 inhabitants and the Republic of Austria a few more than 6,000,000, the Czechoslovakian republic was dominant by the relative size of its population (13,600,000 in 1921, of which in fact 3,800,000 were neither Czech nor Slovak). Yugoslavia (a little over 12,000,000 inhabitants in 1920) and Rumania (17,400,000), the most populous state, were both Balkan and Danubian owing to their geographic positions. The drawing of the borders had stirred up nationalistic feelings and intensified economic difficulties throughout the region.

Because of its divided nature, this area offered the major powers favorable conditions for economic or even political expansion.

However, Soviet Russia was in no position to run any risks at the time, and Germany was cautious as long as she was still subject to disarmament control and the payment of reparations. Although very interested in Greece because of her Mediterranean interests, Great Britain did not intend to assume any direct responsibilities. Only Italy and France among the great powers were active between 1920 and 1930. Italian interests in the Adriatic, touching on Yugoslavia, Albania, and Greece, were inseparable from political action in the Balkans. In the Danubian area these interests had been largely served by the dissolution of Austria-Hungary. French interests were above all political. Economic and financial actions were merely tools. Her principal project was not only to bar the way to future German expansion but to establish "rear alliances" against Germany. Thus Italy's actions in the Danube region clashed with those of France. This antagonism appeared also in Balkan questions.

French Policy and the Little Entente

After the dismemberment of the Austro-Hungarian empire, two solutions had been foreseen to alleviate the consequences of partition and to organize political and economic life in the Danube region. One was to constitute a federation between the countries that were "successors" to the Dual Monarchy, including Hungary and Austria. This amounted to establishing a collaboration between the beneficiaries of the peace treaties and their victims. The other solution was to form a system of alliances between Czechoslovakia, Rumania, and Yugoslavia with the purpose of preventing a possible attempt by the conquered nations to win back territory and of maintaining the territorial status set up in 1919 and 1920. The project of federation, which had attracted the interest of government circles in France and Britain in 1919, was resisted by the governments of the new states which feared that a bond of federation would prepare the way for a new Austro-Hungarian empire. The second eventuality had been considered in February 1920, even before the signing of the Trianon Treaty, by the governments of the countries that were to divide among themselves the territories taken from Austria and Hungary. What role did the major powers play in the choice made between these two solutions and in the formation of the "Little Entente"?

The fear of a monarchic restoration moved Czechoslovakia, Yugoslavia, and Rumania to conclude their alliance. On August 14, 1920, Czechoslovakia and Yugoslavia pledged each other armed assistance in the event that Hungary should attempt an unprovoked attack. The treaties of April 23, 1921, between Rumania and Czechoslovakia, and of June 7, 1921, between Rumania and Yugoslavia, were in response to former Emperor Charles's attempt to regain his throne in Budapest in March of 1921. When the former Emperor made a second attempt at restoration, the three governments announced their intention to resist it by force of arms. The conclusion of such agreements between these states was a logical step, since they all shared an interest in preventing an aggressive return of Magyar nationalism. The actions of French diplomacy in these events merit critical examination, to ascertain whether France, who appeared to be the protector of the Little Entente after 1922, had played this role from the outset.

Judging from Hungarian documentary sources, French policy had wavered for more than a year.

In the spring of 1920, when Premier Alexandre Millerand was Minister for Foreign Affairs, and Maurice Paléologue was Secretary-General of the Ministry, France had favored a plan for a Danubian confederation with Hungary as its keystone. On three occasions French diplomacy had extended to the Hungarian government, by official and unofficial intermediaries, then directly, the hope that it might obtain an adjustment of the borders laid down by the Trianon Treaty, on condition that a dominant share in the Hungarian railroads and in the assets of the Hungarian General Credit Bank be accorded to French financial groups or to large concerns, to Le Creusot in particular. This policy—Paléologue's idea—had been promoted for several months, despite the opposition of certain high officials in the Quai d'Orsay, who suspected, with good reason, that the Hungarian government had secretly retained contact with German military circles.

When Millerand became President of the Republic late in September of 1920, Paléologue was replaced as Secretary-General of the Quai d'Orsay by Philippe Berthelot, a man greatly admired for his intellectual gifts, his tenacity, and his astonishing knowledge of men and diplomatic history. Negotiations with Hungary were immediately dropped. Since 1915, Berthelot had been sympathetic toward Czech leaders.

Does this mean that French diplomacy was immediately in favor of the Little Entente for which Eduard Beneš had just laid the groundwork? Indeed, on the occasion of the first attempt to restore the monarchy at Budapest, Berthelot indicated France's intention to block this move. But Aristide Briand, who had become Premier in January of 1921, had indicated in conversations that he favored restoration. Parliamentary opinion was likewise divided: the right seemingly willing to accept the restoration, while the left was against it. This was not a question of preference for one or another type of regime; it was rather a question of choosing between two roles that the Danubian states might play in Europe. Philippe Berthelot was for the creation of the Little Entente. Aristide Briand did not wish to rule out the possibility of a Danubian confederation and saw the ancient dynasty as the only symbol capable of coordinating these disparate peoples in order to establish a bulkhead against German expansion.

These hesitations did not recur in October of 1921 when the second imperial attempt was made. At that point French policy embarked on the path that it would faithfully follow for fifteen years.

Thus, the foundation of the Little Entente had not been France's handiwork. It had come about through the common desire of the three states to prevent the return of the monarchy and to maintain the territorial status established by the Treaty of Trianon—this at a time when the direction of French policy was as yet unclear. Only after this display of determination did the Little Entente receive France's diplomatic support and become an instrument of the "French system" in Europe. This French system was expressed in the Franco-Czech agreement of January 25, 1924, enlarged upon by a promise of armed assistance on October 16, 1925; in an alliance concluded between France and Rumania on

June 10, 1926; and finally in the treaty of 1927 between France and Yugoslavia. The main threat to the system came from the possibility of the annexation of the Austrian republic by Germany and from Hungarian "revisionism."

The union of Austria and Germany had been forbidden by the treaties of Versailles and Saint-Germain unless authorized by the League of Nations. In a 1922 protocol the Austrian government had promised to maintain the independence of the nation in return for financial assistance from the League of Nations. Despite this promise, the President of the Republic and members of the government, supported by a broad current of public opinion, did not miss an opportunity between 1926 and 1928 to state that Austria was not a viable economic entity, and that the *Anschluss* was a necessity. They did, however, agree that it would be premature to raise this question. The attitude of German officialdom was identical. A moral right should be asserted, the principle of nationalities should be invoked, but the actual demand should be postponed. This explicit refusal to consider the validity of the stipulations of the treaties produced categoric warnings from Italy and France. In May 1925, Mussolini announced that he would "never tolerate" the *Anschluss*. In December 1928, Briand told Stresemann that the union of Austria and Germany could not be effected without a conflict, since France's veto would prevent the Council of the League of Nations from giving its consent. He added that if Germany should attempt to resolve the matter by force, "the result would unquestionably be war."

Protest against the clauses of the Treaty of Trianon placed the Hungarian government in a state of perpetual antagonism with its neighbors, since the adjustment of the borders, which the Magyar people demanded bitterly, was flatly refused by the Little Entente. Italian policy offered some support to Hungarian revisionism, probably in order to control the French hegemony that Italy saw emerging in the Danubian basin. She wanted Hungary to continue to form a barrier against this hegemony and to avoid coming to terms with her conquerors. Budapest accepted this assistance since, being unable to divide her direct opponents, her only hope of obtaining a revision of her borders was with the assistance of a great power.

The Italo-Hungarian commercial treaty of September 5, 1915, favored the importing of Italian agricultural products. Although its terms were rather vague, the friendship treaty of April 1927 marked the entry of Hungary "into the sphere of Italian interests," said the Premier, Count Bethlen. Mussolini's public endorsement of Hungarian revisionism in the spring of 1928 was a direct consequence of the diplomatic agreements. This endorsement was, however, a limited one. *Il Duce* confined himself to saying that "small changes" in Hungary's borders were desirable, and that Hungary deserved a "better fate."

These efforts remained fruitless. The states of the Little Entente declared themselves opposed to any modification, even partial, of the territorial status laid down by the Treaty of Trianon. This was sufficient to frustrate Hungarian demands for the time being. Hungary still seemed to be the "powder keg" of Europe—but the powder was wet.

Thus the policies of the Little Entente had been effective. These countries, which contained 43,000,000 inhabitants, and each of which had a direct diplomatic tie with France, seemed to represent a military force worthy of consideration. However, there was no adequate assurance that the system was viable. Although united in their resistance to Hungarian claims, the partners had not made broader commitments to each other, politically speaking. The Little Entente did not guarantee Yugoslavia against Italian claims. Rumania could not count on her two allies to defend Bessarabia against Soviet Russia. Czechoslovakia received no support from Belgrade or Bucharest in her difficulties with Germany on the question of the Sudetenland. Economically there had been two attempts to establish some kind of collaboration—once at the Portorosa conference in November of 1921, and again at Jachymov in 1927—but they had only resulted in an improvement in rail traffic and in the limitation of import quotas. They did not succeed in setting up a system of preferential tariffs, since this system would have worked to the advantage of Czechoslovakia, an industrial country, while Rumania and Yugoslavia, predominantly agricultural, would have fared badly. Thus the future of the Little Entente was precarious.

Italian Policy in the Balkans

Italian diplomatic actions had quite a different importance in the Balkan area. The region afforded ample opportunity for political manuevering, since the two great nations that had played the dominant role before 1914 were now powerless. Italy's chief aim was to establish a "control" over the Adriatic. Economic motives played a part, of course, but only a minor one. Political and strategic considerations were predominant. In February 1926, Mussolini wrote in the *Popolo d'Italia* that, by assuring the stabilization of peace in that area, Italy would gain a wider freedom of action in "other vital zones of interest"—namely, in the Mediterranean. One must also no doubt take into account the desire to strengthen the prestige of the regime by reversing the conditions that had been accepted by the governments of 1920 and 1921.

The immediate objectives of the Fascist government were, on the one hand, the settlement of the Fiume question which had brought Italy into conflict with Yugoslavia since the spring of 1919; and on the other, the establishment of an ascendancy over Albania and over the eastern banks of the Otrante Channel, gateway to the Adriatic. These designs threatened Yugoslavia's interests, since she did not wish to relinquish the Quarnero coast or to see neighboring Albania under Italian influence. Greece's interests were threatened as well, since she had never withdrawn her claims, dating from 1913, on the southern districts of Albania, Santi-Quaranta, and Argyrocastro, whose people spoke Greek. As it happens, these were the very areas whose geographical situation rendered them of strategic interest for controlling passage in the Otrante Channel. Steps toward the fulfillment of this program extended over the period between 1923 and 1927.

The assassination of an Italian member of the commission formed to determine the Yugoslav-Albanian border gave Mussolini the opportunity to make a show of strength by bombarding Corfu. This measure of intimidation was not addressed solely to Greece.

When one month later the Yugoslav government was invited by the Fascist regime to resume negotiations on the Fiume question, it very likely remembered Greece's recent experience. It reluctantly agreed to discussions that led to the Convention of Nettuno in January 1924, whereby Italy annexed Fiume, while its surrounding region was accorded to Yugoslavia. This Italian success paved the way for an expansion of economic and political influence in all of Dalmatia.

Finally, in the summer of 1924, the *coups d'état* in Albania marking the conflict between Ahmed Zogu, a Muslim, and the Orthodox clergyman, Fan Noli, provided a favorable opportunity for Italy to act. When Ahmed Zogu succeeded in retaining power, he sought financial assistance for reorganizing the administration and the construction of roads. Italy granted this assistance and obtained in return: the acceptance of an Italian military mission to the Albanian army; the creation of a national bank whose assets would be Italian, as would its president; and finally, a corporation backed by Italian banks, which would contract Italian firms for the construction of Albanian public projects. This economic and financial collaboration were only a prelude to political action. By the Tirana Pact of November 27, 1926, Ahmed Zogu received the promise of assistance from the Fascist government in maintaining the political *status quo* in Albania—that is, his own personal rule. In return he pledged himself to conduct a foreign policy that could in no way harm Italian interests. The treaty of November 20, 1927, a year later, established a defense alliance. Finally, by the complementary convention of July 1, 1928, the Albanian government promised to act in harmony with Italy in "all questions pertaining to the Balkan situation." Thus Ahmed Zogu, who assumed the title of King Zog I in 1928, seemed to have placed himself under Italian tutelage.

This Italian penetration into Albania increased Yugoslavia's anxiety. Premier Nincic, who had signed the Nettuno Agreement, resigned in December of 1926; and the new government sought the backing of France. The Franco-Yugoslav treaty of November

11, 1927, although limited to a promise of "concerted action" in the event of aggression, opened a period of serious tension between Italy and Yugoslavia. The Italian press showed its contempt for a country torn by the political and religious controversies between Serbs and Croats, and announced Italy's intention to move into all of Dalmatia at the first favorable opportunity. The Yugoslav press, especially in Croatia, replied with vehemence and threatened the possibility of war.

This Yugoslav resistance encouraged Italian diplomacy to outline the basis for a policy whose essential aim would be to "neutralize" the Balkan states against the eventuality of war in the Adriatic.

The conflicts and controversies that divided these Balkan countries opened up favorable prospects to Italy. Greece and Turkey were engaged for five years in bitter debate because the clauses of the Lausanne Treaty, which had provided for the obligatory migration to Greece of the Greeks of Smyrna and for the optional migration to Turkey of the Turks in western Thrace, provoked serious diplomatic difficulties in their application, which were further aggravated by the sufferings of the uprooted populations. Greece and Yugoslavia discussed at great length the status of the "free port" of Salonika which was supposed to allow the passage of Yugoslav commercial traffic without the imposition of customs duties. Macedonia, where the Treaty of Neuilly had placed the Bulgar population under Serbian domination, was the scene of incessant conflict between the nationalities and the churches. It even became a zone of guerrilla warfare in 1928 when the Macedonian Revolutionary Organization which was based in Bulgaria organized *comitadjis* raids to protect the Bulgars in Macedonia from the Yugoslav "oppression." These *comitadjis* actions, if not encouraged by Sofia, were at least condoned by the Bulgarian government, which declared itself incapable of preventing the raids, since the Treaty of Neuilly had imposed strict disarmament on Bulgaria. The bitterness of these Balkan disputes worked to the advantage of the Italian government.

In September 1926 the Rumanian government, under the leadership of Averescu, whose personal sympathies tended toward the authoritarian regimes, agreed to give Italy a promise of "concerted action" and of diplomatic support—which, if not irreconcilable with the Little Entente pact, had the effect of weakening it. It received in return Italy's recognition of Rumanian rights in Bessarabia. However, the fall of Averescu in the spring of 1927 and the return to power of Bratianu, head of the Liberal party, were not promising for the future of this diplomatic *rapprochement*.

Because of its dispute with Yugoslavia, the Greek government in September 1928 agreed to overlook the Corfu incident and to pledge neutrality in the event that Italy was the victim of "unprovoked aggression."

Bulgaria was the most favorable arena of action for Italian diplomacy, being directly opposed to Yugoslavia over the Macedonian question. Thus the Fascist government refused, in August of 1928, to join in the measures that the representatives of France and Britain took in Sofia to demand the dissolution of the Macedonian Revolutionary Organization by the Bulgarian government.

During these years when German influence had not yet recovered its strength, the opposing interests of France and Italy were the factors that influenced the course of international events in the Danube and Balkan areas. French patronage of the Little Entente caused the Italian government to fear the re-establishment of a "hegemonistic group" (this was the expression used by the Italian press) and to reply by supporting Hungarian revisionism. Rome considered the Franco-Yugoslav treaty of 1927 a direct blow to Italian policy in the Adriatic, and it caused the Fascist regime to broaden its Balkan policy. Thus the Italian action in the Danube basin had been a response to French policy. In the Balkans, on the other hand, it had been "aggressive," but only in its attempt to watch over and encircle Yugoslavia. In effect, Italian and French diplomatic successes had neutralized each other. The subsequent inconveniences of this political and economic subdivision persisted nonetheless, since the rivalry between the two big powers paralyzed all constructive activity.

The Mediterranean
and the Middle East

The Mediterranean, "meeting place for the peoples and civilizations of three continents," had also become a great world sea route since the opening of the Suez Canal.

On the eve of the World War this route had been dominated by Great Britain, who held the two essential "gateways"—Gibraltar and Suez; who guarded the Straits of Sicily with her naval base on Malta; and who, in spite of Russian pressure, had kept closed the northern gateway, the Ottoman Straits. The countries bordering on the Mediterranean had not seriously tried to challenge this British predominance. France, with a strong position in North Africa, had nonetheless respected British interests even before agreeing to an alliance. Italy had long remained in Britain's shadow, and the ascendancy she had gained in the Aegean Sea in 1912 was still precarious. Spain and Greece were powerless. The Ottoman empire, despite the extent of its territories, was too weakened to undertake any action.

The outcome of the World War seemed to confirm Britain's position, since Russia was paralyzed by the civil war, the Ottoman defeat had resulted in the dismemberment of the empire, and Germany's Baghdad railway project had collapsed. Even if the western Mediterranean was not directly affected by the outcome of the war, the eastern Mediterranean was profoundly so. Despite the French presence in Syria and the Italian occupation of southern Anatolia, the British government retained its ascendancy by its protectorate of Egypt, its mandate over Palestine, and its provisional possession —"provisional" for forty years—of the naval base on Cyprus.

Great Britain considered that these aspects of the Mediterranean situation were linked to the problems of the Near East, to the land route to India, which terminated on the coasts of Syria or Palestine, and to British interests in the Persian Gulf. There again, Britain dominated: in 1919, from the Indian subcontinent to the Bosporus, all the strategic points were in British hands.

But European strongholds were to be threatened by Moslem nationalism, especially between 1920 and 1927. These movements also offered the quarreling European powers opportunities that they did not fail to turn to their advantage.

Moslem Nationalism

The movements opposing Western domination sought to establish political communities within Islam, which as yet envisioned no cooperation among themselves. Turkish, Arab, Iranian, and even Afghanistani nationalism were distinguished by their own particular characteristics.

Turkish nationalism found its expression in the movement directed by Mustapha Kemal, which protested against the dismemberment of the Ottoman empire and against the advantages accorded to Great Britain and Greece by the Treaty of Sèvres. Kemal demanded the revision of the treaty, at least wherever it subjected Turks to a foreign domination. Thus he refused to accept the rights of occupation held by Greece in Smyrna, by France in Cilicia, and by Italy in southern Anatolia around Adalia. He also demanded the withdrawal of the inter-Allied contingent—almost entirely British—that was charged with occupying Constantinople and enforcing the new status of the Ottoman Straits. The Turkish government enforced these demands by armed pressure or even war.

The entry of Turkish troops into Cilicia and the Adalia zone led France and Italy to agree to negotiate. The French government surrendered its occupation of Cilicia with the exception of the Sanjak of Alexandretta, where Turks formed only a part of the population. The Italian government abandoned the region of Adalia, although they retained certain privileges for the exploitation of mineral resources.

The Greek troops at Smyrna did not wait for the Turkish attack but launched a preventive offensive which was rapidly broken. The victory of Afium-Karahissar on August 22, 1922, opened the route to Smyrna to Kemal's army, which occupied the region two weeks later without the British cabinet's giving the slightest indication of opposition. The Turkish army then made for the Dardanelles where it encountered an Anglo-French detachment guarding the strait at Chanak. A clash was avoided, but the armistice of Moudania on October 11, 1922, granted Mustapha Kemal the right to reassume the administration of Constantinople and to evict the Sultan. The first part of the program was achieved on November 4; the second on November 17.

Kemal had only to make these successes official by obtaining a revision of the Treaty of Sèvres. The Lausanne conference—which was a result of the armistice of Moudania—brought about this revision. The Turks proved "insolent and intractable," said the head of the British delegation, Lord Curzon. But the British cabinet (Lloyd George had been replaced by Bonar Law) did not wish to risk a conflict under any circumstances. On July, 1923, the new Treaty restored to Turkey sovereignty over all of Anatolia, over Constantinople and Thrace as far as Maritsa (including Adrianople), and over the islands of Imbros and Tenedos which command the entrance to the Dardanelles in the Aegean. It eliminated the system of privileges which foreigners had enjoyed on Turkish territory because of the capitulations. Finally, it disposed of the question of the status of the straits. The Turkish government recognized the principle of free passage established by the Treaty of Sèvres, but obtained the right to deny entry to the ships of a state that was at war with Turkey.

The diplomatic support that Soviet Russia gave the Kemal government does not suffice to explain this success. The Turkish republic would not have been able to destroy the territorial arrangements established in 1920 if it had encountered concerted resistance from Great Britain, France, and Italy. But the victorious countries were divided among themselves. Great Britain, who had benefited greatly from the Treaty of Sèvres, was offered no cooperation by her partners in defending its clauses, since neither France nor Italy deemed it possible to take up arms again, scarcely three years after the end of the World War, in order to defend positions of great interest to Britain but of only secondary importance to themselves. When they yielded on almost all points under pressure from Kemal, the British cabinet protested in vain against the negotiations, which only encouraged the Turks to pursue the fulfillment of their program. In autumn of 1922 the French government had refused to give its troops the order to bar the way to Kemal's army during the incident at Chanak. Why risk a war for the sole benefit of Britain? The British cabinet could undoubtedly have decided to act alone. It did not dare to do so because it was undergoing serious difficulties within the empire: Egypt was demanding independence, and the dominions were refusing to cooperate in an Anglo-Turkish war. Moreover, British policy had reckoned on a Venizelist Greece in the settlement of the Turkish peace. However, King Constantine, who had been exiled since 1917, had regained his throne in December 1920 after a plebiscite and had immediately deposed Venizelos. Thus it was no longer possible to count on the compliancy of the Greek government. It is hardly surprising that Britain tried to throw the blame on her allies for the failure of her policy. But basically this policy—initiated by Lloyd George—collapsed as soon as the Greek trump card was lost.

In the Middle East, British interests were threatened once more by nationalist movements.

In Afghanistan, in 1919 the Emir had obtained the removal of the British quasi protectorate. In order to prepare British public opinion for this setback, the Foreign Office declared that the protectorate was no longer necessary since the "Russian danger" had disappeared. However, when the Communist International began to disseminate its propaganda among the Asian peoples, this outward optimism lost its credibility.

In Iran the British government had enjoyed a sphere of influence in Seistan since 1907. It had acquired the majority of shares in the Anglo-Persian Oil Company, formed six years previously to exploit the petroleum deposits in the zone near the Persian Gulf, and had obtained the right of veto over the management of the company in any question involving political interests. During the war it had set up a military occupation in the zone of influence and in the petroleum-bearing region. Finally, in August of 1919, it obtained a treaty whereby the Iranian government promised to make use of British experts to reform the administration and the army, and of British capital and technicians for the construction of railways, in return for the withdrawal of occupation troops. This treaty, said the *Times,* paves the way for "the reorganization of Persia by British expertise and capital." The Iranian treaty, complemented by the protectorates that Britain had established over the Arab principalities of the Persian Gulf—Kuwait since 1899, the Bahrein Islands since 1892—seemed to ensure British superiority in this area. However, the takeover was slow and difficult, encountering the resistance of Iranian nationalism. In June of 1920, after a change of government, the Shah decided to "suspend" the application of the treaty.

The Arab nationalist movements dominated the scene, from Morocco to Iraq, particularly in the four years between 1922 and 1926.

In Egypt, where in 1919 a vigorous nationalist upheaval had already taken place, the British government thought it wiser to make concessions, even though it had the military means to keep the situation in hand. The declaration of February 28, 1922, announced the relinquishment of the protectorate established in 1914 and proclaimed Egypt's independence, but it reserved to Britain the right to settle all questions pertaining to the defense of the country, to the security of the Suez Canal, to the status of foreigners, and to the Egyptian region of the Sudan, possession of which was essential for controlling the Nile waters. These four "reservations" in effect allowed Britain to retain the upper hand in Egypt. Supported by the great majority of the legislature, Zaghlul refused to accept them. Great Britain was able to force the Egyptian cabinet to yield and accept the "four reservations" by a threatening note and by seizing the Alexandria customs service—a temporary victory.

In Morocco, where in July of 1921 Abd-el-Krim had launched an attack against the Spanish and had formed an independent Riff republic, in April 1925 the Riff tribes attempted to penetrate the upper valley of the Werga to provoke an uprising in French Morocco. The counteroffensive, to which the French government committed 158,000 men (of which 130,000 were natives) under the command of Marshal Pétain, was broken in April 1926 with the surrender of Abd-el-Krim.

In Tunisia, where the Moslem intellectuals were in contact with the Egyptians, the nationalist party—the Destour—did not demand independence. It went only so far as to request, in March 1920, the possibility of government employment for Tunisians, the establishment of a legislative assembly elected by universal suffrage, and ministerial responsibility to the Assembly—a program that would ensure the ascendancy of the native elite. The French government limited itself to bringing about a partial reform in July 1922, which was hardly designed to satisfy the Destour. It announced the creation of a grand council, which, however, would have no political power and would be elected under such conditions that the French colonists and the Tunisians would retain equal representation.

In Tripolitania and Cyrenaica, where in 1919 the Italians had abandoned the reconquest of the interior, in October of 1920 the Italian government signed the Agreement of Regina with Saïd Idriss, head of the Senoussites, which limited Italian sovereignty to the coastal regions and granted an autonomous status to the remainder of the territory. However, with Mussolini's accession to power, the Fascist government broke the Regina Agreement. It undertook a vigorous military action against the Senoussites, which resulted in an important victory in April of 1923—the capture of Saïd Idriss' headquarters—but which nevertheless continued for another five years before the power of Senoussism was broken and the reconquest of Libya was complete.

In Palestine, which was under British mandate, the British government tried to establish a "Jewish homeland," in accordance with the promise given in November of 1917. From Central and Eastern Europe between 1919 and 1926, some hundred thousand immigrants came to join the fifty thousand Jews already established in the country prior to 1914. This Jewish population settled mostly in the towns and cities, where it invested capital and created industries; it also began to take up agricultural activities. But it met with hostility from the Arabs, who formed four fifths of the total population, and who were fearful of the economic and social consequences of this influx of immigrants. In Jerusalem in 1920 and in Jaffa in 1921, the conflicts were bloody. Since the British administration authorized and encouraged the entry of Jews, the Arab opposition blamed the mandate regime. And yet by 1925 this Arab resistance appeared to have died down somewhat.

The exercising of the French mandate over Syria encountered more serious obstacles, for the French administration had to come to grips not only with a movement for Arab independence but with the difficulties arising from the existence of eighteen different religious groups—Muslims, Catholic, or schismatic—divided by religious hatred, differences of life styles, and the memory of bitter wars. On two occasions the French government engaged in important military operations: in July of 1920, in order to conquer Damascus and destroy the Arab Free State which had just been established by Emir Feisal; and in 1925, in order to put down, after a four-month struggle, the Druse insurrection, which reanimated the movement for Syrian independence. Thus, the independence movement had been set back another ten years.

The British mandate over Iraq—that is to say, over the land or river routes of Mesopotamia and over the Mossul oil region—had been accepted by the French government. Early in 1919 France had abandoned the rights established in her favor by the 1916 Franco-British agreement in exchange for an extension of the area granted to her by the Syrian mandate. But British influence met with resistance from Arab nationalism. In August of 1920, in order

to break the independence movement, the British government sent
in an expeditionary force of one hundred thousand men. Although
it was master of the situation, the government considered it opportune to make concessions: in October of 1922, with the Treaty of
Baghdad, the British government agreed to a meeting of a constituent assembly; but in June of 1924 it obtained a pledge from
the Arabs not to claim independence. Was this proof of diplomatic
dexterity? It was quite simply the result of mere bargaining. In the
event of Iraqi intransigence, Great Britain was even prepared to
favor Turkish designs on the vilayet of Mossul, where the majority
of the population was not Arab. As for the Turkish claims, British
diplomacy eliminated them in turn. In order to succeed in this project, she granted rights of exploitation of parts of the Iraqi oil lands
to American interests—as a result of which the Turkish government
could no longer count on support from the United States.

Finally, Arabia was the theater of a struggle between the Moslem
states: the Hejaz, whose King Hussein had since 1915 been allied
to Great Britain: and the Nejd, where Emir ibn-Saud was supported by the religious puritanism of the Wahhabite sect. In 1925
the Hejaz was conquered and annexed by Ibn Saud. Was this to
be the stronghold of a new power that would attempt to practice
a policy of expansion at the expense of the other Arab states and
threaten the positions acquired by Great Britain? Great Britain attempted to avert these threats through diplomacy. In 1927 the
British cabinet recognized the independence of Saudi Arabia but
obtained a promise of nonaggression toward the territories of Iraq,
Kuwait, and the Bahrein Islands, where Great Britain either had
a dominant influence or a treaty of protectorate.

Between 1920 and 1925, from one end of the Arab world to the
other, France, Great Britain and Spain conducted three wars—
the Riff campaign, the Syrian campaigns, and the Iraqi expedition
—in which national or religious resistance movements were defeated. The European countries were able to maintain the advantage without too much difficulty, because these Arab movements
were not coordinated and did not receive support from other
Moslem armies. When in March of 1922 the King of Hejaz wanted
to restore the caliphate abolished by the National Turkish As-

sembly and to become the religious chief of Islam, his claim was rejected by the other Arabs, those of Egypt and of the Nejd. When, after his victory over Hussein, ibn-Saud convened a Muslim congress in Mecca in 1926, the Wahhabite domination over the holy places gave rise to discord among the Islamic peoples and incited the University of Azhar to convoke a rival congress in Cairo. This crisis, which shattered the religious unity of Islam, was doubtless the fundamental explanation for the defeat of the nationalist movements. Nevertheless, the promoters of the Islamic congresses were convinced of one thing: in order to avoid fresh defeat, it would be necessary to re-establish Muslim solidarity and to resist the "disintegration of Islam into secular states." But this desire was to remain unfulfilled.

The Rivalries Among European Interests

There was never any European cooperation in facing the explosive nature of the Islamic countries. In Morocco, where France and Spain had been involved in the same war against Abd-el-Krim, collaboration had been minimal. In Syria, France had not been satisfied with British policy. In the Mossul affair—the most controversial because it had to do with oil interests—Great Britain did her best to eliminate France, while at the same time she offered a share to American companies. These disputes were unpleasant, and yet they did little harm. The only ones of importance were those involving French and Italian interests in the eastern Mediterranean or British and Russian interests in the Middle East.

With the advent of fascism, the Italian government had announced Italy's right to hold a dominant position in the Mediterranean. It is true that this objective had only a remote connection to reality, for it far exceeded this country's potentialities. In short, political action at the time pursued limited goals: the question of Tangiers and the status of the Italians living in Tunisia.

Once France and Spain had divided Morocco between them, the strategic importance of Tangiers had led the British government, in order to maintain its control over the Straits of Gibraltar, to obtain from these two countries the promise that the port would receive international status. The status of Tangiers, left undetermined in 1914, was settled in 1923 in an agreement between France, Great Britain, and Spain. It provided for the neutralization and demilitarization of the city, including the suburbs, but accorded France administrative privileges. The Italian government protested against a settlement that had been made in its absence; in 1926 it received diplomatic support from the Spanish government which, since the accession to power of General Primo de Rivera, looked with increasing disfavor upon the advantages granted France in the 1923 accord. Italo-Spanish diplomacy obtained a revision of the status in 1928. At the same time that Spain acquired the right to appoint the chief of the Tangiers police force, Italy obtained equal standing with Great Britain in the administration of the city. It was a "symbolic" success, which nevertheless left France playing the major role in the affairs of the city.

In Tunisia, Italian public opinion protested against the measures taken in December of 1918 by the French government. The activity of the Italian colony in Tunisia, said the Fascist press, gave Italy a "moral right" to the country, since its prosperity had been for the most part the result of "Italian labors." Italy could not and would not resign herself to abandoning the conventions of 1896 and allowing her colonists to "lose their nationality." She was even determined to claim for them further privileges—namely, equal political rights with the French—with the result that Tunisia became the scene of joint French and Italian domination. The government denied holding the opinions expressed in this press campaign, even though it had in fact inspired them. "These are merely ideals, such as exist among all peoples, but they cannot be part of a positive government program," declared Mussolini in February of 1926. His actions contradicted his words. Italy's real intentions were revealed by Marshal Balbo's voyage to Tunis. As a member of the government bringing greetings to the Italian colony, he pretended to ignore the presence of the French authorities.

Although during the autumn of 1926 this dispute was the occasion for serious diplomatic tension, further aggravated by controversies relating to the activities of Italian political émigrés in

France, the two governments stuck to their positions. French action was limited to an unfulfilled threat to question the status of Italians in Tunisia. Italian diplomacy was unable to restore the 1896 conventions. The Fascist press denounced the "incomprehension" that French public opinion expressed with regard to Italian interests; and in October of 1928 the government demanded equality with France in the field of naval armament—fulfillment of which would have in fact given the Italian navy a superiority over the French in the Mediterranean.

There is a striking contrast between this bitterness, which prolonged and aggravated Franco-Italian relations, and the cordiality of Anglo-Italian relations. And yet Mussolini, the day after the "march on Rome," announced plans for expelling the "parasites" from the area—namely, the countries not bordering on the Mediterranean. Mussolini's impetuosity was tempered by his acquisition of power. British policy was to avoid conflict with Italian interests. Due to the rectification of the frontier between Egypt and Cyrenaica, the Giarabub oasis, center of the Senoussite faction, was now in Italian, rather than Egyptian, territory and as a result facilitated the reconquest of Lybia. In September of 1926, during the visit of the British Minister for Foreign Affairs to Livorno, official Italian declarations emphasized the "cordial" relations between the two countries; in June of 1928 they once again underlined the "traditional and deep friendship" that united them both. This friendship did not, however, prevent the Fascist government, in the same year, from laying the foundations for naval and air bases on the islands of Rhodes and Leros—that is, in the zone where until then the British had held absolute sway, due to their bases in Alexandria, in Haifa in Palestine, and in Famagusta on Cyprus. But when, during the following year at Malta, the British administration wanted to eliminate the use of the Italian language, despite protest from the population, Mussolini avoided posing as defender of the "Italianism" of the Maltese, because he knew perfectly well that on this occasion Great Britain would not yield.

Basically the Fascist government still did not dare to abandon the line of conduct that its predecessors had almost consistently followed since 1861, and clash with British interests.

In the Middle East, where between 1907 and 1914 the British and Russian economic and strategic rivalry had been temporarily stilled, British policy between 1918 and 1919 was unchallenged, since the Bolshevik Revolution and civil war had paralyzed the competition. But the moment the White armies were crushed toward the end of 1919, the Soviet government, while it was re-establishing Russian authority in the Caucasus and Azerbaijan, announced its plan for offering assistance to the Asiatic populations in their fight against British imperialism: the Communist International chose Baku for its meeting place in 1920, the first congress of "oppressed peoples."

Russian policy first directed its efforts toward Iran, adding military assistance to propaganda—the occupation of the Persian port of Enzeli on the Caspian, where Denikhin's small White army had found refuge. This pressure was all the more effective in that the major body of troops available to the Teheran government, the Persian Cossack division, was partially staffed by former czarist officers, who were more susceptible to the traditions of Russian imperialism than to anti-Communist sentiments. Economic interests worked in the same manner, for Persia needed to re-establish trade with Russia which prior to 1914 had bought her dried fruit or raw cotton and sold to her beet sugar and manufactured goods—the bulk of the Iranian import market. In October of 1920 the new Persian Premier, after having suspended the application of the treaty concluded in 1919 with Great Britain, agreed to enter into negotiations with the Soviet government.

There then developed a nationalist movement against this Russian pressure identical to that opposed to Great Britain in the past. The leader was a Teheran journalist by the name of Zia Ed-din. These nationalists criticized the Shah for not having been able to resist foreign intervention. The military *coup d'état* that took place on February 21, 1921, brought to power a "Kemalist" type of government under the leadership of Colonel Riza Khan.

This government pursued a teetering policy—so far as it is possible to get a clear idea of it.

Its first action, five days after having gained power, was to sign a treaty with Soviet Russia. The Moscow government agreed to withdraw the troops occupying Enzeli, to renounce the privileges that czarist diplomacy had acquired in Persia, and not to interfere in the interior affairs of the country; the Persian government promised that its territory would not become a "base of action" against Russia to the advantage of a third power—Great Britain. British political circles did not hide their anxiety: the Minister of Foreign Affairs, Lord Curzon, declared in the House of Lords that the Teheran government had thrown away the chance of "re-establishing her fortune" with the aid of Great Britain and preferred to accept the "endearments" of the Soviet government, prelude to a "strangulation." And yet the British cabinet did not make a move: it withdrew the last troops—some twelve thousand men—still based in Iran.

But the application of the Russo-Persian treaty soon ran into serious difficulties: the untimely activity of the Russian legation, which subsidized three Communist-inspired newspapers in Teheran; the controversy over fishing rights in the Caspian Sea; the embargo that the Russian government imposed on the importation of Persian dried fruits. Furthermore, in 1925 the Persian government sought a *rapprochement* with Great Britain, offering advantages to the Anglo-Persian Company. Soviet diplomacy replied by trying to provoke communist movements in Persia; but her lack of success induced Russia to abandon this tactic and to sign a treaty of non-aggression with the Teheran government in October of 1927.

In short, the new Iranian dynasty having stripped the sovereign of his power, Riza Khan formally dethroned him in 1925. Riza Khan succeeded during these ten years in avoiding British and Russian pressure, which immediately threatened national independence. Riza would have liked to consolidate these results by a reorganization of public funds, calling on foreign capital that would be neither Russian nor British. This is why in 1927 he asked for American experts—the Millspaugh mission—but all he received was advice. Economic and financial independence, the necessary condition for political independence, did not materialize. The future remained, therefore, uncertain.

Afghanistan, which gained her independence in 1919, became another field of rivalry between Russian and British interests. King

Amanullah inaugurated a program of modernization and secularization inspired by the Turkish example. In the organization of communications and in the organization of his army, he called on technicians and officers sent by the U.S.S.R., with which country he signed a treaty of nonaggression in April of 1927. The penetration of Russian influence was therefore becoming quite marked. A few months later, Amanullah was dethroned by a revolutionary movement, which in October 1929, after minor vicissitudes, brought to power Nadir Khan, who dismissed the Russian experts and suspended the reform programs. The Soviet press hastily announced that this Afghan revolution, the cause of which appeared to have been the hostility of the religious leaders toward the "modernization" program, was in reality the work of Great Britain. Was it pure chance that Nadir had been brought to power by the tribes inhabiting the Indo-Afghan border?

And yet the new sovereign avoided accepting British patronage and even declined the financial assistance Great Britain offered him. Following Riza's example, he tried to maintain a policy of balance. And the British cabinet was satisfied for the moment, for it had checked Russian influence.

Could it not be said that the striking characteristic of the development of these nascent nationalist movements and these international rivalries was Britain's continued influence in this part of the world? British policies—those of Lloyd George in the Aegean and of Lord Curzon in Persia—had failed when they embarked upon new adventures; but they had managed to retain the essence of their previous successes in the Middle East and in Egypt, despite the Moslem movements and despite the Soviet threat. And yet this success was to be only temporary. Nevertheless it demonstrated a continuity and a flexibility, proving that diplomatic action can on occasion succeed in delaying the free play of underlying forces.

Nationalism in the Far East

The First World War weakened Western influence in Asia, both economically and politically: Japan gained an ascendancy in the Far East, and the nationalist movements, which acquired significant momentum in 1919, announced an "awakening" in Asia. Relations between the great European nations or the United States with the countries of Asia during the years that immediately followed the peace treaties were marked by two particular trends: the halt of Japanese imperialism and the Chinese attempts at national emancipation.

The "Sudden Halt" in Japan

In June of 1919 the Japanese government won a diplomatic victory when the Treaty of Versailles gave her the German territories of Shantung: the great victorious powers, without taking into account the Chinese nationalist movement, had given up their intentions of intervening in the settlement of the Sino-Japanese disputes. This victory, however, was precarious, not only because it met vehement protest from political and religious circles in the United States but also because of the sudden change in British policy.

Even before the signing of the Versailles Treaty, the Hearst press, which was against the policies of President Wilson, had declared that the Japanese claims in China were unacceptable. In August of 1919 the leaders of the Senate opposition at the Versailles conference condemned the American delegation at the peace conference, with all the verbal exaggeration of political debate, for having agreed to a "shameful transaction," to a "capitulation": Japanese policy aimed at "closing the Chinese market," and it would not be long before it would be "threatening the world"; it would force America to declare war in order to "save civilization." Woodrow Wilson's attitude was even denounced by Secretary of State Lansing, who accused the President before the Senate Committee for Foreign Affairs of having delivered Shantung to the Japanese. This campaign was supported by the "religious" newspapers through the influence of the Protestant missionaries in China, who insisted that there were vigorous nationalist manifestations in China, and that in Korea there were indications of violence on the part of the Japanese administration against the promoters of an independence movement. In refusing to ratify the Treaty of Versailles, the Senate absolved the United States from commitments subscribed to by President Wilson on the subject of the Far East; at the same time it encouraged China's resistance to Japanese policy.

Upon the coming to power of the Republican administration in 1921, the United States exerted direct pressure upon Japan. President Harding decided that the construction programs started during the Great War, with the idea of increasing the size of the navy, would continue, since Japan, said the American press, should not remain "master of the Pacific." Harding declared that the United States government would not recognize the Japanese occupation of the Russian maritime province. And yet the American government had no desire to push Japan "to the wall," because, even before showing its teeth, it had caused Congress to propose an international conference to examine the questions of the Far East and the Pacific.

Apparently its tactics were to threaten Japan with an arms race in which the United States, with its superior industry, would clearly have the advantage; or to offer to abandon this race, but on the condition that the Japanese government renounce its territorial ambitions on the Asian continent. The final goal, declared the American press, was to obtain a revision of the "scandalous war benefits" gained by Japan between 1914 and 1918.

The success of this action depended to a large extent on the attitude Great Britain would adopt. The Anglo-Japanese alliance, signed in 1902, had been renewed for another ten years in July 1911. It is true that at this time Great Britain stipulated that she would not get involved to the extent of armed intervention in a conflict between the United States and Japan. Yet she had promised to give diplomatic support to Japan for the safeguarding of her "special interests." Was it to Britain's advantage to prolong the existence of this treaty?

Since 1915 Japanese political maneuvers had been harmful to British economic interests in China. Moreover, the main reason behind the alliance had disappeared, since Russian expansion in the Far East had been paralyzed by the revolution of 1917. But if the treaty of alliance were abandoned, the British cabinet would have good reason to fear Japan's support of the Hindu nationalist movement in the name of "Pan-Asianism." It was hard to weigh the advantages and disadvantages of this situation. But most important were the future relations between the United States and Great Britain. In May of 1921 the chairman of the Senate Foreign Relations Committee expressed the desire of seeing Great Britain renounce the Japanese alliance. On June 23 the Secretary of State clearly stated that the renewal of the alliance would give encouragement to the Japanese "military" party to the detriment of American interests. He added that the abandoning of this alliance would be tangible evidence of an Anglo-American understanding on Far Eastern and Pacific questions. These declarations were accompanied by a threat that was hardly veiled. The attitude of the United States toward the southern Irish nationalist movement would depend on that of the British cabinet toward Japan.

On the day after this announcement the British Imperial Conference decided not to renew the 1911 alliance.

Subject to direct pressure from the United States and abandoned by Great Britain, the Japanese government resigned itself to accepting the international conference. And yet it could not escape the fact that during these debates, in which all the participating countries would have interests conflicting with its own, it would find itself forced to relinquish some of its possessions. But how could it avoid this situation? The eventuality of an armed conflict, which Japanese military circles mentioned during the spring of 1921, was rejected by the majority of the Japanese population, which was especially preoccupied with the economic, financial, and social crises that were shaking the whole country. In June of 1921, during the Chambers of Commerce conference, business circles appealed for a cut in taxes and, as a result, in military and naval expenditures; they also criticized the "adventurous" policy being pursued in eastern Siberia. In July and August social stability was seriously threatened by worker movements that, particularly in Kobe, took on a revolutionary aspect. This desire for peace and the social unrest called for a cautious policy.

The conference that convened in Washington between November 12, 1921, and February 6, 1922, tackled the questions both of the Far East and the Pacific and of naval armament. Soviet Russia, whose government had not yet been recognized by the other great powers, had been left out of the conference, despite the importance of her interests in Siberia and Manchuria. The United States was assured of Great Britain's cooperation and therefore did not fear France's or Italy's favoring Japanese supremacy in the Chinese empire or in the Pacific. Isolated and reduced to being on the defensive, the Japanese delegation was forced to concede.

The question of the Pacific was the object of a "Treaty of Four," signed on December 13, 1921, whereby the Japanese government joined with the United States, Great Britain, and France in promising, for a period of ten years, mutual respect for the *status quo* in "island possessions."

The question of China was tackled on February 6, 1922, with the "Treaty of Nine," according to whose terms the signers committed themselves to respecting the "sovereignty, the independence, and the territorial and administrative integrity of the state of China," as well as to an "open door" economic policy.

Finally, the question of naval armament was settled with the "Treaty of Five" on February 6. Japan agreed that the proportion of ships of the line be fixed at 3 for Japan, 5 for the United States and Great Britain, and 1.75 for France and Italy. The Japanese offered vigorous resistance to this point but subsided when the United States threatened to accelerate the arms race and build four times as many ships as the Japanese shipyards were able to construct.

And yet these were not the only concessions that the Japanese were forced to make. Under strong pressure from the United States, the Japanese delegation promised China, in an accord signed on February 4, 1922, that she would give back the "rights and interests" that Germany had possessed in Shantung prior to 1914, and that had been transferred to Japan through the Treaty of Versailles. She completely renounced her demands for the advantages she had gained from the Sino-Japanese agreement of May 1915 and was content to obtain participation in the exploitation of the mining region of Han-Yeh-Ping, the right for Japanese colonists to acquire lands in Manchuria, and an extension of the lease on Port Arthur. The Japanese government also announced its intention to evacuate, after a short delay, the maritime province and all points along the Siberian coast where her troops had taken up positions: this meant therefore the end of the "Siberian adventure" which had begun during the summer of 1918. It also consented to China's acquiring a vote in the administration of the "East China" railroad—that is, the Trans-Manchurian railroad—a solution that eliminated the influence of Soviet Russia but ensured a return of Chinese influence in an area from which she had been virtually eliminated for twenty years.

Of all the advantages Japan had acquired, legitimately or by force, during the course of the First World War, how many remained to her in 1922?

She confirmed and even extended the privileges she possessed in Southern Manchuria; she kept three Pacific archipelagoes that she had acquired as a mandate at the expense of Germany in 1919: these were important clauses for the security of the Japanese archipelago and for her supply of raw materials. Despite the proportion of 3 to 5 established by treaty over armament limitation, she maintained a naval superiority in the Far Eastern seas because the United States navy was divided between the Atlantic and the Pacific. But she surrendered her foothold in the maritime province and in the leased territory of Kiao-Chou, and also most of the clauses in the Sino-Japanese agreement of May 1915: in other words, she had renounced her expansionist plans in eastern Asia. She did not even get the Washington conference to take her overpopulation into account and to grant her subjects the right to emigrate to the United States or British territories scattered over the Pacific Ocean. In short, the United States, thanks to British cooperation, brought Japan to a sudden halt through simple diplomatic pressure.

Military and naval circles in Tokyo, which had been the chief partisans of the expansionist policy, protested vehemently against the results of the international conference; in June of 1922 they forced the cabinet that signed the Washington treaties to resign. And yet this discontent had no further repercussions, for the industrial, commercial, and financial circles, which were directly affected by the economic crisis and concerned with the social crisis, were too preoccupied with domestic affairs to accept adventurous efforts in the direction of foreign policy which would involve heavy financial outlays.

Exhausted, Japan needed a moment of rest. Through this sudden halt that she had inflicted upon Japan, the United States succeeded in delaying the serious international difficulties that this Japanese policy seemed likely to provoke. This respite was to last for ten years.

The Nationalist Movements in China

However, Western footholds in China were to be threatened by resistance movements that tried to curb the direct and indirect domination of foreigners. This "awakening of China" was one of the great moments in the history of the contemporary world. What were its essential features?

The spring of 1922 heralded a collaboration among the "new" forces. Li Ta-chao offered his cooperation to Sun Yat-sen for working toward the "national revolution." He agreed to join the Kuomintang, without giving up his Communist party membership, of course. Sun welcomed this offer, although he still insisted that Marxist solutions were not applicable to China. Thus, a temporary alliance was established, whose single aim was to restore China to "independence": in other words, to bring about the abrogation of the "unequal treaties" and to eliminate the privileges accorded to foreigners. This collaboration was announced by the "father of the Chinese revolution" in 1923 in a speech addressed to his Kuomintang comrades. It was not to endure longer than Sun himself. After his death in March 1925, the new leaders of the Kuomintang, Chiang Kai-shek and Wang Ching-wei, abandoned this tactic which in their opinion offered Russia possibilities that would be dangerous not only to the interests of Chinese capitalism but to the nation's independence as well.

Despite the dissolution of this alliance, the troops of the two parties maintained an identical aim: to shake off foreign domination. The "anti-foreign" movement, which dated from June 1925, and whose first major manifestation was the boycott of maritime commerce in the port of Canton, grew in strength over a period of two years. It was carried on in conjunction with large-scale military operations conducted by the government of Canton against that of Peking. On two occasions it was marked by serious incidents in central China: the occupation of the British concession of Hankow by armed bands of Chinese, and the attack by troops of the Kuomintang on the consulates and on American and European commercial or industrial enterprises at Nanking. It appeared also in other forms in Manchuria, where it was directed against Japanese interests.

Naturally this movement for national independence and this wave of xenophobia evoke the memory of previous risings, especially the Boxer Rebellion. But the situation was quite different this time. The agitation was inspired not by the secret societies but by the labor unions, supported by a wave of public opinion whose proportions had already been hinted at in the "movement of May

4, 1919." Such were the threats to the positions long held in China
by the great powers.

Having guided the leaders of the Chinese Communist party
toward a collaboration with the Kuomintang, the Soviet government
declared in a manifesto of January 26, 1923, that Sun Yat-sen's
movement of "national independence" deserved its "warm sympathy," and that Russia would renounce the benefits of the unequal
treaties. It had also given assistance to the unification efforts of
the southern Chinese government—that is, to the military operations
that it was organizing against the northern government. The Borodin
mission, established in Canton in October 1923, furnished the
southern army with instructors and offered the Kuomintang technical advisers for the reorganization of the administration or the
management of economic policy. The "liberation" of China, wrote
Lenin in 1923, could become an essential stage in the "victory
of socialism in the world."

The wave of xenophobia that broke out in 1925 encouraged
this hope. In September of 1925, three months after the start of
the Canton boycott, Zinoviev, President of the Communist International, took note of the rapid progress of the revolutionary movement in the Far East. The Borodin mission was helping this
movement along. Borodin even stated his position publicly: in a
speech addressed to the striking workers of Hankow, in December
of 1926, he appealed for a struggle against imperialism. The
twenty-fourth Party Congress in Moscow in January of 1927 saw
in the Chinese revolution the "second home" of the world revolution. It entrusted the young Chinese national government with the
task of thwarting the English attempt to form a bloc of powers
united against China. The Soviet press reported the presence of
Russian volunteers in the Chinese national army.

The Russian strategy began to encounter difficulties at this point,
however, since the Kuomintang openly turned against it. In March
of 1926, Chiang Kai-shek took advantage of Borodin's absence to
expel the Soviet "technical advisers" but took no further steps,
since he did not wish to deprive his army of the services that the
Russian officer-instructors were rendering just as the offensive

against the Peking government was beginning. Even as Kuomintang troops were routing the northern forces from the Yangtze valley and attacking the foreign concessions at Hankow and subsequently at Nanking, thereby carrying out Borodin's wishes, Chiang Kai-shek, at a session of the Central Executive Committee on March 1, 1927, announced his intention to break with the Communist party and the Soviet Union. This program was effected over a period of several months. In April 1927 he opened hostilities against the Chinese Communists in Shanghai. In December he suppressed a Communist uprising by a bloody massacre. On December 14, 1927, diplomatic relations were broken off between the Kuomintang government, which had just set up headquarters in Nanking, and the Soviet government. Russian trade missions in China were closed.

The Russian press cried treason: Chiang Kai-shek was the "executioner of the proletariat," a "Chinese Cavaignac," a "lackey of English imperialism." It denounced the "confusion of the Chinese revolution" and the "banditry" of the Kuomintang troops. In short, it conceded the defeat of five years of Soviet policy in China: the upper echelons of the Kuomintang party had "gone over to the right," and the working and peasant masses were not tightly enough organized to prevent this defection.

The United States and Great Britain had parallel but unequal interests in this Chinese crisis. Great Britain still played a large part in China's foreign economic relations: 50 per cent of her imports and 50 per cent of her capital investments were British. The number of British commercial and industrial enterprises had risen from 590 in 1914 to 1,000 in 1925. The United States played a less important role, but one that was rapidly increasing since the passage of the China Trade Act by Congress in September 1922. This act grouped all American companies in China under a single "corporation" which would be under the control of the Commerce Department and would be exempt from taxes. Washington wanted to ensure the protection of future interests in this fashion.

The policy of the State Department was subjected to diverse pressures. The heads of the large Protestant missionary organizations, which ran ninety-eight missions in China, were prepared to relinquish the rights accorded by the unequal treaties, including that of extraterritoriality, because they considered it expedient to sever all connection between the spreading of the Gospel and economic imperialism. They were supported in this by a certain proportion of the missionaries. Business came out against such a move in its organ, the *Far Eastern Review,* published in Shanghai. Frank B. Kellogg, Secretary of State, felt that it would be impossible in the long run to exercise control over a nation of one hundred million inhabitants. He thought that a conciliatory policy could achieve more advantages in the development of the Chinese economy than the strict enforcement of established rights. The United States had already adopted this line of conduct between 1868 and 1899. Thus, Kellogg announced his intention to enter negotiations on tariff policy and extraterritoriality once China's political unity was restored. On the occasion of the serious incidents at Nanking, even though Standard Oil had considerable interests in that city, he refused to impose sanctions, saying that to do so would be more dangerous than effective. It is possible he acted in this manner out of the conviction that the xenophobic movement was rather a consequence of the Chinese civil war than the manifestation of a deeply rooted tendency. He hoped also that non-intervention would gain him the sympathy of the Chinese nationalists, or at least of the moderate wing of the Kuomintang, and would impede the development of Russian influence.

The British government, although capable of energetic action, remained basically as prudent as the American. The British chargé d'affaires at Hankow negotiated with the Kuomintang. These negotiations resulted in Britain's agreeing to relinquish the concession on February 19, 1927, handing over its administration to the Chinese municipal government. However, at Nanking, British gunboats bombarded the city during the attack on the consulates. But the diplomats were also at work to smooth over the consequences of the incident. "We are thinking of our relations with China in the next hundred years," said the Minister for Foreign Affairs to those who criticized his weakness. True, the ensuing breach in the system of unequal treaties was a serious one, and British businessmen in China were well aware of it. But in return for this setback the British were able to resume the position in China's economy that they had been losing. At the end of 1927 the entire Yangtze region, which was the zone most essential to Britain's interests, was once again open to her commercial activity. Chiang Kai-shek's break with the Soviet government was reassuring: and the work of reconstruction, economic as well as political, that his government was carrying out opened up profitable opportunities to British business, since China could hardly accomplish this task without resorting to Western financial aid.

In short, both Washington and London were betting on the re-establishment of political unity in China under the leadership of the moderate elements of the Kuomintang, who were as hostile to the Communists as they were to the "war lords." This hope was soon confirmed. The taking of Peking by troops of the "nationalist" government on June 8, 1928, re-established the unity of the state, at least in theory. This Chinese government obtained almost immediately the restitution of its independence in tariff policy from the United States, Great Britain, and France.

The most unexpected development in this Chinese crisis was the behavior of Japan. Even though the Canton boycott in June of 1925 was touched off by an incident between Chinese and Japanese, and even though Japanese interests were considerable in the mining and industrial region near Hankow, the Japanese government limited itself to a diplomatic protest and prudently refrained from any direct action. It no doubt considered it expedient to deal cautiously with the Chinese nationalist movement. The statements of the Minister for Foreign Affairs emphasized these expressions of good will, perhaps because business circles in Tokyo fostered the secret hope of British and American influence being eliminated as a result of Chinese xenophobia. Thus Baron Shidehara declared in January of 1926 that Japan would abstain from any intervention in the Chinese civil war. Peaceful coexistence and economic collaboration were to be her guiding precepts.

This unaccustomed reserve and prudence in Japanese policy were applied, however, only in relations with China proper. In Southern Manchuria, on the other hand, Japanese influence grew stronger, because Japanese colonists had been granted the right to buy land there by the Sino-Japanese agreement of February 1922, and because for two years during the vicissitudes of the civil war, between 1922 and 1924, the region had become the fief of a "war lord" who had in effect detached it from the authority of either Chinese government.

This situation was challenged, coincidental with the rise of xenophobia in central China, by an offensive return of the Chinese administration, which began not only to resist Japanese penetration but to attempt to eliminate it altogether. On the instructions of these officials, the Chinese landed proprietors refused to sell to Japanese colonists. The construction of new railroads undertaken by the Chinese directly threatened the Japanese "South Manchurian Company," whose rail network had enjoyed a monopoly in that region since 1905. Finally, a stream of immigration from China's northern provinces developed, especially from Shantung, Hopei, and Southern Manchuria: each year between 1925 and 1929 it brought 1,000,000 Chinese workers to the region. If not checked, this influx threatened to submerge the 240,000 Japanese and 800,000 Koreans—Japanese subjects—who had settled in Southern Manchuria.

Economic as well as military circles in Japan were convinced that the solution to their overpopulation problem as well as to the agricultural crisis and the shortage of iron ore was to organize the exploitation of Manchuria's resources. They also considered that the colonization that Japanese nationals had already accomplished in this country conferred certain rights on Japan.

What means should be employed to protect these interests? In 1927 some felt that it would be necessary to "liquidate" the Chinese administration in the three Manchurian provinces, since this administration was attempting to deprive the Japanese of advantages they should legitimately enjoy. This was the opinion of the military and of the businessmen connected with the South Manchurian Railroad Company, who wished thereby to establish a direct or an indirect domination. This plan was opposed by the partisans of "peaceful" expansion, for whom Baron Shidehara was the spokesman within the government. This group advocated only diplomatic means to accomplish its ends.

Japanese policy wavered between these two tendencies. The hard line seemed to be on the point of gaining ascendancy when Shidehara was forced to resign from the government by the Premier, Baron Tanaka. However, two years later Tanaka was himself eliminated by the Emperor. Shidehara returned to power but was bitterly opposed by the military and by the South Manchurian Railroad Company. Thus, the Manchurian question was hardly likely to die down for any length of time.

The United States and Great Britain had therefore succeeded in putting a halt to Japanese imperialism and in re-establishing their economic positions in China, despite the serious blows they had suffered between 1925 and 1927. Soviet Russia witnessed the collapse of the hope it had conceived in 1925. She had succeeded neither in eliminating American and British influence in China nor in establishing her own. When Chiang Kai-shek announced his plan to "reconstruct" and "modernize" China, after having begun the restoration of political unity by taking Peking, his intention was to make use of the Anglo-American financial and economic institutions to accomplish this task. In this way Britain and the United States could be compensated for the advantages lost by relinquishing the operation of China's customs administration. The Chinese demand for national independence, as it applied to extra-territoriality and to the "concessions," had been taken up again by the Kuomintang but seemed to be suspended for the moment.

The principal reason for this turn of events was undoubtedly the line of action adopted by Chinese business leaders. Having accepted Soviet Russia's assistance for the liberation movement, they began to comprehend the dangers implied in this collaboration. They realized that Borodin's appeal to the workers of Hankow in 1926, although directed against "foreign imperialism," could consequently be turned against Chinese capitalism itself. For this reason they curtailed the anti-foreign movement in order to counter Chinese pressure. British diplomacy immediately took advantage of the situation. This would seem to be the most reasonable interpretation, although it is necessarily a largely hypothetical one for lack of sufficient documentation.

The Kuomintang's leader, who had understood the necessity to come to an understanding with the world's two greatest financial powers, did not, however, feel obliged to exercise the same prudence with regard to Japan. They asserted China's right to sovereignty over Manchuria. The Chinese Nationalist government's efforts to resist the penetration of Japanese influence in 1929 revived the threat of conflict after several years of quiescence. Basically Japan had begun, since the re-establishment of China's political unity, to perceive the future significance of China's revival to Japanese expansion: it would not be advisable for her to wait for this revival to bear fruit.

The International Position of Latin America

The "common denominator" in the Latin portion of the American continent, which had a population of 85,000,000 in 1925, was the Catholic religion. One must also bear in mind, of course, the similar cultural traditions of the countries in this region. This kinship, however, was of little interest to any but the ruling classes. But what contrasts there were from every other standpoint! Brazil, with 41,000,000 inhabitants, dominated all nineteen of the other countries in sheer size. Nonetheless the others had very little in common: the republics of Panama or of Costa Rica, on the one hand, with 442,000 inhabitants and 471,000 inhabitants, respectively; and Mexico or Argentina, on the other, with 14,600,000 and 10,600,000 people, respectively. There were contrasts in geographical conditions, in economic resources, and in the makeup of the populations—depending on the proportion of whites, of Indians, sometimes of Negroes, and of mestizos. There was the linguistic division between Portuguese-speaking Brazil and the nineteen other countries where Spanish was spoken. There were differences in the political maturity of those states that applied constitutional methods, at least partially, and those that knew no other regime than dictatorship, under the cover of an entirely theoretical constitution.

In this unstable region, marked by conflicting nationalisms, the predominant influences, from the economic and financial as well as the intellectual standpoint, had been, by and large, European. The United States held a dominant position only in Central America. Even in Mexico she had not yet succeeded in eliminating British financial influence. Moreover, the protection afforded the South American countries by the Monroe Doctrine did not seem to them sufficient compensation for the anxiety aroused by Yankee imperialism. But the World War had brought about a withdrawal of European influence and had given the United States the opportunity to increase her commerce and investments in South America. From 1915 on, Secretary of the Treasury McAdoo, son-in-law of President Wilson, had continually pointed out the political advantages that would inevitably accompany the development of economic and financial influence in this region.

During the years immediately following Europe's re-entry into world economic affairs, the focal point of Latin America's problems was the struggle between the United States and Europe to gain ascendancy in these countries—primarily an economic and financial rivalry, but a political one as well.

Economic and Financial Relations

In economic and financial areas the distinction must be drawn between the case of Central America, where the United States had already established a solid foothold, and that of South America, where European competition had temporarily been eliminated by the world conflict.

In Central America, where the Yankee hegemony had still occasionally confronted European competition before 1914, the United States takeover was now complete.

For the management of their public finances, all of these small countries readily turned to the services of American banks. In 1919 the public debts of Cuba, Panama, Haiti, and Santo Domingo were already in the hands of these banks. El Salvador, Nicaragua,

Honduras, and Guatemala, which before 1914 had gone to the financial markets of Paris and London by preference, now floated all of their loans on the New York market. Only Mexico and Costa Rica continued to turn to European banks to cover a part of their needs, without overlooking the possibilities offered by United States institutions. Year by year the United States played a growing role in the economic affairs of these republics, both in capital investment[1] and in development of commercial relations.[2] Banana plantations in the nations of the isthmus, sugar cane and cocoa in the Caribbean islands, gold mines in Nicaragua and Costa Rica, silver mines in El Salvador, oil deposits in Guatemala, railroad construction, electrification of most of the cities—all of these projects were the work of companies based in the United States. Several hundred such companies were operating in Mexico. Their investments were channeled principally into the exploitation of oil deposits, in which United States participation, through the Mexican Petroleum Company and the *Companio Transcontinentale de Petroleo,* an affiliate of Standard Oil, was twice that of Great Britain. But they also flowed into silver, copper, and zinc mines in which the American Smelting Company played the largest part, and into railroad companies. The United States share of Mexican imports was 70 per cent; of exports, 75 per cent.

This hegemony that the United States had achieved in Mexican economic affairs was, however, threatened over a period of ten years by a controversy, which is of interest insofar as it demonstrates the close relations between finance and politics.

In a belated effort to ensure the economic independence of the country, Article 27 of the Mexican constitution of 1917 granted to the state the ownership of all subsoil resources. This article further stipulated that the government could expropriate foreign companies by the payment of indemnities. It would, however,

[1] In Panama these investments rose from $5,000,000 in 1914 to $42,000,-000 in 1928; in Costa Rica, from $7,000,000 to $35,000,000; in Honduras, from $3,000,000 to $10,700,000; in El Salvador, from $3,000,000 to $43,-000,000; in Guatemala, from $12,000,000 to $50,000,000.

[2] The United States share of exports was 30 per cent in El Salvador, 35 per cent in Costa Rica, 46 per cent in Guatemala, 50 per cent in Nicaragua, 80 per cent in Honduras and Cuba.

allow that these companies be granted the right to continue their operations through a concession contract, but only if they would expressly renounce the protection of their governments in regard to difficulties over the application of their contracts.

The petroleum companies sought to eliminate this threat of nationalization. When the author of the constitution, Carranza, was overthrown by a *coup d'état,* the new President, Obregón, pledged himself not to apply the right of expropriation to foreign companies that had acquired oil deposits before 1917. He thus refrained from eliminating the dominant influence of the United States in Mexican economic affairs. But in December of 1925 a new Mexican government under Calles announced its intention to apply Article 27. The British companies were resigned to requesting the new concession contracts required by this article. The United States government, without going so far as to threaten armed intervention, gave diplomatic support to her businessmen who refused to comply with the Mexican law.

On March 27, 1928, the United States ambassador, Dwight Morrow, one of the directors of the Morgan Bank, persuaded the Mexican government to authorize a dispensation whereby those companies that had begun to prepare for the exploitation of oil deposits before 1917 would be granted concession contracts of unlimited duration. It was virtually a victory for the economic and financial interests of the United States.

Between 1920 and 1930 the South American economy was marked by the growth of the transformation industries and by the development of new natural resources. Venezuela, whose oil production had begun in 1912, doubled Mexico's production by 1928; and Colombia began to take her place among the oil-producing nations. Thus these South American nations required industrial equipment, technicians, and investment capital. Would they turn to Europe or to the United States for these needs? The European exporters, who had resumed their efforts in 1920, were partially successful from 1925 on. But almost everywhere they encountered and often lost out to American competition.

Before 1914 all the South American countries were accustomed to floating their loans on European financial markets. After 1919,

Colombia and Peru turned exclusively to the United States. In Argentina, Uruguay, Brazil, Chile, and Bolivia, the governments continued to request the financial cooperation of Great Britain but also looked with increasing frequency toward the big New York banks. At the same time American businessmen came to South America to purchase or create business enterprises and invested in the issues of South American industrial or mining concerns, which abounded on the United States financial market. In 1928 these investments reached $616,000,000 in Argentina, where prior to 1914 they had been insignificant; $342,000,000 in Brazil; $60,000,000 in Uruguay. They nonetheless did not seriously challenge British financial predominance in these areas. In the same year they equaled European investments in Chile and Peru. In Colombia, Bolivia, and Venezuela, American investments in large enterprises were considerably larger than those of European countries.

Outside of Ecuador there was no American investment in railways, which were still financed almost exclusively by British, French, and Belgian capital. United States banks were more interested in electrification projects and telephone installations, in certain industrial activities (ranging from metallurgy and automobile construction to the production of canned foods), in coffee or rubber plantations in Brazil, and sugar-cane plantations in Venezuela. But it was primarily the exploitation of mineral resources that attracted the investments: manganese in Brazil, nitrates in Chile, zinc in Bolivia, copper in Peru, and most of all oil, of which the United States controlled from two thirds to three fifths of the total production in Venezuela, Colombia, and Peru.

While the amount of French and German investments had decreased considerably since 1914, and British investments had just kept up to the level achieved before the First World War, American capital invested in South America had climbed from $170,000,000 in 1913 to $2,294,000,000 in 1929.

The rapid growth of this financial influence paved the way to the development of commercial relations. In 1928 the United States' share in South America's foreign trade was 32 per cent, while Great Britain's did not exceed 16 per cent. This commercial penetration was most evident in Venezuela (50 per cent of the imports came from the United States), in Uruguay (30 per cent of imports), and in Brazil (28 per cent of imports, 47 per cent of exports).

In short, Europe's financial and economic role was at a standstill or declining everywhere, while United States influence was progressing by "leaps and bounds."

Political Relations

To what extent did the role that the United States began to play in Latin America's economic and financial affairs pave the way for her political influence?

Contemporary observers noted that the large enterprises run by Americans tended to form "islands" within local economies; and that American businessmen did not seek to make contacts outside the top business circles, since they felt a certain contempt for the Latin people, whose mentality was foreign to them. What really counted, however, was the influence the United States could exert on the governments of these countries by means of loans. True, these loans were negotiated through the banks and not through the Treasury, but Washington indicated in a communiqué published in March of 1922 that it intended to supervise these operations. The banks were requested to "inform the State Department beforehand" when undertaking the floating of a foreign loan, so that the latter might indicate whether or not the matter in question conflicted with "the national interest." True, the government could not oblige the banks to consult it, since it did not wish to take any direct responsibility. However, such consultation was in effect a constant occurrence, as emphasized in the Secretary of the Treasury's report in 1925.

Thus, the United States found an instrument of political pressure in the granting or refusing of needed resources to these Latin American countries. Of course, the lenders were exposed to considerable risks, especially in countries where governments sprang up and collapsed through armed coups. But if one of these countries did not make a "reasonable effort" to pay regularly the interest on its public debt, then Washington would take steps to cut off all grants of credits, even to private enterprises. This was the policy outlined by the Secretary of the Treasury.

Within the framework of these general principles expressing the intentions of the United States government, there was a quite different attitude in relations with Central America compared to those with South America.

"Dollar diplomacy" continued to be the policy in the Central American countries, including those of the Caribbean. Here, material interests were still closely linked to political action, though their methods of operation varied. Banks sometimes determined diplomatic action and sometimes served as an instrument of the State Department's designs. Between 1920 and 1929 this kind of pressure was applied to Santo Domingo, Honduras, and Nicaragua.

In the Dominican Republic, the United States, which had exercised control over public finances since 1905, brought about an armed intervention in 1916 in order to suppress unrest that was endangering American investments. This occupation continued for eight years: the occupation force was not withdrawn until 1924, after the formation of a government considered capable of ensuring public order and fulfilling the country's obligations to United States banks.

In Honduras, when a revolutionary movement in 1923 brought a government to power whose very existence seemed to threaten foreign investments, the United States sent in a naval squadron and an expeditionary force. She demanded "free elections" but did not consider the presence of her troops to be a hindrance to this freedom. It was hardly surprising that these new elections rejected the regime resulting from the *coup d'état,* and brought to power a government friendly to foreign interests.

In Nicaragua the matter was more complicated, although the steps taken to control the situation were basically the same. Since 1911 Washington had been providing the "international police power" the form for which had been set several years previously by Theodore Roosevelt. In November 1923 it announced its intention to withdraw these troops as soon as a government was

formed through "free elections." These elections took place, but
in the presence of the occupation force and according to methods
stipulated by an American official. They brought to power a
government that, as expected, seemed to offer sufficient serious
guarantees to permit the withdrawal of the occupation forces. This
was a mere episode, as the new government was overthrown by a
coup d'état, which immediately called forth new armed intervention from the United States. In 1926, with the situation under
control, the troops were withdrawn, only to be sent back in 1928
to guard against difficulties threatened by yet another *coup d'état.*
The presidential election took place only after a reorganization of
the local police, whose upper echelons were already entirely
American, and after a "revision" of the electoral law under the
supervision of Colonel Stimson, at one time an important member
of the United States government.

How did these practices differ from those before 1914? The
sole difference was that the United States renounced the "quasi
protectorate" method like that applied to Cuba in 1901. But even
though Secretary of State Hughes had denied any imperialist designs in 1922 and had announced his intention to respect the
"sovereignty of the Latin American peoples," the United States
had in fact maintained her political control and her right of intervention throughout the region.

In the South American countries the United States made no
attempt to employ the methods of "dollar diplomacy" in her
political actions. She did not of course overlook the possibilities
afforded by investing capital, although she availed herself of these
methods with discretion. For example, although Peru and Colombia
both called in American experts to reorganize public finances, they
were under no obligation to do so. In countries such as Chile and
Brazil, for example, certain newspapers were in fact controlled
by Americans owing to the conditions under which they were
financed; but these newspapers—the *South Pacific Mail* and the
River Plate American—were in the English language and were
intended only for the business world.

As far as one can gather from the historical information available, the United States seemed to have been counting on the success

of a long-term project: namely, the development of the Pan-American movement which aimed at establishing some sort of cooperation, perhaps even an "association," between the countries of the hemisphere. Before 1914 this Pan-American policy had encountered the opposition of the South American intelligentsia. But the new conditions resulting from the First World War appeared to have weakened this opposition.

Actually the opponents of the United States in these countries were not lacking in support—a fact that became increasingly evident from 1919 on. It is even possible that in the areas where American capitalism had taken root and had come into contact with the proletariat, this confrontation gave rise to an anti-American sentiment that had not previously existed at the popular level. This distrust was strongest in Argentina, where the business leadership retained a "European" orientation, and where Italian immigrants were less susceptible to the benefits of North American civilization. Moreover, the existence of the League of Nations, of which all the South American countries except Mexico and Ecuador were charter members, imparted a sense of "courage" to these governments in confronting the hegemony of the United States. Could they not hope that the Geneva organization might lend them support and perhaps furnish them with a means of circumventing the Pan-American system? This naïve aspiration overlooked the fact that the League had not lost hope of someday obtaining the support of the United States and consequently wished to humor her; it also did not take into account Great Britain's primary concern to avoid at any price opposing herself to the United States government.

Thus a study of the international political relations in this area should focus on Latin America's situation vis-à-vis the United States and Europe. Would the disputes arising between Latin American nations be settled by the League of Nations—that is, essentially by Great Britain and France—or by the Pan-American conference, dominated by the United States? How, moreover, was the Monroe Doctrine to be interpreted?

The settlement of disputes between countries of the Western

Hemisphere seemed to be outside of the jurisdiction of the League of Nations, since in 1923 the governments of all these countries had agreed to sign the Gondra Treaty, according to which any disputes that could not be settled by diplomatic means must be submitted to a Pan-American commission of inquiry. However, this principle was not strictly applied.

The League of Nations did not intervene in a dispute between Chile, Peru, and Bolivia over the territory of Tacna and Arica (39,000 inhabitants). Chile had annexed this Peruvian territory in 1884, since the territory was to her a source of nitrates. When Peru demanded the restitution of her "Alsace-Lorraine," Bolivia came into the picture because the territory was her means of access to the sea. She demanded the port of Arica, the terminus of her only railroad. After having contemplated yielding to the demands of Bolivia, then having attempted to organize a plebiscite in the area, Chile and Peru finally entered into direct negotiations. The agreement of June 3, 1929, called for a partition that gave Chile the port of Arica and restored Tacna to Peru. The difficulties that might arise in the application of the treaty of partition were to be submitted to the arbitration of the United States. Bolivia also turned to this country when she protested a solution that totally ignored her interests.

In the Chaco dispute which set Bolivia against Paraguay, however, the League of Nations was not inactive despite the difficult position in which it found itself. For almost half a century these two states had claimed ownership of this territory which extended between two rivers, the Paraguay and the Pilcomayo. Paraguay declared that since it possessed the mouth of the Paraguay, it had the right to annex the region drained by this river and its tributaries. Bolivia, having failed to gain a "window" on the Pacific coast, wished at least to be able to make use of the Paraguay River in order to find a commercial outlet toward the Atlantic. Behind the smokescreen of these arguments lay the immediate economic advantages—the oil deposits in the Chaco territory.

When the first shots were fired between the opposing posts and patrols in December 1928, the Pan-American conference happened to be in session. It therefore immediately applied the principles laid down in the Gondra Treaty and asked the two states to submit the dispute to a commission that would determine who was to blame. Why did the Council of the League of Nations feel itself called upon in this case to address to Bolivia and Paraguay a "recommendation" that seemed to prepare the way for their application to Geneva for arbitration? The Council took this step at the insistence of Venezuela, who declared that she regarded this dispute as a "test case." If the Council declined to act on a South American question, this would amount to proof of its inability to apply the principles of the League's Covenant in this area; the South American states that wished to escape United States hegemony would lose all hope of finding the least encouragement or the least protection at Geneva: they would thus be forced to resign from the League of Nations. This was the prospect that led the Council to make a gesture—but in such a manner that the United States could not take offense: in offering the services of the League, Aristide Briand, President of the Council of the League, took great pains to explain that if the conflict were resolved through the Commission of Inquiry, he would be the first to offer congratulations. Thus the League gave priority to the Pan-American conference, but only on a provisional basis.

In the end the diplomatic advantage was won by the United States. When in January of 1929 Bolivia and Paraguay were preparing to bring their dispute before the Permanent Court of International Justice which, as a creation of the League of Nations, had not been recognized by the United States, the Pan-American Commission of Inquiry took pains to keep the matter under its own jurisdiction and succeeded in persuading the two states to appeal for an "American" arbitration. This was only the first stage in a long conflict that was to continue until 1938. But it was a significant stage, because it clearly demonstrated how much the United States wished to keep the European powers at a distance and how far the League of Nations wished to placate Washington.

When the Latin American countries realized that the League of Nations was incapable of acting in American matters, they almost all (with the exception of Chile) halted active participation in the Geneva meetings.

But although the United States had little difficulty in eliminating League of Nations intervention in matters pertaining to the Western Hemisphere, she had less success in attempting to have her patronage accepted by the states of Latin America. At the fifth Pan-American conference at Santiago in 1923, the first postwar reunion, and even more so at the sixth in Havana in 1928, resistance was openly expressed.

This opposition first suggested that the Monroe Doctrine be transformed into a "continental declaration" which, instead of expressing only the views and principles of the United States government, would give all the American countries mutual and reciprocal guarantees. This amounted to a manifestation of suspicion toward the United States. Unjustified suspicion, retorted Secretary of State Hughes in a speech on August 23, 1923. The United States, he continued, wanted only to protect the security of the Panama Canal and had no desire to interfere in the internal affairs of the South American states. However, he added, the United States government intended to reserve its exclusive right to interpret the Doctrine and to modify it when circumstances arose that required it to do so. Thus, this response not only recognized the existing state of affairs—that is, that the United States employed methods in Central America that differed from those in South America—but also confirmed the fears of the United States' adversaries, since it amounted to saying that the Monroe Doctrine was "flexible."

The same concerns reappeared in a slightly different form when a committee of jurists—the Rio Commission—attempted to establish the bases for an inter-American international law. The draft statement prepared by these experts embodied the precept of "nonintervention." No American nation would have the right to occupy any part whatsoever of another nation's territory, "even with the consent of the said republic," or to employ coercion to induce this other nation to modify its internal or external policy. This was a transparent allusion to the actions of the United States government in the Caribbean and Central America. Thus it was scarcely surprising that the State Department rejected the project. However, the delegate of El Salvador brought the matter before the Havana conference, where for the first time in the history of

Pan-American conferences, a heated political debate took place in the course of a meeting. Although all of the delegations did not exhibit the same degree of conviction in the matter (the strongest support for the El Salvador delegation came from Argentina, while that of Brazil was more reserved), the delegations were almost unanimous in demanding that the conference confirm the principle of nonintervention and equality of rights among all the American nations. The only two nations that abstained from expressing an opinion were Nicaragua, whose capital had just been occupied by United States forces, and Peru, where the reorganization of public finances was at that moment in the hands of an expert recently arrived from the United States. The State Department tolerated the reading of these declarations in the conference but opposed a vote of resolution. The right of independence, said the Secretary of State, does not preclude the right of intervention, which is still necessary, at least temporarily, "to provide stability in order to maintain independence." Besides which, how could the United States permit a situation to exist in which the property or lives of American citizens might be threatened by a civil war? This refusal was sufficient to defeat the El Salvador proposal.

Immediately after the Havana conference, American public opinion began to have its doubts about the effectiveness of "dollar diplomacy" and to realize that, despite the success of the economic and financial takeover, American political influence was being increasingly disputed. It became clear that the decline of the Pan-American idea could be attributed to Washington's interventionist policy in Central America. Thus, it was felt necessary to reassure the countries of South America. When the presidential elections of November 1928 brought a new figure to power, Herbert Hoover, the administration took into account this new tendency in public opinion. The President-elect considered it opportune, even before his inauguration, to make a "friendship tour" of South America, without overlooking the republic of Argentina, the principal area of anti-American sentiment. The new Secretary of State, Frank B. Kellogg, told the Senate on December 7, 1928, that the Monroe Doctrine was purely defensive. He consequently disavowed the "corollary" established in 1905, when President Theodore Roosevelt affirmed the right of the United States to exercise an "international police power." In his first speech after the inauguration, the new President condemned the policy of "dollar diplomacy," stating that the United States government "should not use troops to obtain or to enforce the terms of contracts between our citizens and foreign countries or citizens." This was to herald a new policy—a "good neighbor" policy—which was to be practiced from 1931 on.

The Organization of International Relations

During the ten years following the First World War, the big disputes—those arising out of the application of the peace treaties and those that came about through the operation of new forces in Asia or in Mediterranean Africa—were settled by compromise. This conciliatory spirit was undoubtedly a result of war weariness, but it also stemmed from an improvement in the economic situation, which calmed impatience in the people. In early 1929 the attitude of the general public toward international relations was inclined to be optimistic. It was, however, a precarious optimism, which left government circles with vague feelings of uncertainty when contemplating events beyond the immediate horizon. The underlying reason for this uncertainty was no doubt the failure of attempts to establish a system of international relations and to provide for resistance against aggression.

The Inadequacy of Collective Security

The Covenant of the League of Nations had laid down the principle of mutual assistance among the member states, but without establishing any definite system of military sanctions against an aggressor. The refusal of the United States to enter the Geneva organization struck a serious blow at the moral authority of the League and was to threaten the effectiveness of any economic sanctions provided for in Article 16 of the Covenant. The advocates of "collective security" in Geneva, who wished to protect the territorial status established in 1919–1920, set themselves the dual task of filling in the gaps in the system through the completion of its legal framework, and of drawing the United States into collaboration with the League. Four times their efforts failed. Why these setbacks?

The Permanent Court of International Justice, founded in accordance with Article 14 of the Covenant, had opened proceedings in The Hague in January of 1922. In accordance with the strictures of Great Britain and France, it had been attributed only an "optional" jurisdiction: that is, it was limited to litigations that were expressly referred to it by the states involved. Although reduced to this secondary role, it had nonetheless given rise to high hopes in Geneva, because it seemed to offer an opportunity to renew ties with the United States. After all, had not the American jurist Elihu Root, who had been Secretary of State during the presidency of Theodore Roosevelt, and who still enjoyed considerable prestige in the Republican party, collaborated as a private citizen in the preparation of the court's by-laws? Moreover, had not Washington agreed to consider the participation of the United States in the new institution in February of 1923? However, in September of 1926, the American Senate, having left the matter pending for three years, refused to ratify the international convention that was to make the United States' membership official. Senator Lodge declared that this would put the United States into the League of Nations.

Meanwhile France had been trying to enlarge upon the Covenant of the League of Nations, this time without any American participation, by means of a "Protocol for the peaceful settlement of international conflicts," sponsored by the Greek and Czechoslovak Ministers for Foreign Affairs, Nikos Politis and Eduard Beneš. The principal article of this protocol imposed the obligation on all member states to "cooperate loyally and positively" in the application of sanctions, even naval or military, if the Council of the League decided on such measures. Thus, it substituted a strict obligation for the mere "recommendation" provided by the Covenant. On October 2, 1924, this text was adopted by the Assembly of the League with the approval of the British government— Ramsay MacDonald's Labor cabinet. However, the return to power of the Conservatives one month later modified Britain's position. It is not possible, declared Austen Chamberlain, to widen the system of sanctions—that is, to increase the responsibilities assumed by the member states—since the League of Nations is weakened by the absence of the United States. Basically, this amounted to abandoning all effort toward making the Covenant more effective.

However, in April 1927 the sponsors of the Geneva organization were once again hopeful of a collaboration with the United States. Briand issued an appeal "to the American nation" in which he suggested the conclusion of a pact between the United States and France which would "outlaw" war. The French statesman's intention was to give evidence of good will and to calm the anti-French sentiments in the United States brought about by the question of war debts. American pacifist circles suggested the enlargement of this French proposal and the establishment of a general pact in which all the states would pledge themselves to settle their differences without resorting to war except in the case of legitimate self-defense. This suggestion, put forward by the Carnegie Endowment for International Peace, was adopted by the State Department. However, the "renunciation of war" formula if applied without reservation was likely to render all military action impossible, even if imposed as a sanction. To circumvent this objection, the Briand-Kellogg Pact in its final form implicitly allowed that recourse to war would be legal against any state violating the Covenant of the League of Nations or the Locarno Pact on the Rhine. On August 27, 1928, it was signed by all countries, including Germany, the Soviet Union, and Japan.

What was its effect in practice? It did not attempt to define either "legitimate self-defense" or "war of aggression" and thus risked being ineffective. Moreover, it did not imply that Washington had modified its attitude regarding European matters and would consider joining in a "defensive war" waged by the League against an aggressor state. "The United States is still just as much opposed as previously to any action which would aim at imposing peace by force and which might involve her in a European war," wrote James T. Shotwell, chief author of the American draft and official commentator on the pact. The Senate Foreign Affairs Committee took care to emphasize, after the Secretary of State himself had done so, that the new treaty provided "neither explicitly or implicitly" for any sanction, and that the United States did not intend to assume any obligations. The Secretary of State noted that the United States had made a gesture of peace, which was all it had wished to do. This gesture was primarily aimed at American public opinion. International politics seems to have played a subordinate role to domestic politics in Frank B. Kellogg's thinking on this matter.

When the French government resumed the initiative a year later, it embarked upon a new course. In his speech to the Assembly of the League of Nations on September 5, 1929, and then in his memorandum of May 17, 1930, Briand suggested the formation of a European "union" or "federation." He was inspired in this by an idea that Count Coudenhove-Kalergi had developed over a period of three years, and that had attracted the attention of the Interparliamentary Union the year before. With "Bolshevism on the one side and Americanism on the other," was it not necessary to draw together the states of Europe? By this suggestion Briand, a statesman whose name was connected with every effort undertaken by the League in eight years, implied that he no longer counted on obtaining United States participation in the defense of peace. Privately he also expressed his doubts on the solidity of the League of Nations. In short, the "Pan-European" plan seemed to him the only one that might permit the establishment of an effective system of security, strengthened and supported by economic cooperation.

But this project—which encountered some difficulties even in the drafting of its outline—aroused the suspicion of the great European powers from the outset. Germany saw in it an indirect means of guaranteeing the borders drawn in Eastern Europe in

1919, since the French memorandum gave evidence of a design to extend the Locarno Agreements over the entire continent. The Soviet Union thought that this federal link, intended to unite the European members of the League of Nations, was aimed at the formation of an anti-Soviet bloc. The British cabinet adopted the attitude of "cordial prudence" recommended to it by its diplomatic service. The realization of the French project, they felt, would curtail the authority of the League of Nations; it would disturb Britain's system of imperial relations which could not adjust to a continental framework; it would, above all, tend to place Great Britain in a difficult situation vis-à-vis the United States, since a European federation might take a political or even an economic stand that would be contrary to American interests.

Thus, with few exceptions, the European governments welcomed the French memorandum with serious reservations. Thereupon the study commission that Briand had established judged it expedient to postpone further examination of political questions, and turned to economic problems. It did not, however, manage to formulate a program. The "European" plan faded away.

The ardent supporters of the League of Nations considered that "collective security" implied the limitation of armaments. The measures imposed on Germany and the other conquered nations were to be the first step toward general disarmament. These expectations were realized to a certain extent in 1922 in the field of naval disarmament, but the question of land disarmament had not yet been touched upon. Only after the signing of the Locarno Agreements in December 1925 did the League Council decide to set up the Preparatory Disarmament Commission.

The commission, which included among its members not only the representative of Germany but also the official delegates of the United States and the U.S.S.R., became hopelessly entangled in preliminary debate during a long series of sessions that extended over five years. What should be considered "armaments": in other words, in what way could countries be compared which would take into account not only the state of their armed forces but also of their demographic resources, the vulnerablility of their frontiers, their economic resources—all important factors in "war potential"? What would be the most effective procedures: reduction of troop numbers and matériel or reduction of credit appropriations for national defense? Would it be possible to make a clear distinction between offensive and defensive arms, and to establish different rules for each? By what methods could the application of these measures be controlled?

On each of these points the French and German opinions were in constant opposition. On the war matériel question, the French delegation asserted the necessity of comparing not only the level of stocks but also their means of production—factories and labor force. On the question of military manpower, however, the number of troops actually in the service would be counted, not including the number of "trained reservists." The German delegation, of course, held the opposite viewpoint, since the Reich possessed an industrial potential far superior to that of France, while she was unable to increase the number of trained reservists since the Versailles Treaty had forbidden recruitment. Great Britain and the United States were able to arbitrate between these opposing arguments. In fact, their actions were largely favorable to the German viewpoint, whether it was a question of trained reservists or of potential for air warfare. The question of controls over disarmament gave rise to further disputes. The French government suggested that an international commission be entrusted with the task of supervising the execution of a proposed disarmament convention. Great Britain and the United States defeated this solution, citing both the practical difficulties and the respect for national sovereignties.

Thus, after five years of work the Preparatory Commission had nothing to show in December 1930 but a mere framework indicating the principles to be followed and a method to be employed; but it failed to specify the number of troops or the level of armaments and did not provide for a means of international control. Even this modest outline was accepted neither by the U.S.S.R., which considered it a product of "capitalist imperialism"; nor by Germany, which criticized it for not granting all the great powers "equal rights" on the question of armaments; nor by Poland, Rumania, and the Baltic States, which judged it necessary to with-hold their signatures so long as Russia did not give hers.

In short, there was no indication at that date whether the policy of collective disarmament would ever amount to anything. "It is less a question of fixing numbers of soldiers, cannon, and machine guns, than of instilling the desire not to use them," declared Aris-tide Briand. Thus, his appeal substituted the hope of a moral dis-armament for the prospect of an effective limitation of arms. This position looked rather like a retreat.

Thus, ten years after the birth of the League of Nations neither the consolidation of "collective security" nor agreement on the principles of a limitation of arms had been achieved. Was the conflict of interests a sufficient explanation for this lack of success? They could have been overcome if the Council of the League had been more resolute, and if public opinion had impelled the gov-ernments to take action. But the two great powers that domi-nated the Council at Geneva—Great Britain and France—never established a harmony of views on the principles of constructing a system for the maintenance of international peace. Moreover, the current of public opinion favoring the work of the League was not sufficiently widespread.

The Failure of Economic and Financial Cooperation

The organizers of the League of Nations considered that eco-nomic and financial cooperation among nations should be one of the means of establishing mutual trust and strengthening the peace, of avoiding the rising tension created by commercial rivalries and the jealousy between "have" and "have-not" nations. Such co-operation became possible when economic and financial conditions improved in Europe beginning in 1924. It depended, however, on gaining the cooperation of the United States, an important pro-vider of raw materials and capital. What was the reaction of gov-ernment and public opinion to these economic and financial relations?

The settlement of the debts owed to the United States by her war allies—these debts amounted to $10,400,000,000—had given rise to debates that during more than six years had often grown quite bitter. The European debtors, primarily France and Great Britain, had wanted to see a link established between Germany's payment of reparations and the repayment of their inter-Allied war debts. The American government, under pressure from the Senate, refused to accept this principle. However, in 1922 it decided to demand that its associates pay their debts according to the terms set by Congress: namely, spreading the reimbursement over forty-seven annual payments with an interest of 4.5 per cent. It later agreed to delay the payment dates and to reduce the rate of interest, which amounted to relinquishing a considerable part of the debt. The reduction was to have amounted to 20 per cent of the sum agreed upon in June 1923 with Great Britain, who had reorganized her public finances the previous year and who earnestly desired to maintain her credit in the interests of the London financial market. The agreements with Belgium and Italy in 1925 set the reduction at about 50 per cent, and those negotiated with the French government in April 1926 set the figure of 53 per cent.

Relations between France and the United States remained strained, however. French public opinion considered the American claims neither fair nor generous. Since the United States did not have an army capable of participating in the European military operations when she became a belligerent in 1917, since she had been absent from the battlefield for a year after her entry into the war, what could be more logical than that she shoulder a part of the common burden through a financial contribution? But American public opinion on the whole did not feel obligated to prove its generosity. Those who had received the loans had made use of them for the purchase of foodstuffs, raw materials, and war equipment in the United States. They had thus contracted commerical commitments. By what legal right could they now free themselves from their debt—that is, transfer it to the American taxpayer?

The United States Congress had a means of pressure at its disposal in this debate—the refusal of any new loan to the French government or to the cities of France, so long as the settlement of the war debt was not accepted. Therefore, the French government, needing American financial assistance to stabilize the franc, decided to sign the agreement of April 1926. But the parliament wished to add a "safeguard clause"—namely, to obtain a promise that the agreement could be revised if France did not receive the expected reparations payments from Germany. This relation between the debt question and the reparations question seemed obvious to the French public, since the reduction in German payments had been the work of a committee presided over by an American.[1] It was, however, deemed unacceptable by the American Congress. Discussion continued until the French parliament resigned itself to ratifying the agreement in 1929 without inserting the safeguard clause. True, this clause remained in the form of a "reservation," but it was contractually invalid.

Thus at the end of this long controversy—the study of which is interesting in that it demonstrates how difficult it is to ask two nations to try to understand their respective points of view—American diplomacy succeeded in imposing its will upon the European debtors with the exception of the U.S.S.R. But this American success was only temporary: whatever the letter of the agreements, the actual settlement of the debts remained dependent on the fulfillment of the reparations payments.

The confusion that economic nationalism and the unequal distribution of raw materials or fuel resources encouraged in commercial relations had been deplored by Wilson's doctrine as the underlying reason for political difficulties. The League of Nations, however, had not shown great assiduity in acting on this problem. When Italy expressed her desire in the first League of Nations Assembly to see the establishment of equal access for all to the great raw material markets, examination of her suggestion was postponed indefinitely. Why had the European economy, despite the recent improvement, been so far outdistanced by the United States, whose economy was astonishingly vigorous? The chief cause of this inequality seemed to lie in the existence of tariff barriers, which hindered free exchange. But how could the European states be persuaded to abandon their protectionist policies, supplemented by quotas and prohibitions?

[1] The Dawes Plan.

The International Economic Conference, which convened in Geneva in May 1927 on the initiative of the Council of the League of Nations, aimed to prepare for a "relaxation" of tariffs and to persuade the United States to comprehend the economic and financial needs of Europe. The results were disappointing. The conference, at which labor organizations were only sparsely represented, recommended the development of the scientific organization of labor and the rationalization of industrial production. It reacted favorably toward the extension of cartels. On the other hand, it touched neither upon the question of international emigration, which was essential for the relief of those regions of Europe where unemployment was endemic, nor upon the war debts, an important factor in monetary stability. As for the tariff system, it merely recommended to the nations that they "reduce excessive tariffs which are harmful to international trade," and obtained no result other than a slowdown in the increase of custom duties.

The economic policy of the continental nations was no doubt largely to blame for the neglect of this question. The governments feared that if they lowered the tariff barriers, they would harm certain industries and increase unemployment and even, in the process, close down industries that would be indispensable to national defense efforts. Public opinion everywhere was more or less indifferent to the theories of the free-exchange economists. But the attitude of the United States was the decisive factor. She refused to permit discussion of the emigration question and the inter-Allied debts. She indicated that far from lowering tariffs, she was contemplating increasing them. How could the European states agree further to open their territories to American products without receiving any return concession?

Conclusion to Book III

According to their critics, the peace treaties had imposed intolerable conditions on the Continent. These critics protested that there were territorial clauses that were contrary to Wilsonian principles and that could lead rapidly to new conflicts; and, furthermore, that there were clauses that according to John Maynard Keynes would complete "the work of destruction" started by the war. To what extent were these prophecies borne out by 1929?

The "revisionism" of the Magyars, of the advocates of Austro-German union, of the German minorities in Poland and Czechoslovakia, often incited verbal protests; it gave rise to repeated incidents which encumbered the agenda of the League of Nations Council; it continued to assert itself through declarations of principle that were made with an eye to the future; however, it did not produce immediate results. The resistance of the Little Entente, supported by French diplomacy, neutralized the Hungarian demands which threatened to touch off the "powder keg" of Europe. The staunch opposition of the French government sufficed to block the *Anschluss* project. Moreover, the incessant disputes over the status of Danzig went no further than the stage of legal discussions. Of course, the conquered nations never gave up their claims and demands. Hungarian propaganda persisted, the Austrian government repeated on every occasion possible that union with Germany had been merely postponed, and German political circles announced their intention to "bring the Polish question to the forefront" as soon as the reparations question was settled. But they were well aware that they would never obtain a peaceful revision, and that they were in no condition to back up their actions with force. The German government had no intention of going to war with France in 1929 or even with Poland, basically; and even though the supervision of disarmament had been ended in 1927, the Germans still respected the military clauses of the Versailles Treaty, except in certain minor details.

Criticism of the economic clauses of the peace treaties proved to be accurate in part, since the total sum of the German reparations had been reduced on two occasions, once by the Dawes Plan and once by the Young Plan. However, its forecast of Germany's economic future was quite erroneous. The report of the agent-general for reparations, Gilbert Parker, noted that, owing to investments of foreign capital and to extensions of credit granted by American and British banks, Germany was "back on her feet." This was an essential factor in the economic reconstruction of Europe.

Lastly, the appeal for the rising of the proletariat issued by the first Congress of the Communist International in March 1919 failed to provoke a lasting response in Europe. After the unsettling events in the Ruhr in March 1920 and in Bavaria in October 1923, Germany settled down to relative stability. The British Communist party never gained much ground despite the critical unemployment situation which had become endemic and despite the considerable number of workers involved in strike action in 1920 and 1926. In France the Communist electorate, which numbered 875,000 in 1924 (7.9 per cent of the eligible voters) grew to 1,060,000 in 1928 (9.3 per cent). But the party declined considerably in 1929. In Italy the Communists had been unable to prevent the rise of fascism or to hinder its consolidation. When Stalin seized control of the Soviet power structure during the autumn of 1927 he criticized the theory of "world revolution," so dear to Trotsky, renounced this "hooligan policy," and declared that it was possible to "build socialism in one country." For some time the effect of these declarations soft-pedaled the aggressive propaganda of the Comintern.

Despite these positive facts, contemporary observers of international affairs were aware of three signs of uncertainty:

Economically, although German industry and commerce had reached the level considered necessary by Great Britain, this recovery was at the mercy of the flow of international capital. A halt in the flood of American investments was all that would be required to produce a major crisis in Germany. Furthermore, Europe's recovery was far from complete, since Russia had not been reintegrated with the continental economy. How could the balance of economic forces in Europe be achieved if it were cut off from a mass of 160,000,000 consumers?

Socially, the unemployment crisis in Britain, where the number of jobless rose from 935,000 in 1926 to 1,000,000 in 1929, was becoming a permanent condition. In Germany it increased from 123,000 in 1927 to 389,000 in 1929. It was cause of deep concern to Louis Loucheur, French Minister for Economic Affairs, who emphasized the gravity of the situation in a speech in August 1929.

Politically, the "division" of Europe into three types of state— dictatorship of the proletariat, fascist dictatorship, and parliamentary democracy—encouraged suspicion and antagonism, not only between governments, but also among peoples, accentuating the conflicts of national interests. Furthermore, the existence in Moscow, Warsaw, Budapest, Madrid, and Rome of political systems whereby citizens were in fact forbidden to engage in free discussion of international problems created opportunities for adventurist policies. "The unification of the principles upon which the state is founded will no doubt be a great blessing to Europe," wrote Guglielmo Ferrero in 1929—perhaps the most utopian ambition yet.

If we are to judge from public opinion, there is no doubt that the balance shifted toward peace in 1929. After years of great agitation directly following the conclusion of the peace treaties, when periods of social unrest were frequent and nationalistic emotions ran high, public sentiment calmed down with the return of prosperity. The quest for peaceful policies indicated by the Locarno Agreements and the pact renouncing war further reassured the public. In 1929 almost all of the people of Europe approved of the efforts being made to prevent conflict. These currents in public opinion seemed to be the greatest hope for peace in Europe.

General Conclusions

The dominant feature in the world outlook of 1919 was the "decline of Europe." To what extent had Europe recovered her world role ten years after the end of the war, and under what conditions did the relations between the continents progress?

Step by step Europe was continuing to win back her place in the world economy. In 1926 the world's total volume of trade amounted to $61,887,000,000; and Europe's share, including the U.S.S.R., was 45.2 per cent, whereas in 1920 it had fallen to 41 per cent. In 1929, with an over-all figure of $66,708,000,000, Europe's share was 51 per cent.[1] At the same time the nations of Europe had succeeded in maintaining the political footholds on the Asian and African continents that had been so gravely threatened at the end of the Great War.

In the Far East, Japanese expansion had come to an abrupt halt, which was due principally to the efforts of the United States government, but which chiefly benefited the European powers for the time being. The Chinese nationalist movement had been checked in 1926–1927 when it took on the appearance of a xenophobic insurrection. British diplomacy had successfully taken advantage of the anxiety aroused by Soviet propaganda among the

[1] It must not be forgotten that in 1913 it was 61 per cent.

Chinese propertied classes. True, it had been forced to make some adjustments by relinquishing the "concessions" and handing back control of China's customs, but it had saved the essential features of Britain's economic influence. In 1929 Soviet policy, which three years previously had seemed on the verge of succeeding, was now a total failure.

In India, where a movement of resistance to British domination had appeared in 1919, events took a serious turn in 1921 when Gandhi attempted to extract a promise of political autonomy as a preface to independence from the British government by his campaign of "noncooperation." However, the schisms that had arisen within the National Congress since 1924, had weakened the movement. The antagonism between Muslims and Hindus, which had been quiescent since 1916, reappeared after the fall of the Ottoman caliphate at a time when the Hindus feared seeing the Muslims gain too loud a voice in political affairs. In its exercise of voting rights granted by the British government in 1919, the limited electorate demonstrated that it was far from homogeneous. The various "minority" groups that existed within the Hindu population itself showed that they distrusted the majority. And finally, during the two years of Gandhi's imprisonment, when he was unable to keep the leadership of the movement, the slogan of "noncooperation" was challenged. Opposing Gandhi's followers, who refused to take any part in political or administrative affairs, were the moderates who thought it expedient to attempt to cooperate with the British authorities in the interest of the Indian people. In fact, the statute of 1919, which had been suspended for seven years, was applied in 1926, signifying a brief respite in the struggle.

In the Mediterranean region, the resistance movements, both nationalist and religious, which had challenged European domination in North Africa, were all crushed. Morocco and Tunisia were quiet in 1929, and Italy reconquered Libya. Even in Egypt, where British domination had experienced critical moments between 1919 and 1924, the Nationalist party, although retaining a large majority in all elections, tolerated a government led by moderates. In Syria and in Iraq, France and Great Britain respectively, after several years of difficulties, had succeeded in imposing their mandates.

The use of arms had played a role in this consolidation of European interests in Morocco, Libya, Iraq, and Syria. But in India and Egypt even recourse to force did not suffice to maintain British domination, any more than it did to stem the tide of Chinese nationalism. In all of these events the cause of European influence or domination was greatly served by the differences of opinion within the nationalist movements between intransigents and opportunists. Nationalist resistance to the propaganda of the Communist International was similarly helpful. Chiang Kai-shek destroyed Soviet influence in China by force. Gandhi openly disavowed communist ideology. In March of 1924, Zaghlul had the chiefs of the Communist party arrested, as the party had made some progress among Jewish circles in Egypt.

These, then, were circumstances that refuted the prophecies of those pessimists who in 1925 had foreseen the "twilight of the white nations," and that encouraged those who still believed in Europe's vitality.

However, despite these facts, there were causes for anxiety.

European interests were not immediately threatened by Japanese imperialism in the area of intercontinental relations. The attitude of the United States, on the other hand, was the cause of serious concern to a large segment of European public opinion.

True, the political expansion of the United States did not cause alarm among Europeans; only Latin America had reasons for concern. But United States economic policy aroused feelings of annoyance which were sometimes bitterly expressed.

The question of freedom of the seas was at the forefront of these concerns. If, in the event of a European conflict, Britain wished to exercise the right of blockade against another state within the framework of the sanctions provided for by the Covenant of the League of Nations, would the United States, not a member of the League, agree to honor such a blockade and allow her maritime commerce to be controlled by British cruisers? The conclusion of a pact renouncing war opened the way to a solution.

The United States could promise to prohibit her citizens from engaging in any commercial relations with a nation that violated the pact. But would the State Department honor such a pledge?

Another aspect of this anxiety was economic and financial imperialism. American observers were aware of the increasing "unpopularity" of the United States in these areas. The settlement of the war debts was the focal point of this controversy. How could the American Congress continue to demand payment of these debts while at the same time, through its tariff policies, it set about obstructing importation into the United States, thereby depriving the debtors of a means of discharging their debts? The Republican administration was criticized in American intellectual circles for its "inconsistencies" and its "lack of logic."

Contemporary observers of international affairs were attracted to the idea of organizing Europe's economic life by forming a customs union which would provide a means of opposing the United States position and induce her to lower her tariffs. The failure of Aristide Briand's "European" project spelled an end to this hope.

Finally, attempts at establishing a system for promoting peace had been unsuccessful. True, the Covenant of the League of Nations had been complemented by two great "regional arrangements"—the Washington treaties and the Locarno Agreements—which were of unequal significance (the mutual guarantee clauses contained in the Locarno Agreements were absent from the Washington treaties), but both of which implied a promise of "concerted action" on the part of those who had signed. True, the pact renouncing war had been signed by the two great powers whose abstention had weakened the League of Nations. All this led certain statesmen closely linked with the work at Geneva—Eduard Beneš, for example—to declare their optimism. It was their hope that the League of Nations was about to enter into a "constructive" era. However, the activities of the League were criticized in Paris, where conservative quarters feared that the Preparatory Disarmament Commission was about to pave the way for German rearmament; in Berlin, where the nationalists considered it an instrument of the victors, designed to prevent either the union of Austria with Germany or the revision of the German-Polish border; and in London, where the Conservative press considered it dangerous to the unity of the empire. Even more serious was the problem that arose with each crisis in the Council of the League, where opinion was divided between the partisans of military sanctions and supporters of moral sanctions. How valuable would the Geneva system be in the event of a serious problem? This doubt was the "great obstacle" in the way of disarmament, according to Paul Mantoux at the conclusion of seven years as director of the League's political services.

Thus, those observers most attached to the spirit of the Geneva organization did not share the optimism that Mantoux believed it appropriate to express. "Atmosphere of disappointment," "loss of confidence": these were the words that came from their pens. The League of Nations, noted Hugh Spender, "is nothing in itself," since the success of its efforts depends entirely on the good will of the member states in "making their foreign policies conform to the principles of the Covenant." The debates take place, said George Scelle, "in a sort of dead-end atmosphere" and do not succeed in erecting a barrier against tendencies dangerous to peace. It has not yet found a "stable basis," wrote Alfred Zimmern. "The nature of the cooperation between its members changes from year to year, sometimes from month to month."

Where was the remedy to be found? Some looked to a thorough remodeling of international institutions. They proposed the adoption of a "supranational concept" whereas the Covenant of the League had confirmed itself to establishing "a juxtaposition of sovereignties." The others did not believe that the most serious difficulties were organic, but noted that the effectiveness of the system depended entirely on the state of mind of the governments, determined by the attitude of the peoples. According to them, the League had "not yet received the support of public opinion, without which it cannot survive."

A feeling of doubtful satisfaction, a will toward optimism which did not however succeed in overcoming a feeling of precariousness —this was the spirit of the times. But nothing foretold an imminent crisis. However, in the autumn of 1929 a surprising event took place in the very country where stability seemed to be most assured: the economic crisis that broke out in the United States was to extend throughout the entire world.

Bibliography

GENERAL TITLES

The collections of diplomatic documents, which are so abundant for the period between 1871 and 1914, are much rarer for 1914–1929.

For the period 1914–1918, only American and Russian archives have been partially open to historians, who have published volumes of correspondence: in the United States, *Papers Relating to the Foreign Relations of the U.S.A.: The World War*, Washington, 1928–1940, 13 vols. (the volumes on Russia, 1918, are particularly important); in Russia, *Mejdounarodnia Otnochenia v epokhou imperialismy, 3rd series, 1914–17*, Moscow, 1930. The Italian collection *I documenti diplomatici italiani*, cited below, will, in its fifth series, offer several volumes on the period 1914–1919, but so far only one volume has been published (1954); it concerns the first months of the war (August 2–October 16, 1914). Three other volumes have been published on the period 1919–1929.

Finally, the German Commission of Inquiry, which in 1919 made a study of "the causes of the defeat," has published a selection of documents from its report *Das Werk des Untersuch ungsauschusses der verfassunggebenden deutschen Nationalversammlung und der deutschen Reichstags*, Berlin, 1928, 31 vols. All these publications—neither Great Britain nor France are represented yet—are very fragmentary. One has therefore to try and fill in the holes with the study of firsthand accounts. They will be cited in my work below.

For the period of 1919–1930, three large collections are in the process of being prepared for publication; they are as follows:

I. *Documents on British Foreign Policy 1919–1939*, 1st series, London, 1947 (10 volumes have appeared on the period of 1919–1929).
II. *Papers relating to the foreign relations of the U.S.A.*, Washington (23 volumes have already appeared).
III. *I documenti diplomatici italiani*, Rome, 1953, 6th series (1918–1922 [one volume has already appeared: November, 1918–January, 1919]); 7th series (1922–1935 [two volumes have already appeared: October, 1922–February, 1924]).

There are still no such similar publications in France, Germany, or Russia.

The general works that were of particular use are as follows:

General history for the period between 1914 and 1945

Albrecht-Carrier, R. *France, Europe and the Two World Wars*, Geneva, 1960.
Beloff, M. *The Great Powers. Essays in Twentieth-Century Politics*, London, 1959.
Chambers, F. *The Age of Conflict, 1914–1943*, New York, 1944.
Crouzet, M. *L'epoch contemporaine. A la recherche d'une civilization nouvelle (Histoire generales des civilizations*, Vol. VII) 2nd ed., Paris, 1959.
Ezgang, R. *Europe in Our Time: 1914 to the Present*, Boston, 1958.
Fabre-Luce, A. *L'histoire de la révolution Européenne*, Paris, 1954 (essay).
Langsam, W. *The World Since 1914*, 5th ed., New York, 1943.
Lhuillier, D. *De la Sainte-Alliance au pacte atlantique*, Vol. II:1898–1954, Neuchâtel, 1955.
Pirenne, J. *Les grands courants de l'histoire universelle*, Vol. VI:1904–1939, Neuchâtel, 1955.
Salvatorelli, L. *Storia del Novecento*, Milan, 1957.

The First World War

Renouvin, P. *La crise européene et la première guerre mondiale*, 3rd ed., Paris, 1948 (Peoples and Civilizations, Vol. XIX).
La revue d'histoire de la guerre mondiale (17 vols. appeared from 1926–1929 under the direction of C. Bloch and P. Renouvin) published a large number of articles.

For the years 1919–1929

Barbagallo, C. *Storia universale. Evo contemporaneo, 1919–29*, Turin, 1954.
Baumont, M. *La faillité de la paix, 1918–1939*, 3rd ed., Paris, 1951

(Peoples and Civilizations, Vol. XX, which is by far the most important volume of the work).

Carr, E. H. *International Relations Between the Two World Wars,* Paris, 1947.

Duroselle, J. B. *Histoire diplomatique de 1919 à nos jours,* Paris, 1953, 2nd ed., 1957.

Gathorne-Hardy, G. M. *A Short History of International Affairs, 1920–1938,* London, 1938.

Giraud, E. *La nullité de la politique internationale des grandes démocraties, 1919–1939,* Paris, 1948.

Rain, P. *L'Europe de Versailles (1919–1939), Les traités de paix, leur application, leur mutilation,* Paris, 1945.

The Survey of International Affairs, published by Arnold Toynbee (London, 1925, 14 vols.) is of monumental importance, particularly on account of its chronicles and bibliographical notes.

The major works relating to the foreign policy of a particular country (for the period as a whole) are as follows:

The United States

Bailey, T. *A Diplomatic History of the American People,* 3rd ed., New York, 1946.

Bemis, S. *A Diplomatic History of the U.S.,* New York, 1936; and *The United States as a World Power, 1900–1950,* New York, 1950.

Nevins, A., and L. Hacker. *The U.S. and Its Place in World Affairs, 1918–1943,* Boston, 1943.

Rae, J., and T. Mahoney. *The U.S. in World History, from Its Beginning to World Leadership,* New York, 1949.

Japan

Akagi. *Japan's Foreign Relations,* Tokyo, 1936.

Ishida, S. *Japan Among Foreign Powers. A Survey of International Relations,* New York, 1940.

Russia

Potemkine, V. *Histoire de la diplomatie,* Vols. I and II, Paris, 1956.
There are no works of the same variety on the other major powers.

Economic questions have given rise to a number of studies:

Clark, C. *The Conditions of Economic Progress,* London, 1940.

de Jouvenel, B. *L'economie mondiale au XXième siècle,* Paris, 1944.

James, E. *Histoire de la pensée économique au XXième siècle,* 2 vols., Paris, 1955.

Memorandum sur la production et le commerce, 1913 and 1923–27, League of Nations Press, Geneva, 1929.

Pommery, L. *Aperçu d'histoire économique contemporaine, 1890–1939,* Paris, 1945.

Richardson, J. *Economic Disarmament,* London, 1939.

Svennilson, I. *Growth and Stagnation in the European Economy, 1913–1945,* Geneva, 1954 (important).

Truchy, H., and M. Bye. *Les relations économiques internationales,* Paris, 1948.

Among the economic histories of Europe, see in particular S. B. Clough and C. A. Cole, *Economic History of Europe,* 3rd ed., Boston, 1952.

Demographic questions, on the other hand, have hardly been studied at all. But see in particular M. Reinhard, *Histoire de la population mondiale,* Paris, 1949 (the first essay deals with the period 1700–1947).

It has been necessary to limit this bibliography and those for each chapter to somewhat modest proportions. In a work of synthesis, any other method would have made the lists too long and quite unusable. The author has therefore primarily kept the studies containing more recent research or those that offered new interpretations. Of other works, he cited only those that had been most useful to him. Firsthand reports were rarely indicated, and when they were not to be found, especially in the case of questions referring to the treaties, they were adequately explained. In order to complete the list of titles given in this volume, one has but to turn to W. L. Langer and E. Armstrong, *Foreign Affairs Bibliography* (Vol. I.:1919–1930), New York, 1942.

CHAPTER 1: THE UNDERLYING FORCES

On economic questions

The large *Economic and Social History of the World War,* published by the Carnegie Foundation under the direction of J. T. Shotwell (126 vols., New York, 1922) is essential.

The works relating to the war economy of each major power often supply useful information on the history of international relations; for lack of space they have not been quoted here.

However, for relations between the coalitions, the following should be read:

Gratz and Schüller. *Die äussere Wirtschaftspolitik Oesterreich-Ungarns. Mitteleuropäische Pläne,* Vienna, 1926.

Lyddon, W. *British War Missions to the U.S. 1914–1918,* London, 1938.

Petit, L. *Histoire des finances extérieurs de la France pendant la guerre*, Paris, 1929.

On the role of the blockade

Duttwyler, H. *Der Seekrieg und die Wirtschaftspolitik der neutralen Staaten*, Zurich, 1945.
Guichard, L. *Histoire du blocus naval*, Paris, 1929.
Lank, F. *Der Wirtschaftskrieg und die Neutralen, 1914–1918*, Berlin, 1940.
Siney (N.C.). *The Allied Blockade of Germany, 1914–16*, Ann Arbor, 1957.

On submarine warfare

Gibbon, R., and M. Prendergast. *The German Submarine War*, London, 1931.
Laurens, A. *Histoire de la guerre sous-marine Allemande*, Paris, 1930.
Michelson, N. *Der U-Bootskrieg, 1914–1918*, Leipzig, 1921.
Salter, Sir A. *Allied Shipping Control*, Oxford, 1921.

On the role of social matters

Dolléans, E. *Histoire du mouvement ouvrier*, Vol. II, Paris, 3 vols., 1952–53.
Fainsod, M. *International Socialism and the World War*, Cambridge, Mass., 1935.
Halévy, E. *L'ere des tyrannies. Études sur le socialisme et la guerre*, Paris, 1939.
Van der Slice, A. *International Labor, Diplomacy and Peace, 1914–1919*, Philadelphia, 1941.

On nationalist movements

Boehm, R. *Europa irredenta*, Berlin, 1925.
Ruyssen, T. *Les Minorités nationales de l'Europe et la guerre mondiale*, Paris, 1923.

CHAPTER 2: THE WAR IN EUROPE (AUGUST, 1914–FEBRUARY, 1917)

On the foreign policy of the belligerents

Pingaud, A. *Histoire diplomatique de la France pendant la guerre*, 3 vols., Paris, 1935–1945.

Potemkine, V. *Histoire de la diplomatie*, Vols. I and II, Paris, 1956.
Smith, J. C. *The Russian Struggle for Power, 1914–17. A Study of Russian Foreign Policy during the First World War*, New York, 1956.

It is impossible to give a complete list of references, therefore the particular importance of a few among them are as follows:

Poincaré, R. *Au service de la France: Neuf années de souvenirs*, 11 vols., Paris, 1925, and succeeding years.
von Bethmann-Hollweg, T. *Betrachtungen zum Woltkriege*, 2 vols., Berlin, 1919–22.
Grey, E. *Twenty-five Years*, London, 1924.
The biographies of Wilson by R. S. Baker, *Woodrow Wilson, Life and Letters*, 4 vols., New York, 1931; and of Briand by G. Suarez, 5 vols., Paris, 1941–55, are interesting.

On the intervention of Italy

Galli, C. *Il Ministro di San Guilano e la politica estera italiana all'inizio della prima gerra mondiale*, in the N. Riv. Storica, May, 1955.
Toscano, M. *Il patto di Londra, Storia diplomatica dell' intervento italiano, 1914–1915*, Bologna, 1934; and *La Serbia e l'intervento in guerra dell'Italia*, Milan, 1939.
Volpe, G. *Il popolo italiano tra la pace e la guerra, 1914–1915*, Milan, 1940.

On the Balkan questions

Cosmin, N. *L'Entente et la Grèce pendant la grande guerre*, 2 vols., Paris, 1926.
Frangulis, N. *La Grèce et la crise mondiale*, 2 vols., Paris, 1926.
Jaschke, G. *Der Turanismus der Jungtürken. Zur osmanischen Aussenpolitik im Weltkriege*, Leipzig, 1941.
Mühlmann, C. *Das deutsch-türkische Waffenbündnis im Weltkriege*, Leipzig, 1940.
Notovic, F. *Diplomaticeskaia borba v gody pervoj mirovoj voiny* (The Diplomatic Struggle during the First Years of the World War), Moscow, 1947.

On the Belgian question

Pirenne, H. *La Belgique et la guerre mondiale*, Paris, 1928.
Wullus-Rudiger, J. *La Belgique et la crise européenne*, Villeneuve-sur-lot, 1944.
General Van Overstraeten published the *War Diaries of Albert I*, Brussells, 1923.

On the Far East question

La Fargue, T. *China and the World War*, Stanford, 1937.
Li, T. Y. *Woodrow Wilson's China Policy*, New York, 1952.
Renouvin, P. *La question d'Extrème-Orient, 1840–1940*, 3rd ed., Paris, 1953.
Toscano, M. *Guerra diplomatica en Estremo Oriente. I trattati delle ventun domande*, 2 vols., Milan, 1950 (important).

On the war aims of the belligerents

Charles-Roux, Fr. *La paix des empires centraux*, Paris, 1947.
Gatzk, H. W. *Germany's Drive to the West. A Study of Germany's Western War Aims during the First World War*, Baltimore, 1950.
Howard, H. N. *The Partition of Turkey, a Diplomatic History, 1919–1923*, Norman, 1931.
Kerner, J. "Russia, the Straits and Constantinople," in the *Journal of Modern History*, 1929, pp. 400–415.
Renouvin, P. "Constantinople et les detroits," in the *Revue du droit international*, 1930, pp. 578–591.
Toscano, M. *Gli accordi di San Giovanni di Morienna*, Milan, 1936.

On the neutrals

Olivar Bertrand, R. "Repercusiones, en España, de la Primera Guerre mondiale," in *Cuadernos de historia diplomatica*, Vol. III, pp. 3–51, Saragossa, 1956.
Rüchti. *Geschichte der Schweiz wahrend d. Weltkrieges*, Berne, 1928.
Vandendorsch, A. *Dutch Foreign Policy since 1815. A Study of Small Power Politics*, The Hague, 1959.

CHAPTER 3: THE UNITED STATES ENTERS THE WAR

On the practice of neutrality

The report of the Senate Investigation Committee presided over by G. Nye, *Report of the Special Committee on Investigation of the Munitions Industry*, Washington, 1935–1936, is essential material.

The *Lansing Papers*, 2 vols., Washington, 1929–1942, also contain exceedingly important information.

Bailey, T. *The Policy of the U.S. Government Toward the Neutrals, 1917–1918*, Stanford, 1942.
Morissey, A. M. *The American Defense of Neutral Rights, 1914–1917*, Cambridge, Mass., 1939.

Orvik, N. *The Decline of Neutrality, 1914–1922,* Oslo, 1953.
Savage, S. *Policy of the U.S. Toward Maritime Commerce in War,* 2 vols., Washington, 1936.
Williams, W. C. *William J. Bryan,* New York, 1936.
George, A. and J. *Woodrow Wilson and Colonel House. A Personality Study,* New York, 1956.

On the entry into the war

Millis, W. *Road to War,* London, 1935.
Notter, H. *The Origins of the Foreign Policy of Woodrow Wilson,* Baltimore, 1937.
Spencer, S. S. *Decision for War, 1917, The* Laconia *Sinking and the Zimmermann Telegram as Key Factors in the Public Reaction against Germany,* Ringe, 1953.
Tansill, C. C. *America Goes to War,* Boston, 1938.
Tuchman, B. *The Zimmermann Telegram,* London, 1959.
Witke, C. *German-Americans and the World War,* Ohio University, 1936.

On the attempts at peacemaking in Europe

Beneš, E. *Souvenirs de guerre et de révolution,* 2 vols., Paris, 1925.
Briggs, M. *George D. Herron and the European Settlement,* Stanford, 1932.
Charles-Roux, Fr. *La paix des empires centraux,* Paris, 1947.
Epstein, K. "The Development of German-Austrian War Aims in the Spring of 1917" in the *Journal of Central European Affairs,* April, 1957, pp. 24–48.
Fester, R. *Die Politik des Kaisers Karls und der Wendepunkt des Weltkrieges,* Munich, 1925.
Gwyn, D. *The Vatican and War in Europe,* London, 1941.
Loiseau, I. "Une mission diplomatique près du Saint-Siège, 1914–1919," in the *Revue des Deux Mondes,* May 1, 1956, pp. 54–73.
Mamatey, V. *The U.S. and East-Central Europe, 1914–1918,* Princeton, 1957.
Martin, L. *Peace Without Victory, Woodrow Wilson and the British Liberals,* New Haven, 1958.
Meinecke, F. *Kühlmann und die papstliche Friedenskation,* Berlin, 1928.
Passivirta, J. *Suomea istenaïsvyyskysymis, 1917* (The Problem of Finnish Independence in 1917), Helsinki, 1947.
Prince Sixtus of Bourbon-Parma, *L'offre de paix séparée de l'Autriche-Hongrie,* Paris, 1920.

Wullus-Rudiger, J. A. *La Belgique et la crise européenne, 1914–44*, 2 vols., Villeneuve-sur-lot, 1944.

CHAPTER 4: THE COLLAPSE

On Russia's separate peace

Carr, E. *The Bolshevik Revolution, 1917–1923*, 3 vols., New York, 1953.
Fokke, A. "Na scien i za koulissam bretskoi tragikomedi," in the *Arkhiv Rousskoi Revoloutsii*, 1930, pp. 5–207.
Gankin, O., and H. Fisher. *The Bolsheviks and the World War: The Origins of the Third International*, Stanford University, 1940.
Gatzke, H. W. "Zu den Deutsch-russischen Beziehungen im Sommer, 1918," in *Viertelj fur zeitgeschichte*, January, 1955, pp. 67–99.
Hahlweg, W. *Lenins Ruckkehr nach Russland, 1917*, Leiden, 1957 (German documents).
Makareva, P. M. "Japonskaja intervencija ma russokum Dalnem Vostoke, 1918–1922" in *Pripodav ist*, Skole, 1948, pp. 19–42.
Morley, J. W. *The Japanese Thrust into Siberia, 1918*, New York, 1957.
Pares, B. *The Fall of the Russian Monarchy*, New York, 1939.
Pipes, R. *The Formation of the Soviet Union, Communism and Nationalism, 1917–1923*, Cambridge, Mass., 1954.
Sukhanov, N. *The Russian Revolution, 1917* (translation), London, 1955.
Volkswart, J. *Brest-Litovsk*, Stutgaart, 1937.
Warth, R. D. *The Allies and the Russian Revolution, from the Fall of the Monarchy to the Peace of Brest-Litovsk*, Durham, 1954.
Wheeler-Bennett, J. *Brest-Litovsk, the Forgotten Peace*, London, 1938 (important).
White, J. A. *The Siberian Intervention*, New York, 1952.
Williams, W. A. *American-Russian Relations*, New York, 1952.
Zeman, Z. *Germany and the Revolution in Russia, 1915–1918*, London, 1958 (documents taken from the German archives).

On the Bulgarian armistice and the collapse of Austria-Hungary

Birman, M. A. *Revolujucionnaja Situacija v Bolgarii, 1918–19*, Moscow, 1957.
Briggs, M. *George D. Herron and the European Settlement*, Stanford University, 1932.
Fellner, F. (ed.). *Das Politische Tagebuch Joseph Redlichs, 1908–1919*, 2 vols., Graz, 1953.
Kerchnawe, H. *Der Zusammenbruch d. oesterreich-ungar. Wehrmacht im Herbst 1918*, Vienna, 1921.

Mamatey, S. "The U.S. and Bulgaria in World War One," in the *American Slavonic and Eastern European Review*, April, 1953, pp. 232–57.

Opočensky, J. *Umsturz im Mitteleuropa. Der Zusammenbruch Oesterreich-Ungarns und die Geburt der kleinen Entente* (translated from the Czech), Hellerau, 1932.

On the defeat of Germany

Berlau, A. J. *The German Social-Democratic Party, 1914–21*, New York, 1949 (important for the "stab in the back" question).

Schwertfeger, A. F. *Die Politischen und militarischen Verantwortlichkeiten im verlauf der offensive von 1918*, Berlin, 1928.

von Kühlmann, R. *Erinnerungen*, Berlin, 1953 (firsthand report).

On the collapse of the Ottoman Empire

Howard, N. *The Partition of Turkey, 1913–1923*, Norman, 1931.

Kedourie, E. *England and the Middle East. The Destruction of the Ottoman Empire, 1914–1921*, London, 1956.

On the armistices

Alberti, General. *L'Italia e la fine de la guerra mondiale*, 2 vols., Rome, 1924 (on the Villa-Giusti armistice).

Larcher, A. *La guerre Turque dans la guerre mondiale*, Paris, 1923 (on the Moudros armistice).

Laurens, A. *Le commandement naval en Méditerranée*, Paris, 1931.

Lhopital, Commander. *Foch, l'armistice de la paix*, Paris, 1938.

Rudin, H. *Armistice, 1918*, New Haven, 1944 (on the whole, the best book).

Weygand, General. *Le onze Novembre*, Paris, 1932 (on the Rethondes armistice).

von Epstein, F. "Zwischen Compiegne und Versailles. Gcheime Amerikanische Militardiplomatie, 1918–1919," in the *Vierteeljahreshefte fur Zeitgeschichte*, October, 1955.

CHAPTER 5: THE DECLINE OF EUROPE

On the economic situation

To the books listed in the general bibliography should be added *An Inquiry into Production*, published by the Internation Work Bureau, 8 vols., Geneva, 1923–25. Also, see A. Demangeon, *Le declin d'Europe*, Paris, 1920.

On the currents of new political thought

The basic texts are:

Lenin, V. *The State and the Revolution,* new ed., Paris, 1946; and *Imperialism, the Supreme State of Capitalism,* new ed., Paris, 1945.

Spengler, O. *The Decline of the West* (translated from the German; the first edition appeared in 1918).

On the movements resistant to European influence

In addition to the general picture outlined by M. Muret in *Crépuscule des nations blanches,* Paris, 1925, and by N. Keyserling in his *La révolution mondiale* (translation), Paris, 1933, see:

Antonius, G. *The Arab Awakening. History of the Arab National Movement,* London, 1938.

Fischer, L. *The Life of Mahatma Gandhi,* New York, 1950.

Grousset, R. *Le réveil de l'Asie,* Paris, 1924.

Heyd, U. *Foundations of Turkish nationalism; the Life and Teachings of Ziya Gokalp,* London, 1950.

Nanda, B. *Mahatma Gandhi, A Biography,* London, 1959.

Rossi, E. *Documenti sull'origine e gli sviluppi della questione araba, 1875–1944,* Rome, 1944.

The bibliographies of the books mentioned above will offer further information.

CHAPTER 6: THE PEACE SETTLEMENT

The most important documents are those relating to the deliberations of the Big Four; minutes of these meetings were collected and assembled by Sir Maurice Hankey and published in *Papers Relating to the Foreign Relations of the U.S., 1919. The Paris Peace Conference,* 2 vols. New York, 1942; and notes of Paul Mantoux. *Les Délibérations du conseil des quatres,* 2 vols., Paris, 1955.

Among the more important materials—and there are quantities of it—are: for France: A Tardieu. *La Paix,* Paris, 1920; for the British Empire: D. Lloyd George. *War Memoirs,* London, 1934; for the United States: Lansing. *The Peace Negotiations, a Personal Narrative* (memoirs), London, 1921; and C. Seymour. *The Intimate Papers of Colonel House,* New York, 1920; for Italy: L. Aldovrandi-Marescotti. *Guerre Diplomatica, Ricordi e frammenti di diario,* Milan, 1937.

Among the general studies, the main ones appear to me to be:

Brown-Scott, J. B., and J. T. Shotwell. *The Paris Peace Conference, History and Documents,* New York, 1934.

Ferber, F. *Das Diktat von Versailles,* 2 vols., Essen, 1939 (particularly on the applications of the treaty).

House, E. M., and others. *What Really Happened in Paris. A History of the Peace Conference by the American Delegates* (translation), Paris, 1923.

Lucknau, A. *The German Delegation at the Paris Peace Conference,* New York, 1941.

Marston, F. S. *The Peace Conference of 1919: Organization and Procedure,* London, 1944.

Temperly, H. *A History of the Peace Conference of Paris,* 6 vols., 1920–21.

Torre, A. *Versailles, Storia della Conferenza della Pace,* Milan, 1940.

Zeigler, W. *Versailles: Die Geschichte eines missgluckten Friedens,* 2nd ed., Hamburg, 1933.

On the Polish question

Blocizewski, J. *La restauration de la Pologne et de la diplomatie européenne, 1914–1923,* Paris, 1927.

Recke, W. *Versailles: Die Polnische Frage als problem der europaischen Politik,* Berlin, 1927.

On the Russian question

Kennan, G. *The Decision to Intervene,* Princeton, 1958.

Pierre, A. "L'intervention française en Russie méridionale," in the *Monde Slave,* 1927, pp. 143–160.

Stein, B. E. *Die Russische Frage auf der Pariser Freidens konferenz, 1919–1920,* Leipzig, 1953.

Strakhovsky, L. *Intervention at Archangel. The Story of the Allied Intervention, 1918–1920,* Princeton, 1944.

Volkoy, F. D. *Krah anglijkoj politik interventsii, 1917–1924* (The Failure of the English Policy of Intervention), Moscow, 1954.

On the Danubian questions

Almond, N., and R. Lutz. *The Treaty of Saint-Germain,* Stanford University, 1935.

Deak, F. *Hungary at the Paris Peace Conference,* New York, 1942.

Holzer, E. *Die Entstehung des jugoslavischen staats,* Berlin, 1929.

Kybal, V. *Les origines diplomatiques de l'état tchecoslovaque,* Prague, 1929.

Opočensky, C. *Umsturz im Mitteleuropa. Der Zusammenbruch Oester-*

reich-*Ungarns und die Geburt der Kleinen Entent* (translated from the Czech), Hellerau, 1932.

On the territorial disputes in Europe

Wambraugh, S. *Plebiscites since the World War. With a Collection of Official Documents,* Washington, 1933 (exceedingly useful).

Anjel, J. *Manuel géographique de politique européenne. T. I. L'Europe centrale,* Paris, 1936 (exceedingly useful).

Gould, S. W. "Austrian Attitudes Toward Anschluss (October, 1918–September, 1919)," in the *Journal of Modern History,* September, 1950, pp. 220–31.

Grauzinis, G. *La Question de Vilna,* Paris, 1927.

Harder, H. A. *Danzig, Polen under Volkerbund,* Berlin, 1928.

Herre, P. *Die Sudtiroler Frage,* Munich, 1927.

Moodie, A. *The Italo-Yugoslav Boundary,* London, 1945.

Smogorzewski, C. *La Pologne, l'Allemagne et le corridor,* Paris, 1930.

Tapie, V. *Le Pays de Teschen,* Paris, 1936.

Uhlig. *Die bessarabische Frage,* Berlin, 1928.

On the Chinese question

In addition to the works already mentioned on page 341, see R. H. Fifield. *Woodrow Wilson and the Far East. The Diplomacy of the Shantung Question,* New York, 1952.

On the Middle East question

Howard, N. *The Partition of Turkey, a Diplomatic History, 1913–1923,* Norman, 1933.

On the "mandates"

Logan, R. *The African Mandates in World Politics,* Washington, 1948.

Macaulay, N. *Mandates; Reasons, Results, Remedies,* London, 1937.

Margalith, A. M. *The International Mandates,* Baltimore, 1930.

On the question of reparations

Burnett, P. *Reparation at the Paris Peace Conference, from the Standpoint of the American Delegation,* 2 vols., New York, 1940. See also titles cited in Chapter 9.

On the policies of the various governments

Albrecht-Carrier, R. *Italy at the Peace Conference,* New York, 1938.
Baker, S. *Le President Wilson et le reglement franco-allemand* (translation), Paris, 1924.
Lansing, R. *The Peace Negotiations. A Personal Narrative,* New York, 1921.
Nicolson, H. *Peace Making,* London, 1933.
Noble, G. *Policies and Opinions at Paris, 1919,* New York, 1935.

On the elaboration of the Covenant of the League of Nations

Fleming, D. F. *The U.S. and the League of Nations, 1918–1920,* New York, 1932.
Miller, D. H. *The Drafting of the Covenant,* 2 vols., New York, 1928.
Scelle, G., and R. Lange. *Les origines et l'oeuvre de la Societé des Nations,* Copenhagen, 1923.
Winkler, H. *The Development of the League of Nations Idea in Great Britain, 1914–1919,* London, 1948.

CHAPTER 7: DISSENSION AMONG THE VICTORS

On France

Beau de Loménie, E. *Le débat de ratification du Traité de Versailles,* Paris, 1945.

On Great Britain

Keynes, J. M. *The Economic Consequences of the Peace,* London, 1919; and the critique of this work by E. Mantoux. *The Carthaginian Peace,* London, 1943.
McCallum, *Public Opinion and the Last Peace,* London, 1944.

On the United States

Bailey, T. *Woodrow Wilson and the Great Betrayal,* New York, 1945.
Bonsal, S. *Unfinished Business,* New York, 1944.
Daniels, J. *The Wilson Era, 1917–1923,* Chapel Hill, 1946.
Debyser, F. *Le Sénat des Etats Unis et le Traité de Versailles,* Paris, 1932.
Paxson, L. *American Democracy and the World War,* Vol. III, New York, 1936.

CHAPTER 8: THE NEW INFLUENCES

General aspects (in addition to the works listed in the general bibliography)

de Jouvenel, B. *D' une guerre à l'autre: Vol. I. De Versailles à Locarno. Vol. II. La décomposition de l'Europe liberale, 1925–1932,* 2 vols., Paris, 1941.
Pirou, G. *Economie libérale et économique dirigée: Vol. I. Economie libérale,* Paris, 1946.

On international economic relations (in addition to the general works on pp. 337–338.

Damalos, B. V. *La réorganization de l'économie mondiale; les tentatives infructueuses de la S.D.N. et les efforts actuels de l'O.N.U.,* Paris, 1947.

On national economic conditions

In the United States:
Anderson, B. *Economics and the Public Welfare. Financial and Economic History of the U.S., 1914–1946,* New York, 1950.
Faulkner, H. *American Economic History,* 5th ed., New York, 1942.
Franck, L. *Histoire économique et social des Etats Unis de 1919–1949,* Paris, 1950.
Mikesell, R. F. *U.S. Economic Policy and International Relations,* New York, 1952.
Soule, G. *Economic History of the U.S.* Vol. VIII. *Prosperity Decade (1917–1929),* New York, 1947.

In Great Britain:
Gregg, P. *A Social and Economic History of Britain, 1760–1950,* London, 1950.

In France:
Combe, P. *Niveau de vie et progrés de technique en France 1860–1939,* Paris, 1955.
Gignoux, J. *L'économie française entre les deux guerres, 1919–1939,* Paris, 1942.

In Germany:
Bruck, W. F. *Social and Economic History of Germany from William II to Hitler,* London, 1938.

In Japan:
Lockwood, W. *The Economic Development of Japan. Growth and Structural Change, 1868–1938,* Princeton, 1954.

In Poland:

Zweig, F. *Poland between Two Wars. A Critical Study*, London, 1944.

In Russia:

Dobb, M. *Soviet Economic Development since 1917*, 2nd ed., London, 1949.

Prokopovicz, S. N. *Russlands Volksirtschaft unter den Sowjets*, Zurich, 1944.

Wenger, L. *L'essor économique de l'U.R.S.S. depuis la Révolution de Octobre 1917 jusqu'à la guerre germano-russe de 1941. Essai de synthèse d'une documentation statistique*, Paris, 1945.

On national politics

In Germany:

Baumont, M., and M. Berthelot. *L'Allemagne, lendemains de guerre et de révolution*, Paris, 1922.

Benoist-Méchin, J. *Histoire de l'armée allemande*, 2 vols., Paris, 1936.

Eyck, E. *Geschichte der Weimarer Republik*, Vol. I, Zurich, 1954.

Göhring, M. *Bismarck's Erben, 1895–1945*, Wiesbaden, 1958.

Gordon, H. *The Reichswehr and the German Republic, 1919–26*, Princeton, 1957.

Rivaud, A. *Le relèvement de l'Allemagne, 1918–1938*, Paris, 1938.

Schüddekopf, O. E. *Das Heer und die Republik. Quellen zur Politik der Reichswehrführung*, Hanover, 1955.

Vermeil, E. *L'Allemagne contemporaine, sociale, politique, et culturelle, 1890–1950*, Vol. II, Paris, 1953.

Wheeler-Bennett, J. *The Nemesis of Power. The German Army in Politics, 1918–1945*, London, 1953.

In France:

Ackermann, M. *Quelques aspects de l'opinion public en France sur le problème allemand, 1920–1940* (typed thesis), Paris, 1953.

Chastenet, J. *Les années d'illusions, 1918–31*, Paris, 1960.

Howard, J. E. *Parliament and Foreign Policy in France, 1919–1939*, New York, 1948.

In the United States:

Grassmuck, G. L. *Sectional Biases in Congress on Foreign Policy, 1921–1941*, Baltimore, 1951.

In Great Britain:

Biggs Davison, J. *The Uncertain Ally*, London, 1957 (on relations with the United States).

Medlicott, W. *British Foreign Policy Since Versailles, 1919–1939*, London, 1942.

Wolfers, A. *Britain and France Between Two Wars: Conflicting Strategies of Peace Since Versailles*, New York, 1940.

In Poland:
Rose, A. *La politique polonaise entre les deux guerres*, Neuchâtel, 1945.

In Italy:
Alatri, P. "Le origini del fascismo. La classe dirigente italiana," in *Belfegor*, 1950, pp. 129–147, 271–80, 377–403.
Christopoulos, G. *La politique exterieure de l'Italie fasciste*, Paris, 1936.
Salvatorelli, E., and G. Mira. *Storia del fascismo: l'Italia dal 1919 al 1945*, Rome, 1952.
Salvemini G. *Mussolini diplomatico, 1922–1932*, Bari, 1952.
Vaussard, M. "Comment Mussolini devint impérialiste," in *Revue des Deux Mondes*, January 15, 1959, pp. 305–17.

In Sweden:
Tingsten, H. *The Debate on the Foreign Policy of Sweden, 1918–1939* (translated from the Swedish), London, 1949.

In the U.S.S.R.:
Beloff, M. *The Foreign Policy of Soviet Russia, 1929–41*, London, 1947 (the introduction to the work).
Degras, J. *The Communist International, 1919–1943*, Vol I: 1919–1922, London, 1956.
Fischer, L. *The Soviets in World Affairs*, 2 vols., New York, 1930.
Miliukov, N. *La politique extérieure de l'U.R.S.S.*, Paris, 1931.

On the national minorities:
Azcarate, P. *League of Nations and National Minorities*, New York, 1945.
Kaeckenbeck, C. *The International Experiment of Upper Silesia, 1922–1937*, London, 1942.
Ladas, S. P. *The Exchange of Minorities*, London, 1932.
Politis, N. "Le problème des minorités," in *L'esprit international*, January, 1935, pp. 3–21.
Wambaugh, S. *Plebiscites Since the World War*, 2 vols., Washington, 1933.

On Islam:
Gibb, R. A., and others. *Whither Islam? A Survey of Modern Movement in the Moslem World*.
Glubb Pasha. *Britain and the Arabs, 1908–1958*, London, 1949.
Masignon, L. *Le problème islamique* (speech), Paris, 1921.
O'Leary, L. *Islam at the Cross Roads. A Brief Survey of the Present Position and Problems of the World of Islam*, London, 1923.
Stoddard, L. *Le Nouveau Monde de l'Islam* (translation), Paris, 1923.
Zingarelli, I. *Il kisveglio dell'Islam*, Milan, 1928.
XXX: *L'Islam et la politique contemporaine. Conférences organisées par la société des Anciens élèves de l'Ecole libre des Science politiques*, Paris, 1927.

On the nationalist movements in the Far East

Brandt, C., and B. Schwartz. *A Documentary History of Chinese Communism*, Cambridge, Mass., 1952.
Brown, D. M. *Nationalism in Japan*, Berkeley, 1955.
Chesneaux, J. *Sun Yat-sen*, Paris, 1959.
Kao Chung-Ju. *Le mouvement intellectuel en Chine, 1919–1925*, Paris, 1957.
Léger, F. *Les influences occidentales dans la révolution de l'Orient: Inde, Malaisie, Chine, 1850–1950*, 2 vols., Paris, 1955.
Szu Yu-teng and J. Fairbank. *China's Response to the West. A Documentary Survey, 1839–1923*, Cambridge, Mass., 1954.

CHAPTER 9: THE GERMAN QUESTION

On the general aspects

Jordan, W. M. *Great Britain, France and the German Problem, 1918–1939*, London, 1943.

On the roles played by statesmen

Chastenet, J. *Raymond Poincaré*, Paris, 1948.
Laroche, J. *Au quai d'Orsay avec Briand et Poincaré, 1913–1926*, Paris, 1937.
Petrie, C. *The Life and Letters of Sir Austen Chamberlain*, 2 vols., London, 1934–1940.
Stresemann, G. *Six années de politique allemande. Les papiers de Stresemann* (translated), 3 vols., Paris, 1932–1933.
Suarez, G. *Briand, sa vie, son oeuvre* (6 vols.), Vols. V and VI, Paris, 1938–1941.

On the reparations question

Antonucci, A. *Le bilan des Réparations et la crise mondiale*, Paris, 1935.
Bergmann, C. *Der Weg der Reparationen*, Frankfurt, 1926.
Calmette, G. *Receuil de documents sur l'histoire de la question des Réparations, 1919–1921*, Paris, 1922.
Schacht, H. *Das Ende der Reparationen*, Oldenburg, 1931.
Seydoux, J. *De Versailles au plan.*
Weill-Raynal, E. *Les Réparations allemandes et la France*, 3 vols., Paris, 1949.

On the occupation of the Rhur

Wentcke, P. *Rhurkampf*, 2 vols., Berlin, 1930–1932.
Fierain, A. *La presse française et l'occupation de la Ruhr* (typed memoir), Paris, 1953.

On the German disarmament question

Benoist-Mechin, J. *Histoire de l'armée allemande*, 2 vols., Paris, 1936.
Morgan, General J. H. *Assize of Arms. Being the Story of the Disarmament of Germany and Her Rearmament, 1919–1939*, London, 1945.

On the question of Austrian unity

Auerbach, B. *Le rattachement de l'Autriche à l'Allemagne*, Paris, 1927.
Bell, M. *Post-war German-Austrian relations. The Anschluss Movement, 1918–1936*, Stanford University, 1937.
Shepherd, G. *The Austrian Odyssey*, London, 1957.

On Germany's eastern policy

Holtje, C. *Die Weimarer Republik und das Ostlocarno Problem, 1919–1934*, Wurzburg, 1958.

CHAPTER 10: RUSSIA AND EUROPE (1920–1929)

On the general aspects (in addition to the works by Miliukov, p. 351, and Potemkine p. 337)

Eudin, X., and R. North. *Soviet Russia and the West. A Documentary Survey*, Stanford University, 1957.
Rubenstein, N. *Sovetskaja Rossija i kapitalisticeskie gosudarstva v gody perechoda ot vojny k miru, 1921–1922* (Soviet Russia and the Capitalist States in the Years of Transition between War and Peace), Moscow, 1948.
Schuman F. L. *Soviet Politics*, London, 1941.
Seton-Watson, H. *Eastern Europe Between the Wars, 1918–1941*, Cambridge, 1945.
Stein, B. E. *"Russkij Vopros" v 1920–21* (The Russian Question in 1920–1921), Moscow, 1958.

On German-Russian relations

Carr, E. *German-Soviet Relations Between the Two World Wars*, Baltimore, 1951.

Castellan, G. *Le Réarmement clandestin du Reich, 1930–35*, Paris, 1954 (Chapter 5 offers information on the period between 1920–1930).

Freund, G. *Unholy Alliance. Russian-German Relations from the Treaty of Brest-Litovsk to the Treaty of Berlin*, London, 1937.

Gatzke, H. "Russo-German Collaboration during the Weimar Republic," in the *American Historical Review*, April, 1958, pp. 565–597.

Hallgarten, G. W. "General von Seeckt and Russia, 1920–22," in the *Journal of Modern History*, March, 1949, pp. 28–34.

Hilger, G., and H. Meyer. *The Incompatible Allies*, New York, 1953.

Kochan, L. *Russland und die Weimarer Republik*, Dusseldorf, 1956 (translation of an English work that appeared in 1952).

Korbljakov, I. *Ot Bresta do Rapallo*, Moscow, 1954.

Kuler, H. *Die Aussenpolitik der Weimarer Republik, 1918–1923*, Aschaffenburg, 1957.

Schnieder, T. "Die Probleme des Rapallo-Vertrags," in *Arbeitsgemeinschaft für Forschung des landes Nordrhein-Westfalen*, Heft 43, 1956.

Von Stockhausen, M. *Sechs Jahre in der Reichskanzlei, von Rapallo bis Locarno. Erinnerungen und Tagebuchnotizen.*

Basch, A. *The Danube Basin and the German Economic Sphere*, New York, 1943.

Hantos, E. *Die Neuordnung des Donauraumes*, Berlin, 1935.

Machray, R. *The Struggle for the Danube and the Little Entente*, London, 1938.

Paslovsky, L. *Economic Nationalism in the Danubian States*, New York, 1925.

Toscano, M. "L'accorde revisionista franco-ungherese del 1920," in *Politica*, January–April, 1943, pp. 323–95.

Werkmann, J. *Aus Kaisers Karls Nachlass*, Berlin, 1925.

On the Balkan questions

Ancel, J. *Les Balkans face à l'Italie*, Paris, 1928.

Howard, R. N. *The Balkan Conferences and the Balkan States*, Berkeley, 1936.

Marcovitch, L. "La France, l'Italie, et la Yougoslavie," in *Esprit International*, April, 1930, pp. 163–80.

Mousset, A. *L'Albanie devant l'Europe*, Paris, 1927.

CHAPTER 12: THE MEDITERRANEAN AND THE MIDDLE EAST

General aspects

Driault, E. *La question d'Orient, 1918–1937: la paix de la Méditerranée*, Paris, 1938.

Rondot, P. *Destins du Proche-Orient*, Paris, 1959.
Siegfried, A. *Vue générale de la Méditerranée*, 5th ed., Paris, 1943.
Toynbee, A. *The Islamic World Since the Peace Settlement*, London, 1927 (very important).
Yale, W. *The Near East, a Modern History*, Ann Arbor, 1958.

On the Turkish nationalist movement

Arnold, T. *The Caliphate*, Oxford, 1924.
Giannini, A. *L'Ultime Phase della questione orientale, 1918–1932*, Rome, 1933.
Nicholson, H. *Curzon, the Last Phase, 1919–1925*, London, 1934.
Pallis, A. H. *Greece's Anatolian Adventure and After, 1915–1922*, London, 1937.

On the Arab and Berber movements

Bentwich, N. *England in Palestine*, London, 1932.
Cataluccio, F. *Storia del nazionalismo arabo*, Milan, 1939.
Fontaine, P. *Abd-el-Krim. Origine de la rébellion nord-africaine*, Paris, 1958.
L'Huiller, F. *Fondements historiques des problèmes du Moyen-Orient*, Paris, 1958.
XXX *Great Britain and Egypt, 1914–1951*, London, 1952.

On Afghan nationalism

Barton, Sir W. *India's North-West Frontier*, London, 1939.

On the rivalries between the major powers

In the Mediterranean:
de Mulhacen, M. *Politica mediterránea de España, 1704–1951*, Madrid, 1952.
Passamonti, E. *Negoziati mediterranei anglo-franco-italiani, della guerra di Libia al conflitto mondiale*, Verbania, 1941.
Silver, P. *Itali, Francia, Inghilterra nel Mediterraneo*, Milan, 1939.
Solni, A. *Italia e Francia nei problemi attuali della politica europea*, Milan, 1931.

In the Middle East:
Fatemi, N. *Diplomatic History of Persia, 1917–1923*, New York, 1952.
Lenkowski, G. *The Middle East in World Affairs*, New York, 1952.

CHAPTER 13: THE NATIONALIST MOVEMENT IN THE FAR EAST

General aspects

Buss, C. A. *The Far East,* New York, 1955.
McNair, H., and D. Lach. *Modern Far Eastern International Relations,* New York, 1950.
Renouvin, P. *La question d'Extrême Orient, 1840–1940,* 3rd ed., Paris, 1953.

On the Washington conference

Archimbaud, L. *La Conférence de Washington,* Paris, 1923.
Buell, R. L. *The Washington Conference,* New York, 1922.
Ichihashi, Y. *The Washington Conference and After. A Historical Survey,* Stanford University, 1928.
    The British, American, and French governments have published collections of documents relating to the work of the conference, which seemed superfluous to mention here.

On the policies of the major powers

Borg, D. *American Policy and the Chinese Revolution,* New York, 1943.
Clark, G. *Economic Rivalries in China,* New Haven, 1932.
Griswold, A. *The Far Eastern Policy of the United States,* New York, 1938.
Moore, H. L. *Soviet Far Eastern Policy,* Princeton, 1945.
Pollard, M. *China's Foreign Relations, 1917–1931,* New York, 1933.
Sapoznikov, B. G. *Pervaja grazdanskaja revoljucionnaja vojna v Kitae, 1924–27* gg. (The First Civil War in China, 1924–1927), Moscow, 1954.
Varg, P. *Missionaries, Chinese and Diplomats. The American Protestant Missionary Movement in China, 1890–1950,* Princeton, 1958.
Whiting, A. S. *Soviet Policies in China, 1917–1924,* New York, 1955.

CHAPTER 14: THE INTERNATIONAL POSITION
OF LATIN AMERICA

General aspects

Inman, S. G. *Latin-America; Its Place in World Life,* New York, 1944.
Rippy, E. *Latin-America in World Politics; an Outline Survey,* New York, 1928.

On relations with the League of Nations (in addition to the general histories on p. 348)

Galeano, V. *L'Amérique-Latine et la S.D.N.*, Paris, 1927.
Kelchner, W. *Latin-American Relations with the League of Nations*, Boston, 1929.
Perez-Guerrero, M. *Les Rélations des États de l'Amérique Latine avec la S.D.N.*, Paris, 1936.

On relations with the United States

Bell, M. *The Problem of Panamerican Organization*, Stanford University, 1934.
Bemis, S. *The Latin American Policy of the U.S.: An Historical Interpretation*, New Haven, 1943.
Feis, H. *The Diplomacy of the Dollar. First Era: 1919–1932*, Baltimore, 1950.
Gantenbein, J. W. *The Evolution of our Latin-American Policy. A Documentary Record*, New York, 1950.
Halsey, F. *Investments in Latin-America*, Washington, 1918.
Stuart, G. *Latin-America and the U.S.*, New York, 1938.
Winkler, M. *Investments of U.S. Capital in Latin-America*, Boston, 1930.

On South American conflicts

Dennis, J. W. *Tacna and Arica—An Account*, New Haven, 1931.
Kirkpatrick, E. *The Chaco Dispute, the League and Panamericanism*, Geneva, 1936.
de Lastra Bernales, J. *Historia Diplomática de la cuestión de Tacna y Arica*, Santiago, 1951.

CHAPTER 15: THE ORGANIZATION OF
INTERNATIONAL RELATIONS

On the organization of peace in general

Rappard, W. *The Quest for Peace since the World War*, Cambridge, 1950.

On the role played by the League of Nations in international relations

Knudson, J. *A History of the League of Nations*, Atlanta, 1938.
Ray, J. *Commentaire du Pacte de la S.D.N.*, Paris, 1930.

Walters, F. P. *A History of the League of Nations,* 2 vols., London, 1952 (all in all the most important work on the subject).
Zimmern, A. *The League of Nations and the Rule of Law,* London, 1936.

On the reform plans of the Covenant of the League of Nations

Alvarez, A. "Les Groupements continentaux et la réforme du conseil de la S.D.N." in *L'Esprit International,* 1927, pp. 44–63.
Baker, J. N. *The Geneva Protocol,* London, 1925; and *The League of Nations at Work,* London, 1926.
Brugiere, P. *La Sécurité collective, 1919–1945,* Paris, 1946.
Hudson, M. O. *The World Court, 1921–1931,* Boston, 1932.
Le Brun-Keris, G. *Les projets de réforme de la S.D.N.,* Paris, 1938.
Scelle, G. *Essai sur la crise de la S.D.N. et ses remèdes,* Paris, 1927.
Wehberg, H. "Le Protocol de Genève" in *Receuil des Cours de l'Académie de Droit Internationale,* 1925, Vol. II, pp. 5–149.

On the Paris Treaty and the role played by the United States

Ferrell, R. *Peace in Their Time: The Origins of the Kellogg-Briand Pact,* New Haven, 1952.
Flemming, D. *The U.S. and World Organization: 1918–1933,* New York, 1938.
Shotwell, J. T. *Le Pacte de Paris,* Paris, 1930.

On the question of disarmament

Chaput, R. A. *Disarmament in British Foreign Policy,* London, 1934.
Latmer, H. *Naval Disarmament,* London, 1930.
Lyon, J. *Les problèmes du désarmement,* Paris, 1934.
Wheeler-Bennett, J. *Disarmament and Security Since Locarno, 1925–1931,* London, 1932.
XXX *L'U.R.S.S. et la conférence du désarmement,* Paris, 1932 (documents with a preface by A. Lounatcharsky).

On economic and financial aspects

Moulton, N., and L. Pavlovsky. *World War Debts Settlement,* London, 1927.
Rappard, W. "Le nationalisme économique et la S.D.N." in *Receuil des Cours de l'Académie de Droit International,* 1937, Vol. XI, pp. 167 ff.

Index

[359]